# The Case Book of a
# MEDICAL PSYCHOLOGIST

BY Charles Berg, M.D. (LOND.), D.P.M.

FELLOW OF THE BRITISH PSYCHOLOGICAL ASSOCIATION,
PHYSICIAN TO THE BRITISH HOSPITAL FOR FUNCTIONAL
MENTAL AND NERVOUS DISORDERS, PHYSICIAN TO THE
INSTITUTE FOR THE SCIENTIFIC TREATMENT OF DELIN-
QUENCY, LATE HON. PHYSICIAN TO THE TAVISTOCK CLINIC

W · W · NORTON & COMPANY · INC · *New York*

Four months before he died, Professor Sigmund Freud wrote the following letter about these Case Book articles:—

May 16th 1938

**PROF. SIGM. FREUD**

20 MARESFIELD GARDENS.
LONDON. N.W.3.

TEL: HAMPSTEAD 2002.

Dear Dr Berg

Long and serious illness made it impossible for me to give your letter of April 6th an earlier reply. Even now I could not read all the reprints you sent me. I have to say, I liked what I had read. You will understand, that I entertain certain suspicions against the technique of analysts who have made the popularization of analysis their aim. It appears to me a very difficult if not an impossible task. The man in the street is not likely to swallow and digest our conception of an unconscious mind nor will he be ready to agree to the emphasis we put on the primary urges.

Psychoanalysis might never become
popular.
Yet I am to glad to say, I
think you are doing
good work.
Yours sincerely
Sigm. Freud

# CONTENTS

## WAR NEUROSES

# PREFACE TO FIRST EDITION

WHEN it was suggested to me that I should write a series of case sheet articles as an introduction to the practical application of modern psychology, I essayed the task with mixed feelings. On the one hand I felt with Freud (*vide* facsimile of his letter) that it was hardly possible to present analytical material in popular form, particularly the enormous proportion of sexual material which emerges during the treatment of patients: and yet, on the other hand, I felt that, case material being the irrefutable data on which clinical psychology is based, it was just this evidence which was required for a recognition of the fundamental truths underlying the theory.

Psychology, particularly clinical psychology, appears to be too full of unacceptable theories to influence the lay reader, save in the direction of scepticism; but in the verbatim utterances of patients we can present the simple data, and often leave the listener to his own theories.

Whatever the disadvantages of this psychological exposition here at least we have a live process: live people expressing their relatively uninhibited thoughts and feelings, mostly in the exact words which they used in the consulting-room.

The theoretical explanations attached to each case sheet have for the most part been reduced to a minimum, but, nevertheless, enough has been included not only to interest the general reader, but in its accumulation through the series of cases to provide the would-be practitioner with an easy, practical, and I hope even an entertaining introduction to the subject.

I hope, too, that the understanding reader will forgive the more obvious omissions, and agree that it is as well that I have placed a limit upon the indiscretion of premature interpretation, the more so perhaps in that many actually practising the therapy are not themselves prepared to accept the deepest interpretations of psychoanalysis. The critic is sure to miss the analytical significance of the sniff or pooh with which he would test and reject the broaching of some of these latter.

There are a sufficient number of cases of war neurosis to demonstrate that these patients differ in no essential particular, except ease of curability, from the average case with which the medical psychologist has to deal. Any case of psychological illness may have a traumatic precipitating factor, and it makes little difference to the nature of the case if that factor be war or peace.

The final chapter of the book is an attempt to summarize the essentials of analytical technique and theory together with its general applications in as brief a space as possible.

Though the book is meant to appeal to every class of reader, I should be very pleased if some of my colleagues also find interest and relaxation on this familiar ground.

These articles have appeared in various journals, and for permission to publish them I am indebted to the editors of *The International Journal of Psycho-Analysis*, *The British Journal of Medical Psychology*, *The Medical Press and Circular*, *The Psychologist*, and *The Practitioner*.

CHARLES BERG

HARLEY STREET
LONDON, W.I

## PREFACE TO SECOND EDITION

A SECOND edition of this work having been called for in spite of, or perhaps because of, its freedom from the usual anxiety-ridden pursuit of perfection, my feeling is that I had best let it remain very much as it was at its original carefree inception.

I have taken the opportunity of making a few minor improvements and of substituting for the last three articles in the section on War Neuroses a long analytical case paper of a more advanced nature.

On re-reading the material it has been borne home to me that other and even more hidden aspects of our subject remain untouched, and I have been encouraged by the success of the present volume to commence a further collection of case papers illustrating some of these and carrying the study to a more advanced stage, at the same time embodying a criticism of the so-called normal mind, and of its cultural institutions. I propose to issue this in due course.

CHARLES BERG

HARLEY STREET
LONDON, W.I

# ANXIETY—THE FOUNDATION OF NERVOUS ILLNESS

THE phenomenon of anxiety ranks first in importance in the study of all nervous and mental disorders. Anxiety is the raw material out of which all neurotic symptoms are made. The mind simply cannot tolerate more than a certain quantity of anxiety without doing something about it. It is as though the feeling of anxiety was so uncomfortable that the sufferer had to pin it on to some idea or to change or convert it into some other symptom.

These symptoms are almost limitless. They could be classified under two main headings: mental and physical.

Mental symptoms of anxiety may vary from vague feelings of uneasiness to fears and phobias of the most complicated, rigid, or changeable variety.

I had a patient who seemed to be uncertain whether she was afraid of knives or sex, blood, meat, her legs giving way, losing her hair or her teeth, burglars, getting appendicitis, or her mother dying! These and a hundred other phobias seemed to chase each other across the kaleidoscopic screen of her mind.

One thing was certain; she was always afraid of *something*, she was always in a state of anxiety.

The physical symptoms of anxiety can be classified under almost every organ or function of the body. For instance: disturbances of the heart, such as palpitation or irregularity; disturbances of breathing, such as rapid breath or asthmatic attacks; disturbances of the skin, such as sweating; disturbances of the digestive system, such as dyspepsia, diarrhœa, or constipation; disturbances of the muscles, such as tremblings, shakings, weakness, or spasm; disturbances of sensation called paræsthesias, which can include hot and cold feelings, indescribable sensations, numbness or hypersensitiveness, or even acute pain.

Other common symptoms are: giddiness, either of heights or in open spaces, feelings of inferiority, fear of going to sleep, congestion in the head, loss of control of various functions.

It will be seen that the symptom of anxiety has its ramifications in every nook and cranny of nervous and mental illness. Therefore in writing such an article as this I must confine myself to its simplest and least organized form, lest we find ourselves attempting a comprehensive study of all mental and physical phenomena.

In morbid anxiety (as distinct from ordinary fear of a real danger) any one or more of these symptoms, physical or mental, may be experienced without the others. For instance, a person suffering from a state of morbid anxiety may complain merely of feelings of mental apprehensiveness, or she may present herself with the single symptom of palpitation of the heart, sometimes without any corresponding mental state.

It may be apparent from this summary, and from the instance of the case mentioned, that it gets us nowhere to recite a million different *forms* that anxiety can take. To continue to do this would be like skating on the surface of the problem. It would get us no nearer to the deep and fundamental *source* of the symptom of anxiety.

Let us therefore turn for a moment to consider the mechanism or physiology of normal fear.

If we observe the animal in the forest, be it rabbit or bird, or if we consider the life of the cave man or the soldier in the firing-line, we shall observe at least some of the symptoms of anxiety. All life seems to be on the alert for the perception of danger.

Let us see what effect this has upon the functions of the animal.

A cat is allowed to become accustomed to sleep after its meal behind the screen on an X-ray table. A barium meal opaque to X-rays is given, and inside the resting cat the movement of its stomach can be detected ryhthmically digesting its food, some of this food passing on with digestion into the intestine.

A dog is now brought into the laboratory and barks at the tethered cat. The observer at the X-ray screen will see that immediately the stomach stops its functioning. The sphincter, or circular muscle, at the exit of the stomach closes down firmly. The stomach becomes limp, its secretions stop, and the whole process of digestion is arrested. Another form of activity is prepared for.

This is a mechanism provided by nature for the protection of the living creature faced with a danger situation.

If the matter is gone into further it is found that, as a result of the fright, adrenalin from the ductless glands of the cat is secreted into its bloodstream. The blood vessels of its digestive apparatus contract, and the blood that was formerly engaged in digestion is now diverted to the brain and central nervous system, muscles and skin.

In this condition the animal can leap ten times as far. Therefore it must be admitted that the mechanism is useful to the preservation of life. Moreover, it could sustain its physical activity, for glycogen or starch stored in the liver is simultaneously converted into sugar and circulates in the bloodstream to feed the muscles with the energy requisite for sustained activity. At the same time the extra heat and waste products generated are liberated into the vascular skin and other excretory organs. The heart beats faster. The breathing is accelerated. Even the hair tends to stand on end.

Now, the difference between the cat and the neurotic patient is that with the cat the presence of the dog is not perpetual. She eventually gets out of danger, gets into a position of safety where she can digest her food and even sleep peacefully. In spite of all their frights, cats do not suffer from anxiety neurosis; but stockbrokers do.

One of our famous physicians when lecturing would always get in his favourite little quip: "When stocks go down in New York, diabetes goes up." Note the mechanism just referred to, whereby the blood sugar is increased in a danger situation.

But to try to explain anxiety neurosis on such grounds as this without going any more deeply into human psychology is to try and play *Hamlet* without the prince. It does not tell us the difference between cats and neurotics. The difference is that, while animals in a natural state, or soldiers at war, have their battle or conflict in an external drama, that drama has its intervals, its periods during which the curtain is rung down, and even its periods when the theatre is deserted and the players and audience rest peacefully in bed.

The soldier comes back from the battle-line out of the reach of shells and sleeps the sleep of peace. Not so the neurotic. His drama, his conflict, goes on for ever within his conscious or unconscious mind. There is no rest for him.

He is not like the experimental cat on the X-ray screen whose stomach is digesting his food in the absence of any alarm. For him the dog is there all the time, more or less. The sphincters of his stomach and intestines are contracted more or less all the time, leading eventually to visceroptosis and even to ulcer, his heart tends to palpitate, his system is constantly prepared for battle with the unseen, unconscious enemy.

If he does sleep, he is wrestling with a ghost, or being chased by a bull. This ghost or bull is merely a dramatization of unconscious primitive animal forces within his own unconscious mind, forces which he has opposed, repudiated, dissociated, or repressed. He has refused to recognize them as part and parcel of his own nature, and to allow them adequate liberty of action.

Instead of riding on the horse or bull, which is the powerful instinct drive within him, and enjoying the exhilaration thereof, he has stood in its path and tried to stop it. He has tried to go contrary to his own animal nature. He has pitted himself unduly against the forces of nature, even believing that God would have him do so, forgetting that God's laws are Nature's laws, and that the laws he ascribes to God are the creations and projections of man's own ideas.

Thus he gets illness, the creation of man, instead of health, the creation of Nature.

If we pause to ask why the neurotic must so oppose himself to his nature, why he must struggle with ghosts in the night, we often find on analysis that these are elements or impulses in his own instinctive nature for which he or the organization of society has not provided.

Usually it means that these very primitive or infantile instinct impulses have in early life been prevented from developing into a more mature form, such as that of the normal adult instinct for loving and procreation. They have been prevented by fear or an overmoral infantile strictness from reaching a form or a maturity which would enable them to be released by such a normal process as marriage.

The process which prevents this natural development or maturization is still at work within him. The instincts, or their primitive components, are still being opposed by an infantile morality. This is the conflict which goes on day and night.

Always there is the fear that some animal impulse will get the better of his control, that his ego or reason will be overwhelmed.

If, however, one or other of these instinct impulses should break out, even in phantasy, or unconscious phantasy, the temporary relief of tension is swiftly followed by a revival of the infantile morality forces; fear and repression are increased; self-reproach, recrimination, and even punishment follow; and his last state may be worse than his first.

This drama is largely or completely an unconscious one (revealed to him only by the process of mind analysis), and the only parts of it which reach his consciousness are the effects or feelings belonging to it. These *feelings*, such as fear, as he becomes aware of them, he attaches to concepts or ideas belonging to his conscious way of thinking.

The original symbols to which anxiety is attached may be very simple anatomical ones, such as sexual organs, but immediately other symbols, such as trains or tunnels, may be substituted for them. Thus we get any conceivable phobia.

Or if displacements of *precautionary* measures against the danger predominate we get such symptoms as fear of stepping over a line, compulsion to touch or fear of touching, compulsive handwashing, or compulsive thinking. In obsessional neurosis this process can go to such lengths that the original source of the trouble is completely lost sight of.

Thus the sufferer gets off the track of understanding his own illness.

To follow such processes would take us far away from our original thesis of anxiety and its source.

In some cases the neurotic may not become consciously aware, even of the affects or feelings belonging to his unconscious dramas. The energy of them may be debarred from reaching consciousness, and may be diverted into bodily innervations such as that of the heart or stomach. And he goes to the doctor (sometimes equally innocent in these matters) complaining of palpitation or dyspepsia, paralysis or pain.

The position may be elucidated in this way: the sufferer from morbid anxiety, no matter what he pins the symptoms on to, does not know the *source* of the feeling. That is to say, he is not *conscious* of the source of his anxiety. In other words the source of anxiety is unconscious. It lies in his unconscious mind.

When the content of his unconscious mind is revealed by analysis, it is found to contain two principal unconscious elements. The first is derived from a layer of the mind which can hardly be distinguished from body. It is the dynamic energy of life derived from bodily combustion. This energy is more or less organized into patterns for discharge, which are called the innate instincts. These instincts operate normally in such a way as to discharge or reduce accumulated tension. The pinnacle of their organization serves the purpose of perpetuating the species.

The second important element discovered in the unconscious mind had its source in the earliest instruction, prohibitions, etc., designed to make the primitive creature conform to the rules and regulations of the social order in which it was to live. In the course of the earliest education, particularly the control of instinct, dynamic energy which formerly belonged to these instincts was diverted to oppose or control their expression.

Here we have the essence of the conflict or battle which is being continuously waged, and merely the thunder of which reaches the conscious level.

How a compromise within the normal limits is ever reached may be regarded as a more wonderful phenomenon than the partial failure observed in nervous illness.

We are, of course, none of us entirely free from the tyranny of morbid anxiety—a witness of the struggle that our biological nature has had to bring itself into even workable conformity with the demands of civilization or the social state. He who suffers illness or incapacity through this source has merely been less successful in his efforts of adjusting his deeper natural needs to the standards demanded.

Often it is because the standards set him, or the standards he set' himself, were too extreme to be practicable—at least for him.

He is frequently a man with an ideal of living which is beyond his own strength—the spirit is willing but the flesh is weak. In so far as he conforms to this ideal his inherited animal nature is tortured and keeps having its revenge. In so far as he abandons this ideal and gives more liberty or gratification to the primitive forces within him he is severely punished, by an excessive conscience or conscientiousness.

A practical point to remember is that conscience or conscientiousness is usually infinitely more exacting or severe than reality, society, or reason demands.

## SELF-CURE BY ASTHMA

WHEN I was very young and inexperienced, an elderly lady consulted me for asthma.

I was for the time being engaged in general practice, and the function expected of me was to treat symptoms with the appropriate medicine. My enquiring turn of mind often provoked surprise, or even resentment, but when I learnt that the first attack of asthma had occurred only three years ago, I could not resist persuading the patient to describe the circumstances in which it arose.

Once her tongue was loosened, and she warmed up to the subject, she even forgot the symptom (asthma) altogether, and poured into my willing ears a host of grievances against life in general and her family in particular. Some practitioners would probably have cut short her verbosity, but already I had an inkling that this *free association of thought* was telling me the real *complaint*, and that the symptom (asthma) was merely its latest *form*.

Piecing her story together, it reads like this:

Years and years ago, as a young wife, she had been the apple of her husband's eye and the mother of a dependent and adoring family. She reigned as queen in her domestic domain. She was beautiful, loved, and valued. At that time she enjoyed health and happiness: there was no asthma. For many years she had grow accustomed to this perfect situation.

It was only recently, as she had grown old, that tragic changes had insidiously undermined her position. Her husband had become less affectionate, less heedful and less needful of her love. He had taken to spending the greater part of his leisure at his club. Her children had grown up, and found companions and attachments outside the home. She felt that they, too, had less need of her, and certainly they showed less respect and obedience. Where her word had been law, and her opinion wisdom, she was now neither listened to nor obeyed. Besides, there was usually nobody to listen or obey. She felt herself neglected and unloved.

Things reached a climax when, some years ago, she had complained of her daily loneliness, and even hinted that she felt nervous left in the house alone. Thereupon her husband had purchased an Alsatian dog to keep her company. This was too much! She felt that insult had been added to injury. She asked for company, and they brought her a dog! A dog was good enough for her, while her society was not good enough for them. When, after a time, she voiced her indignant protests, the others had grown fond of the animal. When she ventured to mention that she was afraid of it, they exploded with incredulous laughter.

The crisis arrived one day when her demand for its removal led to a heated argument with her husband. She became exasperated. She worked herself up into a frenzy. She lost her control, and suddenly she found herself unable to speak—and *gasping for breath.*

She noticed the look of anger in her husband's face, just as he was turning away, abruptly change into one of consternation and alarm. He caught her as she collapsed. He carried her to her bed; cancelled his club appointment; and summoned the doctor. Her children, too, rallied round her bedside. There were flowers, a nurse, doctor's visits, bottles of medicine, and, above all, the anxious solicitude of all the previously neglectful members of the family.

The dog was sent away, and her slightest wish became an absolute command.

At last, her kingdom was restored to her. She was again the queen of her home. Moreover, when she did resume her ordinary duties, there was that bottle of medicine in the centre of the table at every meal, the ghost at the feast, warning every person that mother must on no account be upset.

Possibly the family had found this situation, continuing over three years, less delightful than the patient had found it. They were getting heartily sick of the whole thing. Therefore they had prevailed upon her to seek the assistance of a new doctor.

She had accordingly come to me for her bottle of medicine; for, if one suffers from asthma, one must necessarily be doing everything to cure it. It was obviously my function to take my appointed rôle in this unconscious conspiracy: to provide the medicine: and to accept a weekly remuneration. The patient clearly indicated that she would be amply satisfied by this course:

"Oh, Doctor, I really mustn't take up any more of your time. Somehow or other, you have got me to tell you all my troubles, but, you know, I didn't come to do that. Of course, you cannot help me there. In any case, things are much better than they were. I am not so neglected, and the family do take some notice of what I say. Indeed, they have all become most considerate to me since the time when I first got ill.

"I came to you only on account of my asthma. Just give me a bottle of medicine to cure that, and forgive me for wasting your time."

I looked steadily and thoughtfully at her for some little time, and then said:

"I am afraid I cannot give you anything better than your asthma."

"Good gracious, Doctor, what do you mean? I don't want to keep that; the attacks are most distressing."

"But not so distressing as continuous neglect. In fact, they only come when you are neglected or crossed in any way. They are more effective than a club in keeping your husband and family in order. I can give you no more powerful weapon. Take my advice! Keep your asthma!—only do not use it more than is necessary."

The patient rose—more bewildered than indignant.

I never saw her again.

Months later a member of her family told me:

"I don't know what you did to mother. Since she saw you she has not had a single attack of asthma. . . ."

The conclusions I am about to draw will astonish the reader who is rejoicing that he has found at last a simple and understandable explanation of such illnesses. Too many facile explanations of nervous illness already fill journals and text-books. The untruth and unsoundness of these lies in their *omissions* rather than in their statements. They mislead the inexperienced into believing that the *apparent* cause of the illness is the whole explanation of why it happened.

Such case-histories are apt to convey the impression that psychogenic illness has a more simple explanation than is actually the case.

The member of the patient's family above referred to not only said that his mother had had no further attack of asthma: he added:

". . . but sometimes she seems more depressed and miserable than she used to be."

Such is the sad lot of increasing age, and such is often the ignorant interference of inexperienced youth! In making the advantage of her illness plain to her, in exposing the process to her conscious mind, I had robbed her of the facility of using this weapon, by which she had reinstated herself into the emotional life of her family.

Orthodox medicine would have aided and abetted the plot with its accompanying self-deceit. But perhaps we should remember that, however much she was the gainer thereby, her family certainly felt themselves to be losers. They were already complaining against the restrictions to their liberty which her illness involved.

Was this curing the patient, or was this curing the family and robbing the patient of her cure (asthma), which she had inadvertently found as a "cure" for her more grievous complaint?

What should the physican do?

He should certainly not make such a deep interpretation at a first interview, thereby robbing the patient of an adjustment (or necessary symptom) without at the same time being in a position to offer her any compensatory satisfaction in place of it.

This case-history is given to enable me to point out and to correct a misconception.

I have made it short and understandable by limiting myself to the *epinosic gain* in the illness. Epinosic gain (the secondary gain achieved by an illness) can be at the most only a precipitating, exacerbating, or maintaining factor, while the real causes reside much deeper in the psyche of the invalid.

These are infinitely more difficult to understand by those who are not acquainted with the ways of the unconscious mind and its conflicts.

The truth about this case is that the patient had a hysterical disposition. This is the foundation upon which her illness was built. The *form* it took may have been partly determined by the immediate circumstances: the husband's and family's alarm at the shortness of breath which accompanied her hysterical attack. This concern of her family, contrasting so favourably with their previous neglect, no doubt acted also as a precipitating factor.

But already, before this precipitation (the outbreak of the illness), she had accumulated within herself the most uncomfortable and intolerable tensions. These tensions were failing to obtain their normal relief by a satisfactory love life, such as she had enjoyed in the many years of health and happiness, before her husband and family began to neglect her.

In other words, she was uncomfortable, distressed, and unhappy, not only because she had emotionally lost her husband and family, but because she had in her disposition a very strong need to possess them emotionally. Had she been adequately treated by analysis, it might have been revealed that she had an unduly strong possessive instinct.

Possibly in her infancy she had held on to pleasure with her mouth; she now had a strong need to hold on to her husband and family.

Failing to do this, her frustrated passion reverted to an auto-erotic level, and she *held* her breath.

The fact that this seemingly restored an objective love situation temporarily relieved the distress. Once the ties with which she bound her family were broken, the distress was confined within her psyche, whether it were manifested by hysterical attacks or not.

The asthma brought back the family, and thereby bettered her condition." As the doctor in this case, I made it more difficult for her to produce this manœuvre, which was only possible through self-deception. Thereby I robbed her of her weapon, without giving her any satisfactory compensation. She was left more or less alone to endure her intra-psychic tensions, and the frustrations of her emotional life. Therefore she was rendered more depressed and miserable than she had been with the asthma.

Her family were relatively freed to pursue their own lives. But perhaps this respite was at the most, only temporary, for a personality strong enough to produce so dramatic a weapon as asthma would not for long be at a loss to find other means to gratify the distressing need. And she will be careful to take her next hysterical symptom to a doctor who, if not more blind to its psychopathology, will at least be tactful enough to pretend to such blindness.

The fight for the gratification of one's needs, particularly one's unconscious needs, is indeed the fight for life itself.

# THE MAN I DID NOT PSYCHO-ANALYSE

A MAN of fifty staggers into my consulting room early one morning and demands to see me. The previous night he had taken a large dose of sedative with the object of never waking again. Now he was frightened at what he had tried to do, and he was feeling very ill.

The story which this man told me is in vivid contrast to what I hear from the majority of nervous patients. He had led an extraordinarily full, vigorous, and courageous life.

Born in Scotland, he had found himself alone in America at the age of sixteen, and had seized life with both hands.

"How did you come to be in America at sixteen?"

"Like this: my mother, a widow, owned a large butcher's shop in Glasgow. I had been out all day with a horse and van in a driving rain and sleet storm. I finished my round soaking wet. As I got in my mother said, 'This order has to go to the Golf Club' (three miles away). I said I would saddle the mare. She said, 'You will take it now, and walk it.' I did.

"It was a fifty-pound load. When I got to the place, still in the rain and sleet storm, they found it was not their order. She had given me the wrong basket. Half-way back with the load I met the boy who had been sent after me with the right order. I wanted him to take it on and deliver it. But no: he said he had instructions from my mother to change baskets with me, and that I was to deliver it myself.

"When I got back at last, I walked straight into the shop. The place was full of customers. Mother was in the cash desk. I strode over to her in my dripping clothes and said: 'Check my money.' She said, 'I will see you in a minute.' I said, 'You will see me now.' Perhaps I shouted it. Anyhow, all noise stopped. You could have heard a pin drop. She checked my money at once. I said, 'Now you can give me £20.' She threw over twenty sovereigns, and told me to get out. I did. And I sailed for the States within a week."

I have told this story to emphasize the man's character. There are no nervous self-suppressions or mother-fixations about him. He could tolerate a considerable amount of discipline and hard knocks. But when he reached the limit of his endurance he did not curl up and die. He turned upon his oppressors and forged a new life for himself.

The story of his American adventures is equally characteristic and vigorous. This go-ahead people stimulated him to even greater go-aheadedness. He out-Americanized the Americans.

So well did he work for his employer, a wholesale butcher, that when he wanted to start up a business of his own he found people eager to lend him the necessary capital.

He chose a restaurant in a suburb of Boston, a restaurant which had had five successive proprietors and had failed five successive times. Therefore it was going cheap. He was strongly advised against it. The disadvantage was that it was suburban. Nevertheless, within twelve months Boston came out to the suburb to lunch and dine at his restaurant.

Putting his heart and soul into the work, he neglected no detail— not even the psychology of his employees. They worked as a team: results were excellent.

Eighteen months later a large building opposite was in the process of completion, and the builders offered it to him for the obviously necessary extension of his business. This gave him an opportunity to have kitchens, storehouses, etc., built exactly according to his own requirements. They were models for every *restaurateur* to see.

Before long he was feeding over fifteen hundred people at each meal. An exciting quantity of capital was accumulating.

This was his real mission in life. Previously, more by misadventure than design, he had married, produced a family, lost interest, and embraced the excitement of hard work and good business.

The wife in whom he had lost emotional interest became a useful helpmate in his business endeavours.

Then everything disappeared with the Wall Street crash, including half a million dollars!

He started again in Australia. He provided for the wife and family left in America, and then forgot them. She divorced him.

Back in Scotland, rather alone and still in the thirties, out of sheer loneliness he became linked to a companion of his infancy, now a widow. It was natural to marry her and live in her house.

In London he became the manager for the proprietors of a new business venture. All went well for some time. He had no say in the direction of the company. It was his duty merely to expand it, and this he did with phenomenal success. But troubles accumulated. The directors' way of business was not his way. There were methods of debt evasion and of dividend payment, the object of which was to create a profitable muddle.

My patient had to deal with this muddle, and yet avoid clearing it up. He did not enjoy his business rôle. Making excuses for the inexcusable conduct of the directors did not suit his psychological make-up.

He endured it for some time. What broke him was something quite different.

His wife had now reached the age of forty-eight, and insidiously her attitude towards him underwent a curious change. She exerted an unfamiliar supervision over all his actions and revealed suspicion of any unaccounted half-hour.

He said to me: "I was in harness all the time. I was unable to think my own thoughts or to lead my own life in the slightest particular. Added to this I felt the business was not making further headway. Everything seemed to be frustrated.

"But, doctor, the chief trouble was that my wife was directing the traffic all the time. Everything I did, or did not do, was subjected to the closest cross-examination, and there was a continuous process of nagging going on. It was as though I were under constant suspicion. I had to account for my minutest act or thought.

"This state of affairs was new to me. It only began about eighteen months ago. The effects of it were very curious. I do not know quite how to describe them.

"I am a one-woman man, doctor. While I have one woman, I don't look at any other. I could not live with my wife and be unfaithful to her in the slightest degree. But this incessant nagging and suspicion of hers, which began eighteen months ago, resulted in my feeling a certain revulsion towards her. In consequence I have had no sexual inclination towards her, and have experienced instead only an increasing degree of irritability.

"She would question and cross-examine and argue. I must confess one day I almost lost my control. I seized her by the throat, and might have strangled her. What I did was to push her out of the room and slam the door. I had to have some peace.

"No doubt she was surprised, but it did not cure her. The next day she was nagging again as usual. Somehow or other the feeling grew upon me that I had reached the end of my life.

"What was the good of it all? Nothing was being achieved. I was just in harness, day and night. I was not used to this sort of thing. It was not me or my life. And then a funny thing happened.

"I was walking down Westbourne Grove one afternoon, when I felt a strange feeling as if I were walking high up in the air. I remember nothing more. It was two days later that I recovered consciousness in a hospital.

"With reference to this experience, I heard a doctor say that there was only one disease that could account for it. Accordingly, I was subjected to all sorts of tests and examinations. They even took the fluid—I believe they call it cerebro-spinal fluid—from my spinal cord and had it tested at a laboratory.

"They had to admit to me that all their tests were negative. Nevertheless, they wished me to remain in the hospital for some months.

"I packed up and went home.

"I have struggled along as before ever since. The same muddle at business; the same nagging, suspicions, and cross-examinations at home. This is not the life for me. Bursts of irritability! Fancy me coming to that! I thought, what was the use of it all? Getting drunk occasionally was no solution.

"Suddenly I decided to end it. This reminds me of my sudden decision at sixteen to chuck up my mother's service and to go to America: only this time I was going to Kingdom Come.

"Well, you know the rest, doctor. Here I am. I never thought that I would come to this. Lying on a doctor's settee in Harley Street! Anyhow, I feel much better for having told you all about it. If you will let me, I should like to go on coming here and talking to you until I feel really ready to start again."

For several weeks he came daily. I said little or nothing, but I was intensely interested in what his mind was doing, in his reminiscences, and in watching his energy, after a few weeks of rest, mobilizing itself and taking new shape.

Lately he has decided, of his own accord, not to go back to the firm whose technique was business muddle. He has decided to open a new business entirely on his own. It is not long since he said to me, "I feel very peaceful, as though I am still on a long recuperative holiday." But suddenly he announced:

"I have given myself a test, doctor. Yesterday after I left you I went home and drew up the order forms and the prospectus in full detail of the new business. I worked from noon to midnight, and hardly noticed my meals. I could give you the figures of expenditure, income and profits. The new business will make a return of 300 per cent. I know that I can successfully canvass 500 clients within two square miles of this area."

I have told this story in the man's own words so that the reader may appreciate how easy it is to be influenced by the patient's inordinate enthusiasms and perhaps hoodwinked by his excessive optimism. The sympathetic psychologist will be tempted to accept everything that his patient has said at his own valuation, and to argue his case as follows:

"This man is fifty years of age. His psychological patterns are well formed. They are strong and practical, and, what is more, they have been tested in the hard school of real life. He has succeeded before, and left to himself, with the courage which he clearly possesses to rely upon himself, he will succeed again.

All he requires is an understanding and sympathetic listener to help him to mobilize his energy, and thereby to encourage him to regain his self-reliance. If by my passive receptivity I can fulfil that rôle, I shall have done him inestimable service.

His present wife, who may to some extent have unknowingly served this function, has of late failed him owing to her own psychological changes. It seems likely that the change of life has precipitated a latent streak of suspicions or semi-delusions, which is expressed in the form of cross-examinations and naggings, which have reacted upon him.

At so early an age as sixteen his character was sufficiently well formed to make him intolerant of oppression. He had the vigour of a leader, and that made him unsuitable for the rôle of being badly led.

Frustration to him was the equivalent of death. He would have none of living another's life, which meant the precluding of living his own life, and unless he could break free from frustration and live he was psychologically as good as dead. It was on this account that he broke from his oppressive mother at the age of sixteen and proved that he could live his own life.

Instead of rising to greater and grander climaxes he had recently found his tendency of progressive living frustrated both in his business strivings and, more fundamentally, in his private and sexual life.

Psychologically, to him this was death indeed. The first reaction was a pure psychological blackout—the incident of fugue (memory-blank) which occurred eighteen months ago. The second was a conscious co-operation in this psychological reaction to insurmountable frustration, namely, the suicide attempt.

Talking the whole matter over calmly and understandingly has enabled him to see that the frustration is not insurmountable. He has the same vigour which he had at sixteen, with the addition of much experience behind it. Without so much as a hint or suggestion from me he is proposing to start again, perhaps in a bigger and better way, as befits his greater maturity.

This will again mean life for him—LIFE in capital letters, which is the only sort of life he knows.

I do not want to break down these excellent psychological patterns.

They have been formed in a manner which is well adapted to reality. The analysis and breaking down of them would hardly enable him to form a better adjustment. It is quite possible that, were he analysed, he would find a more natural or primitive relief for his mental tensions.

His irritability would go in favour of more satisfactory and pleasurable outlets. But it would not be helpful to him to get him to make such adjustments at the age of fifty, when he is evidently so formed that he can obtain equivalent excitements and reliefs in the sublimated form of business adventure and success.

He already has prospects of success along these lines, which in the circumstances are the best possible for him and for society."

Unfortunately this is not the whole story from a scientific point of view. It is natural and usual for a patient to blame the external world for the changes that have their real source in the unseen world within the deeper levels of his own unconscious psyche.

The psychologist must maintain his power of impartial judgment, and there are some points in this case which call for deeper reflection.

A man who attempts to strangle his wife and to commit suicide is not admirably well balanced. The business successes he obtained may have been due more to luck and energy than to capacity for judgment. Be this as it may, we must reflect why there should be these enthusiasms and successes interspersed with these mental storms and suicidal depressions. The conclusion forced upon us is that this patient is an example of the cyclothymic temperament, bordering upon, if not actually identical with, the mental illness called manic-depressive psychosis.

The problem arises: should one analyse such a case? The correct answer cannot be given by theoretic considerations alone. The individual, rather than the case as such, has to be considered on his own psychological merits. It is well known to psycho-analysts that cases of manic-depressive psychosis *can* be successfully analysed during the interim period, if one is prepared to continue for an indefinite length of time. This may not always be practicable, for financial as well as psychological reasons. Both were important in this case. We may decide not to analyse him: we may decide that an adequate course of psycho-analysis would be impracticable and that various risks attendant upon the attempt may well prove too costly both to patient and to analyst. In the meantime he is continuing to attend and to express his thoughts with increasing freedom. It may be borne home to us that however much we may refrain from interpreting, from revealing to him the content of his unconscious mind, nevertheless he is, whether we wish it or not, progressing along the initial stages of analysis. Indeed, we may recognize that, having regard to the strength and resistances of his ego defences, this is the best or the only way to introduce him to the deeper stages of the process.

What, then, can we do to forestall the natural and inevitable progress of analysis? Apart from refusing to interpret there is one thing we can do. As his thoughts flow more freely, as his libido or vital energy becomes released from repression, every patient owing to resistances to analysis shows signs of diverting this energy away from analysis into the activities of so-called real life. It is usually the function of the analyst to analyse these resistances and to forestall or circumvent such tendencies, knowing that otherwise analysis will come to a premature termination.

Now, if we decide not to analyse such a case we can adopt the reverse process. We can refrain from analysing the resistances to analysis, and at the same time encourage such tendencies to the development of external interests which the patient reveals.

This was the procedure adopted in this particular case.

## "MARY, MARY, QUITE CONTRARY, *WHAT* DOES YOUR GARDEN GROW?"

THE third case of this series has to do with the problem of the bachelor lady of thirty odd years. It is a problem that exists in every office, in every profession, and in every walk of life.

This example will show us that with the very best intentions in the world, with the most careful planning of our children's lives, we can by dint of succeeding *too* well bring about a condition of illness—a condition that undermines the edifice we had planned.

This is because we plan as idealists, or as lunatics, who turn away from a recognition of material realities. This is because "our very best intentions" leave out of account the nature of the soil upon which we are building; we build our castles, if not exactly in the air, with very little consideration of their foundations.

In short, this is a case where concentration of attention upon the spiritual, ethical, and intellectual ideals has resulted in the biological laws underlying the existence of a living organism, being overlooked.

If a conventional, or even a psychological problem has thereby been solved, a medical problem has certainly been created. And that is more fundamental.

The case is that of a young woman in the early thirties, a school teacher, who presents herself for treatment because she discovers that her *"mind is refusing to function."*

She says:

"I'm becoming more and more *stupid* as the years go by. At the same time my *interest* in things grows less and less. At present I am not interested in anything at all.

"You may think it is due to overwork. Doctors are apt to think that. But I know it is not. If it were due to overwork it would have come on ten years ago when I took a very difficult scholarship at Oxford. Actually, it has come on since I *stopped* overworking—years after. Lately, it has reached such a pitch that I cannot even do my routine class work properly.

"I wonder if I'm at the beginning of a nervous breakdown? Or is it just that I don't like my job?"

"How does the trouble show itself?"

"Chiefly by stupidity. As though my brain won't function—or

won't function fast enough. It gets too slow or gets held up altogether."

"For instance?"

"When I'm teaching the girls, I keep making mistakes or forgetting things I ought to know. But even apart from such disgraceful revelations I commonly feel a girl is thinking faster than I can. She gets the result before I do and there she stands, naturally thinking how stupid I am.

"I find myself in a ridiculous position, as though the class had turned the tables on me when I should be *their* teacher. They will get a contempt for me and all discipline will break down if I go on like this.

"I sometimes think they're laughing at me. Also I seem to have no interest in the work—so how can I expect to get them interested? Should I give it up? Resign?

"I've changed my school twice in the last two years as I thought it was the particular school that didn't suit me. I've been teaching for several years now and I don't know how to do anything else. Is it perhaps that I don't like teaching?"

"What would you like to do?"

"There's nothing else I can do. I haven't been trained to do anything else. And what a training I have had! The best schools, the best tuition, Oxford and good degrees, and then the special training college.

"My father is a poor missionary. To think of the money he could ill afford! He has spared nothing to get me to my present position. I ought to be very grateful. And so I am.

"But am I? If I speak the truth I must confess that my present life does not seem to suit me. Nor does it satisfy me. And it is worse than discontent. It is inefficiency, incompetency, incapability.

"After all my father's planning, after all our successes, I am nothing but a miserable failure. I can't take an interest in anything. I can't enjoy life, *I can't even teach.*"

"Apart from all practical considerations, what would you like to do—I mean in the realms of phantasy?"

"If I could do my work well I would be satisfied. If I could find something—anything—that I could do really well, I should be satisfied. If I could find something that I *liked* doing I should be satisfied."

"What would you like doing?"

"*I've often thought I'd like to do gardening. I'm fond of gardening. If only I could get it to do as a job! I'd like a garden of all kinds—vegetables, fruit trees, and of course the flower part, too. I'd like to do everything myself, but I suppose I'd have to get a man to do the digging.*"

"Whose garden would it be?"

"Of course, it's nicer to have your own garden and look after that. But that's impracticable. So I've usually thought of myself as employed in somebody else's garden—somebody who was away all the time. So that I could arrange everything just as I'd like it.

"But I have thought practically about it, too. I've thought that if I stick to my job and save money, by the time I am fifty-four I may be able to retire. And *then* I shall certainly have my own garden."

(Even if the reader is slow to grasp the symbolism of these ideas perhaps the pathos of the situation will not escape him.)

"Heaven at last?"

"Yes. I suppose I might as well work a bit longer and wait for the real heaven. That's what my father is doing and that's what he'd have me do. Only my faith can't be so strong or so satisfying as his."

"He had you as well."

Here our patient paused for a moment and stared at me, then continued, "*I* have got my father and a certain obligation to him after all he has spent on me.

"If my father died I'd throw up my work to-morrow. I suppose it's a very wicked thought, but do you know, I'd feel *released*. Then at last I'd feel I could do as *I* liked. I wouldn't mind being a housemaid . . . if it were not for father."

Pause.

"In seeking for an alternative to teaching I have thought of a more practical occupation than gardening. With my savings I'd take a six months' course in domestic science. Then I would try to get employment as a housekeeper. Next to gardening I would like best to look after a house."

"Whose house?"

"Oh, perhaps some married couple who were out all the time and left everything to me."

She becomes silent for several minutes. I do not speak  Finally, she continues:

"I suppose you are thinking that it ought to be *my* house. That I ought to get married. That may be. But men were never attracted to me. I suppose I never set out to attract people. I never went in for pretty dresses or parties—social life. Father thought it was more important for me to get on with my studies.

"I was always a 'bluestocking.' If I stop teaching I must get a job. I can't just go out and by a miracle marry a man and become entitled to a home of my own."

C

Pause.

"I could of course put my head in a gas oven. But there's no point in committing suicide unless you are absolutely certain that you won't be in a worse position *after* it. You might be in just as great or even greater torment—only I suppose you'd find yourself without a *body*. That wouldn't be any improvement, would it?"

"So you have found."

"What do you mean?"

"What have you put in the gas oven?"

"Oh! I suppose you mean I've tried to do away with my body. Perhaps I have. Anyhow no one wanted it! My life and my future were properly mapped out. My father meant me to get the most out of our circumstances. I had to attain to the highest ideals . . . and I suppose to reap my reward in heaven.

"I certainly was not supposed to snatch at the lower orders of pleasure, happiness or even relaxation and day-dreaming. These were not only left out but the door was loudly slammed against them."

"Was it the oven door?"

"Yes. You mean I've already performed my suicide act? I've put my body in that gas oven and all that remains outside and alive is my mind? But in that case what is it that keeps interfering with the workings of my mind?"

"What do you think it is?"

"Perhaps it's the wretched body tending to resurrect. . . . Secretly trying to get up from the tomb or gas oven?"

"You did suggest that your suicide was not successful, and only made the situation worse."

"Yes. I can remember that when father warned me against day-dreaming I continued to have one persistent day-dream. It was a dream of having a house and garden of my own . . . and I'd have dogs and cats . . . and a flock of Aylesbury ducks!"

Does one need to be a poet or a medical psychologist to interpret the symbolism unconsciously used by this patient?

Poets have always associated love with a garden, from the time when the first lovers were expelled from their garden of Eden into the harsh, uncomfortable world. And this is a garden in which our patient would grow things—useful things as well as pretty, fruit trees as well as flowers. And naïvely if reluctantly she adds, "But I suppose I'd have to get a man to do the spade-work"—before the garden yielded up its fruit!

Whatever incredulity the reader may have about the value of symbols, the medical psychologist with his experience has no doubt

of their value as the cypher in which the patient clearly expresses to him (if not to herself) the contents of her unconscious mind.

If a young woman says to me "I'd like to get married and have babies," I might doubt the veracity of her statement. She might be boasting. She might be compensating for inferiority feelings by claiming a maturity which she does not possess. But if under analytical conditions of free association she says, "I'd like to have a garden and grow living things in it (fruit trees and flowers)," then I have no doubt that she would like to get married and have babies.

Similarly, a "house" is the symbol for a body, particularly a female body. "To be a housekeeper and look after a house" in addition to its obvious conscious implications, reveals an unconscious desire to turn her attention to her own physical person—to let her body come into its own.

The dogs and cats and Aylesbury ducks that she would keep are the living things, living and life-giving emotions, materialized into the physical realities for which the maternal instinct in her is craving.

Such interpretations are, however, unnecessary in her case, for she gradually comes to them herself. "I suppose you're thinking (i.e. she is thinking) that I ought to get married."

Three questions present themselves in connection with this case:

1. Why does she not marry?

2. Will such knowledge as she will learn from her analysis make her worse instead of better?

3. What practical lesson can be learnt from it all?

As the answers are all very closely related, I do not propose to draw a hard-and-fast line between them. It is not unusual for a person, particularly if being trained for an academic life, to be educated away from the primitive instinct pleasures and away from sexuality. But that in itself does not usually succeed in an asphyxiation of the biological drive which is an integral part of life itself. However much emphasis is laid on man's artificial cultural values it does not usually result in ruling out nature's primitive pleasure values.

In extracting the golden eggs of culture we do not usually destroy the goose of reproductive life that lays them—though it must be admitted that we occasionally maim her.

It requires a process deeper than ordinary education or training to effect serious injuries at a deeper level. It requires emotions and instincts such as those of fear to curtail seriously the healthy working of other instincts.

Admittedly, these can be *affected* by external influences. Mothers are commonly to blame for the non-marriage of their sons and

fathers are commonly to blame for the non-marriage of their daughters.

I am using the word "blame" rather loosely, for psychology does not *blame* anyone; it recognizes that a person's acts, like the acts of any organism or *organ*, are predetermined by heredity, development, and environment. From a scientific point of view it would be as inappropriate to "blame" the human race for propagating its species.

In general the inherited instinct survives all efforts to suppress it, whether by parents or by training; it can only be slightly influenced or guided. It is as natural for the parent to cling to her child—to keep him at the breast, as it were, as it is for the child's developing maturity to cause him to break away and find a mate.

But parents *can* cling too tightly—usually through the absence of a more appropriate love attachment—as for instance in the case of a widower. Also, with or without the operation of this parent-influence, fear of sexuality may be aroused in the developing mind to such an extent that it occasions a flight from passion and an undue repression of all such elements.

That such a fear existed in the unconscious mind of our patient was revealed in her deeper analysis. She had a dream in which it was shown that passion was identified with an air raid, the explosion of bombs and the blowing to pieces of her body. The school children had to be evacuated to safety. The "children" symbolized the primitive or sexual elements in her composition, and they had to be removed to a place of safety—or repressed.

When the origin of all these fears is laid bare and their development revealed to her, she will be in a position to abandon this particular mode of dealing with her instincts. In any case, it has failed as a "cure," for these unconscious elements keep resurrecting, endeavouring to push up into her consciousness, sufficiently to interfere with her "will to teach."

Eventually, she may be in a position to tolerate courtship. She may even decide to put herself in the way of it. For she is still in no way unattractive and is also a most worthy and able person whom any man would be fortunate to have as a partner.

But what if this good luck does not come her way? Must she throughout life be the victim of a conflict between nature's urge and society's convention? There are those who go farther and insist that if she solve this problem in the conventional way, namely, by marriage, they will no longer permit her to teach. May she then remain a teacher only so long as she is not mentally well enough to teach?

There are some who think such a situation calls for an alteration in our social conventions. Well, so do war and other forms of death, poverty, dissatisfaction, and a thousand and one things upon which the stupidity of man insists.

Nature has always been cruel to her failures. Her penalty for failure is the death penalty—extermination. The generation just before the extermination may feel the process in the form of a death agony of their instinct-life instead of a gratification of it. Nature may maim before she kills.

To come back to our patient and the question of the effects of treatment upon her. It should be emphasized that illness is not the direct effect of circumstances but the result of an *inner* inability to utilize the circumstances around.

Persons may have all the advantages of a married life and yet be frigid and starved of emotional satisfaction and relief. On the other hand, if the inner emotional urges are not unduly repressed it takes an extraordinary amount of external hardship to create illness.

However, medical psychology does not rest upon a foundation of theories. On the contrary its theories, so far as they have been formulated, rest upon the factual observations of clinical experience. The fact here is that although her environment, her habits, and her continence have in no wise altered, this patient is already considerably improved. She is better adjusted, her symptoms are far less troublesome, and she is happier. Also she is justifiably more hopeful of the future.

If this patient, having been freed from her repressing fear, does not obtain her "man to dig the soil," nor her garden, house, or Aylesbury ducks, she will nevertheless be in a position (psychologically) to "adopt" her class of young children, instead of finding them uninteresting and uninterested.

A vital, healthful, stimulating, and gratifying situation will arise in whatever walk of life she finds herself. She has admitted, "Even if I could do my work *well*, I would be satisfied."

At worst the human children could and would produce in her as much satisfaction as the Aylesbury ducks.

---

*Postcript for Psychiatrists*

If the question arises as to whether this case has a schizophrenic element much as the preceding case had a foundation of manic-depressive psychosis, I would suggest the view that we are merely asking whether it took one or more generations of mental strain to *acquire* it, and that the incipient stages of such a process may consist of just such failures of adjustment as here portrayed.

## MEN WHO FEAR MARRIAGE

THE medical psychologist is frequently being consulted by men suffering from a state of acute anxiety on the eve of marriage. The cynic may laugh and say, "Well they may! They have every reason for their misgivings and anxieties."

My experience is that these "reasons" are merely excuses to hide irrational but deeper internal sources of the anxiety feelings. Such cases, at least those of them who consult a psychologist, have something fundamentally wrong with the instinct basis of the urge to marry. What they are fearing is whether they really have the need for this marriage or whether they will be able to utilize it when it does take place.

Unfortunately, they usually go the round of optimistic friends inside as well as outside the medical profession. These optimists think that all the hesitating bridegroom requires is a push forward. "You will be all right," they say, with a slap on the back. "Go on, do it. Take the plunge, be a man."

I remember one unfortunate victim of such advice. He told me that although he had felt very much of a man before, it disappeared with the engagement, and at the wedding he felt like "a lamb being led to the slaughter." He has never had the slightest manly feelings since. After two years of misery he and his wife parted.

The "slap-on-the-back" type of treatment can influence only the conscious mind. It cannot reach those unconscious levels in which are the *sources* of our behaviour—and of our symptoms.

The back-slappers, like others with too ready psychological advice, are prescribing appropriate treatment for *themselves*; they have given neither time nor attention to the unfortunate person seeking their advice. Their mental process is just a reaction to the thought of what would suit themselves in a similar predicament.

They treat the patient, not as though he is himself (for they do not know *him*) but as though he were themselves. They overlook that "what is one man's meat is another man's poison."

The hesitator, or sufferer, is in a state of inner *conflict*. Something deep down within him has caused him to feel that this marriage may be of no value to him, that he may not be able to use it; that it may be an empty and uncomfortable shell.

These subterranean feelings have broken through to the surface

sufficiently to cause upheavals in the well-concreted roads and buildings of the city of conscious and conventional living. They are powerful underground forces that so disturb the conscious levels. Yet our optimist comes along and flattens down the upheaval with his slap on the back and says—"See, now it's all right!"

But no city has yet been built which can hold down the volcanic pressure within the depths of the earth. The disaster is liable to come after marriage if held off before, unless adequate attention is paid to the sources of the disturbance, and unless the conflict is brought to the surface and dispelled.

The psychologist then, unlike other would-be advisers, must have no preconceived theory based upon his own psychology, but must be an unbiased observer and student of the troubled mind that has consulted him.

These cases of hesitancy and misgivings before marriage can be due to an infinite variety of causes. In all cases the real source of the anxiety is unconscious, however thoroughly the victim may attempt to pin this anxiety on to plausible realities. In addition, there are certain factors common to a large variety of cases. They are of very frequent occurrence, but it would be a mistake to regard them as essential or universal.

We shall see one such common factor in the case about to be described. We shall see also at least one of the curious ways in which it can exert its influence.

A young man comes to me because his mind is troubled. Curiously enough he at first says nothing about marriage. (How often do we encounter this attempt to ignore the relevant factors in a situation —even conscious ones!)

He complains of periodic fits of most utter black depression. He says he is completely "baffled" regarding his work, his prospects and the whole of his future life. For no reason that he can discover he has periodic feelings and thoughts of suicide.

I sit and wait for more enlightenment. Finally he can avoid it, or put it off, no longer. It comes out:

"It is all so utterly silly, doctor, for I ought to be the happiest man in the world. I am expecting to be married in four months' time."

When a man who is to be married in four months' time keeps thinking of suicide, what does it mean? He himself says—"I ought to be the happiest man in the world." In other words, marriage ought to stand for the liberation of something, the coming to life of something which has been suppressed—happiness.

But to him, if we read the language of his unconscious, it says the opposite—suicide, death. What is wrong here?

If, instead of finding out what is wrong, we optimistically encourage him blindly to take the plunge, we may find we have been reckoning without the unconscious.

The patient himself is apt to adopt these tactics. He says:

"On account of my increasing depression, my fiancée and I talked it over and decided to expedite the marriage. I went off to look for a suitable house. The result was the worst panic I have ever had.

"I recovered from that, laughed at myself and again tried to make arrangements for the marriage. The same thing happened. That was really the beginning of this nervous breakdown.

"We have now gone to the opposite extreme and put off the wedding pending my treatment with you, and I immediately feel better.

"It isn't as though I didn't love her. On the contrary. She is several years older than me, but I never had any use for very young women. I loved her almost as soon as I got to know her five years ago. She seemed to be a very superior type of person; too good for me. I was very happy in that love. Perhaps I would have been content to let that state of affairs continue unchanged.

"But I have always envied married people. I have always wanted a home of my own, a wife of my own, and a family of my own. Yet when I go to get it there is this panic and thoughts of suicide. What is the matter with me? I should not have thought I was so abnormal. I even enjoyed the long engagement period. I did not particularly want to alter it.

"Do most people when they fall in love marry when the passion is at its height and do their thinking afterwards? I never had much passion though I was genuinely in love. I seem to be doing nothing but think and think about it. It gets me nowhere.

"I was always a shy boy and I may be a little shy of my fiancée. When I am going to meet her I experience a curious succession of emotions. First there is a feeling of exhilaration and elation. Then, when I get near the place, this gives way to anxiety or even to panic. Her appearance may reassure me, but after I leave her there is this extraordinary fit of depression.

"I have always been particularly shy of women older than myself, yet these are the only women who have ever attracted me. Is it strange to be attracted to and shy of the same type of woman?"

No, it is not strange. On the contrary. *But it is a sign of conflict,* for attraction is a pleasant emotion and shyness may be very uncomfortable or unpleasant. To experience these two at the same time is, in some degree, a common experience. What young man has not blushed at the meeting of his loved one!

None of our patient's symptoms are very strange. He merely throws into a high light the common conflicts of which we are all the victims more or less. Every neurotic symptom, on deeper investigation, teaches us that we all have the seeds of it within our own constitution. It is only when it reaches some extreme degree of severity that it stands out uncovered. Our attention is focused upon it, and lo! we discover that it is everywhere, in all persons.

Perhaps the strangest thing about him is that his preference is for older women. Having had our attention arrested by this deviation from the norm, we may detect minor deviations in some of his other statements. Does the average bachelor envy married people? Does he want a home of his own, a wife and family?

Some, like our patient, may, but I do not think that it is usual for a male to want these things *in the abstract*.

It seems to me that something is missing, lacking or inadequate. Perhaps he wants these possessions to compensate himself for the feeling of something missing. He himself says, "I never had much passion though I was genuinely in love."

I strongly suspect that the envy is the infantile envy of the boy of his father, that the home he wants is the old home of his childhood, that the "wife" is the mother of his childhood and that the family, likewise, is a desired compensation for a feeling of inadequate virility.

Is our patient a little bit feminine? Has he, in addition, an over-strong mother-fixation?

He tells us. Listen to this:

"The first time I became engaged was when I was in the early twenties. I lived with mother and father and never saw any girls of my own social class. I helped at a Mission Hall and became very friendly with the lady who ran it. While my parents were abroad on a long holiday I fell in love with this lady and we became engaged. I was most excited and pleased with myself.

"I wrote to my people about it and they came rushing home. There was a nice fuss and bother; they kept dinning it into my head that she was nearly fifty years old. Her age had never occurred to me; I had never thought of it. Between my parents on the one hand and this woman on the other, it was a wonder I didn't have a nervous breakdown."

[*Note.—The reason he had no nervous breakdown at that time was because the commotion was in the real world, outside the mind. In the present instance a similar commotion is going on inside his mind.*]

"I was carted round to priests and clergymen and, finally, to a psychologist. He was the only one who did not attempt any advice or persuasion. I talked to him daily for some weeks and then, for no reason that I can properly understand, I broke off the engagement myself, although it nearly led to an action for breach of promise.

"I left the psychologist and, almost at once, I became engaged to a woman of my own age. Nobody seemed to mind that very much. In fact, that was about my own attitude also—I did not mind it very much. For some unknown reason I never felt we were absolutely *together*. I would prefer to go off and spend my summer vacation at the home of my elder sister (aged fifty) without the girl.

"That seemed to me perfectly natural. I enjoyed it better when I was on my own; I didn't feel so lighthearted when I was with the girl. I always treated her with great respect. I didn't mind being engaged to her until she and her parents tried to fix the day for the marriage.

"It seemed to me they wanted to rush it. I wanted to go slower. I kept putting it off. Then I found myself losing interest in her. I realized that she was alien to me and to my family. If I had to go and meet her I would get late, my feet and legs would be heavy. Finally, it somehow just 'frittered out.' That was many years ago.

"My position now is a very different one. My feelings towards my present fiancée are also very different. I am really in love with her. She is not so old as the first woman nor so young as the second, which suits me. What is all this fuss and panic about?

"There is no indifference when I am going to meet her; on the contrary there is elation. Why is this succeeded by anxiety and panic when I get to the meeting-place, and why is there this terrible depression afterwards?"

*The answers to these questions, like the answers to all neurotic symptoms and to all unaccountable behaviour, lie in the patient's unconscious mind and in his forgotten childhood and infancy.*

At the next session he says:

"I had a dream last night that a middle-aged woman was looking at me and I felt most uncomfortable. I had forgotten this dream, and, indeed, was unaware that I had dreamed at all until in some way the dream was repeated as a real experience on my way to see you.

"I was at the railway-station looking at the bookstall. I noticed a paper or two with pictures of a woman's figure. Then I glanced up and saw a middle-aged woman staring at me. I blushed crimson and could have sunk through the floor. Then I remembered that I had dreamed something like this last night."

It is interesting here to notice the relationship between unaccountable behaviour, symptoms, such as blushing, and dream material. All have their origin in the unconscious mind or in the forgotten past. Free association of thought released a flood of forgotten or half-forgotten memories. (I shall alter the sequence.)

"My mother and father did not get on well together. Something had gone wrong in their emotional relationship; they were cold to each other like me and my former fiancée. In consequence, mother turned more to me than to my father. I often asked her why she lived with him. *I* was her favourite.

"It was a very strict household. Mother thought I was better and nicer than all the other children in the district and did not like my mixing with them.

"However, as a very little boy I joined the 'gang' on the sly. We formed a 'secret circle' in which the staple talk was all about sex. When I got home I would feel all hot and bothered because I had been listening to prohibited things. Mother would say, 'Where have you been?' and I always answered, 'Nowhere!' I dare say I blushed then.

"Some time later I had got a girl member of this gang in our garden. She was older than me and we were trying some experiments together. We thought we were hidden in the bushes.

"Suddenly there was a sharp hammering on the window. I looked up and saw my mother's face, with a horrified expression on it, staring at me. I felt as though my inside would fall out. I felt like I felt in the dream of last night and like I felt when I saw the middle-aged woman at the bookstall staring at me.

"Mother said she would tell my father, and for days I was in fear and trembling—terrified. *I got the same sort of panic that I got when I am about to meet my fiancée.*

"It may be since then that I have been such a very good boy. I have always stuck to my mother. It is only comparatively recently that I have been attracted to any other woman. They are always older than myself. I have little or no passionate inclination towards them. But why should I get this horrible depression?"

The final answers to these questions take us deeper than we have ventured in this article. They take us to the infant's emotional relationship to his mother. Enough has been said to show us the direction of the relevant thoughts and memories. Those recorded are later emotional experiences, *screen memories*, which serve both to hide and reveal the earlier emotional patterns.

The psychopathology is, briefly, as follows: there is a strong emotional fixation to the mother-image. This image stands for two diametrically *opposite* emotional reactions. In the first place, she is all that is attractive and desirable. He has no interest in a woman unless she is older than himself. It should be noted, however, that this is *not* an essential element in mother-fixation. Even a young woman may symbolize the mother (or elder sister) image.

In the second place, this mother-image is the one that spells horror at all things sexual.

Feelings of elation, like sexuality, have their source in the unconscious. Thus we see this patient hurrying with alacrity and elation towards number one mother-image (his fiancée) only to discover as he approaches it, number two mother-image horrified at his elation or potential sexual purpose. It is again as though he were discovered at the prohibited act.

Elation gives place to anxiety. Sexuality is under the cloud of mother-image number two incorporated with mother-image number one in the person of his fiancée. Thus his love for an older woman can only be enjoyed under conditions of asexuality, at the expense of cutting off any potential virile inclinations.

He says, "I am not a passionate man." A marriage without virility may indeed be a failure. He has cause to feel depressed, though the cause does not belong to the conscious reasoning level of his mind. Where is that family going to come from, those children he envisages? His guilt-feelings before the mother-figure will not let him produce them. Guilt-feelings and impotence together cause extreme depression and lead to ideas of suicide.

It is the story of Œdipus all over again. Œdipus put out his eyes when he discovered that it was his mother with whom he had been consorting. Our patient was inclined to put out his sexuality, or even his life.

We all have an Œdipus complex. It is the severity of its domination over us that counts. Differences between tolerable health and ill health are, at bottom, differences of degree rather than of kind.

The more this conflict within him was brought into consciousness, the less this patient became the slave or victim of it.

Its hold over him grew less. He ceased to blush when middle-aged ladies looked at him. At a quite superficial stage he realized that if he did not marry his present fiancée, it was practically certain that he would never marry at all, and he did so want a home, a wife, and a family.

He presently came to realize that in choosing this lady he had effected a compromise between the very young woman, who did not attract, and the older mother-figure who could not bear him a family. He came to realize in a deeper sense (which is very different from knowing it consciously) that this woman was *not* his mother and automatic unconscious incest taboos eventually ceased to operate.

Occasionally a slight flavour of them crept into his marital relationship, for it is difficult to retain the mother-image that attracts in the person of his wife, and at the same time, to keep its Siamese twin, the mother-image that forbids, from occasionally creeping into the picture.

We all suffer, more or less, from difficulties similar to those of this patient. The details may be different and we may deal with them in very different ways.

For instance, we all know the man who, unlike this patient, instead of bringing his passionate life and his mother love to the same door, makes a division or cleavage between them. Such a man either lives with his mother and has his other life apart, or he may have a wife who is a mother-image, and find illicit attraction elsewhere.

The patterns of these and many other types of behaviour can be traced back to the earliest mother-relationships, though, admittedly, heredity factors may predispose.

Regarding neurosis on the eve of marriage; the above types of illness should not be confused with another common type of breakdown at this juncture of a man's life.

I refer to cases of so-called pure anxiety neurosis. These are young men who, unlike our patient, possess an abundance of passion and a relative intolerance of holding it without psychic injury.

A conflict is set up between their nature on the one hand and the material or reality plan. They have planned according to common sense. They have arranged to marry the year after next but in the meantime (their instincts never having heard of common sense) a conflict is set up.

Eventually a breaking-point may come with the breaking up of the sexual and nervous health. That which was formerly attractive or too attractive may become repellent. At the same time a crop of anxiety symptoms may arise.

Such cases are not of very special psychological interest, for they may have very little psychological content.

The case we have here discussed at some length in this article is of greater interest, not only because of its abundance of psychological content, but because similar mechanisms have their place in almost all conflicts in connection with an imminent marriage.

Moreover, we see here that a neurosis or a conflict having its source in the unconscious mind, may have far-reaching effects, not only upon the individual but also upon his rôle as a link in the biological chain. He may live free from illness and yet there is something wrong if he fails to perpetuate his kind, whether such failure be due to non-marriage, to failure in marriage, or to marriage to a mother-figure too old to bear him children.

I am pleased to say our patient was not such a one. He recovered from his nervous breakdown and got married. This was all several years ago and he is now the father of two children.

## CONVENTION AND PASSION

A WOMAN in the middle thirties is sent to me by a doctor on account of a phobia that she will harm people, stab them in the back. She complains also that, for some inexplicable reason, the word "leprosy" keeps recurring in her mind, causing her sensations of horror.

The patient's appearance is in sharp contrast with that of a number of nervous sufferers. She appears particularly smartly dressed, slim, and brisk in her movements. She has a penetrating eye and a gripping handshake. Obviously her nature is vigorous and passionate. Her conversation reveals that she has, in addition, a clear mind and a sharp intelligence. She almost radiates efficiency.

Therefore she is particularly distressed, if not indignant, that she of all people, should be tormented by the intrusion of these unwelcome, silly and horrible impulses, phobias, and that blood-curdling word "leprosy."

She says:

"I was perfectly well and happy, Doctor, until three years ago when I had an attack of influenza. During that illness, while I was feverish, I had several bad dreams. It was a few months after this that I developed a number of nervous symptoms, which in the course of several months settled down to these absurd impulses and fears, which have remained with me ever since, and against which all my efforts to fight and kill have proved unavailing.

"The first symptoms included extreme lassitude: I could hardly walk upstairs. I used to get palpitations of the heart and dreadful headaches at the back of my head. Insomnia followed: then more terrifying dreams. I would awake at night with a desire to scream. I thought I was going mad. I read something in a book about leprosy, and then I could not get that *word* out of my head.

"I had a terrifying dream:

"*I was going to Charing Cross Station in a taxi and passed a man with his hands out begging. He was headless, and I knew he had leprosy.*

"*Another dream I had was that my employer was staring at me with a strange look in his eyes, and I felt he was going to harm me.*

"This dream also has had a lasting effect, because now if he comes behind me I get an awful frightened feeling. It is absurd, but I cannot get rid of it.

"Then there was a third dream:

"*I dreamed he had his back to me, and he was bending over doing some-thing, and I stabbed him in the back.*

"The sequel to this dream has been my most persistent symptom. I shortly developed a sort of desire or impulse to stab him in the back, and, of course, an ever-present fear of doing so. I dare not even see a pair of scissors lying about at the office. It is most odd, as I am really *very* fond of this man.

"I have always had such a clear and efficient mind that it seems to me a most brutal tragedy that I should be afflicted with these symptoms, 'leprosy' and wanting to kill. A doctor that I saw years ago put it down to sex repression, but that is not true. Besides fear of going mad, I have had ideas of suicide.

"Now I have been sent to you as a last resort, but, to be candid, I have no faith in this psychological treatment. I believe it is all nonsense, but I have now had these symptoms for nearly three years, and something has got to be done about them."

Conscious of the fact that this is a vigorous and passionate nature, and recognizing a confirmation of this in the nature of her symptoms, I asked her the following pertinent question.

"Is there any satisfaction of your nature or impulses which you were enjoying three years ago, and which you have since been deprived of?"

She says:

"I don't think so. The only thing that happened three years ago was that I gave up my own flat and went to live with my father and stepmother.

"That reminds me that at first it was my father that I 'wanted' to stab. But it soon became my employer. In phantasy I have pictured myself killing him, stabbing him in the back with the bread knife. He was bending over, and I actually visualized myself raising my arm, bending over him, and stabbing him! This picture keeps recurring. Occasionally it gives place to the thought of suicide. Then I would picture myself looking in the glass and cutting my throat."

*Doctor:* "Have you any grievance against your father or your employer?"

"As a child I idolized my father until I came to realize that he made mother very unhappy. I thought that, indirectly, he might have been the cause of her early death. Then I hated him. But now the impulses are not about him, but about my employer, who has always been very good to me. I have been perfectly happy with this employer for the past fourteen years, until this trouble started three years ago. We have always been so much in tune with each other.

"He runs his own business, and says that its success is entirely due to me, my efficiency and the help I have been to him. Of course, I have helped him with every ounce of energy and ability I possess, for I have loved him ever since I was twenty-two.

"But that can't have anything to do with my illness, and I would rather not talk about it, if you don't mind."

Here I had again to explain to this patient that her part of the work was free association of thought, and no thoughts whatsoever which crossed her mind must be withheld from me. There must be nothing sacred or secret. Frankness and free expression of thought were essential to the success of the treatment.

She says:

"Oh, well, if you must have it, I will tell you. I didn't break his marriage up. It was already cold and dead before I met him. I was quite willing for his wife to divorce him, but she would not. She said: 'If you want to become his mistress, you stew in it.' This was years ago, when I was only twenty-two. I felt he was the only man I could love in my life. We have been very happy all these years, until the onset of this wretched illness."

At this point I found it necessary to repeat a former question.

"Is there any satisfaction that you were getting before three years ago, which has since been lost to you?"

She says:

"Well, of course, as I have told you, I had my own flat up to that time, and he could visit me freely and stay as long as he pleased. Since I have gone to live with my father and stepmother we naturally only meet at business, and there is not very much opportunity for love-making, nor is it so satisfactory. But I don't see what that has got to do with my symptoms, except that, as you have pointed out, there seems to be a time-coincidence. Now I am afraid of the future, afraid of losing my mind. It has been a good intelligent mind up to now. I am indignant that these impulses and phobias and this horrible word should keep intruding."

*Doctor:* "Perhaps you have always opposed your impulses and feelings very strongly."

"Well, I know I have always had strong feelings—strong feelings of repugnance towards nasty things; and I know I am capable of strong feelings of love. Love means sacrifice, caring for people. I have felt of this man on some occasions that I love him so much I could eat him."

**D**

*Doctor:* "And now perhaps you are saying: 'I love him so much I could stab him.' "

"Oh, no! That is nonsense!"

*Doctor:* "Unless it is that you are saying: 'I hate him so much I could stab him.' "

"I know I have had very strong hatreds for certain things, but I can't believe that I have ever hated him.

"I dislike animals. I can't bear them to touch me. I can't bear hair or furs. I had the idea once that leprosy was carried by furs, and I don't believe I have ever got over that idea. Certainly, I have never been able to wear furs. I can't handle them or touch them."

*Doctor:* "What else do you dislike handling?"

"Soil: worms: spiders. I have always been fussy about touching things that were not quite clean. The idea gives me a nasty feeling, a cold horror, and that word 'leprosy' comes to my mind. I could never stroke a kitten, and if an animal brushes against me I go hot and cold with fear, like I go hot and cold with fear at those thoughts I have had. Can it be connected with the fact that when I was very much younger I disliked anybody touching me, and I could never stand sentimental displays?

"I used to get a similar feeling of fear, a sort of cold horror, with one or two men I met in my youth up to the age of twenty-two. I think of a beastly type of man. I think of men who take advantage of you when they are dancing with you. If either of these men even touched my arm when he was dancing with me I would get a feeling of cold horror, like I get at the thought of 'leprosy.' One of these men also had a nasty habit of holding me too close, and he stroked my arm in a horribly suggestive way."

*Doctor:* "What would it suggest?"

"Oh, something nasty—intercourse, I suppose."

*Doctor:* "What does the curved back that you want to stab suggest to you?"

"A curved knife: the long curved packing needle that I once thought of stabbing my lover with. Oh, doctor, you make me think of most horrible things. I can't tell you what I thought of then.

"When I was about nineteen, I went to see a film about venereal disease. I was as white as a ghost after it. I felt everything was pretty dreadful. Dirt and sin and sex are all the same—like venereal disease, and now I come to think of it that is the feeling I get when I think of 'leprosy.'

"I was horrified at all such things, and I was very much 'don't-touch-me' at that time. And yet it was just about then that I was so much in love with this man that I gave way to him. My father had wanted me to marry somebody he thought suitable, but the thought nearly drove me mad. I couldn't have borne him—even to touch my elbow, and yet I willingly gave way to this man.

"He was already married. I don't think I really wanted intercourse, even with him. I don't think I should ever have wanted sexual intercourse on my own account. But I loved him so much I couldn't have refused him anything. I couldn't love him like that mentally without wanting to be kissed and fondled. I did like it when he first kissed me. But I didn't like the other part at first. I didn't see why he wanted to bring sex into it.

"Although I learnt sometimes to appreciate that too, even now more frequently than not my feelings are against it. But, of course, I still could not refuse him anything. It is often against my feelings, and yet it is my nature never to refuse him."

*Doctor:* "What association of thought do you get to these feelings?"

"The memory of those horrid men I have spoken about, who touched my arm suggestively. I remember now how I was forced at an early age to kiss my father against my inclination. I hated it."

*Doctor:* "So now at last we have the hate we were looking for. What association do you get to this?"

*Patient:* "The cold horror. The feeling I get when I think of 'leprosy.' That headless man in the dream. Some atrocity being committed. Dirtiness. Sexual intercourse. The impulse to stab. And the fear I have of it."

*Doctor:* "So your resistance to being touched, which was so evident in the dancing experiences before you were twenty-two, has not disappeared. It seems to be there still, in spite of your love of this man. While, on account of your love, you allow him to do what he pleases to you; you at the same time frequently retain your old revulsion, the feeling of cold horror, and the idea of 'leprosy,' which, it seems, is another name for venereal disease. Although you cooperate with him in doing violence to your resistance, it seems that your resistance returns with a vengeance after the act. And then you wish to stab him *or it* in the back."

### PSYCHOPATHOLOGY

It is, of course, impossible in a short paper to give all the material and free associations of thought which this patient produced in the course of the twelve sessions which led to the disappearance of her symptoms. Put briefly, the psychopathology of her condition may be described as follows:

Here is a woman gifted with a great deal of vitality, with an innate capacity for strong impulses, feelings and passions. It is fundamental in the nature of psychic economy that the energy of these must find some form of expression and relief. Normally such relief would be obtained largely in love, sexuality and orgasm. But in this case we observe that from quite an early age a considerable portion of this energy has gone over on to the other side, and taken shape as a strong resistance to such primitive modes of relief.

As a girl she is horrified when men hold her closely in dancing, or touch her arm "suggestively." Instead of feeling pleasure or strong tendencies to respond, she experiences a strong feeling of the opposite nature, namely a cold horror.

She has, it seems, already become frightened of what must be her own original nature—shall we say the tendency within her to original sin? She already feels that this would be disastrous, horrible, "leprosy." Thus, her secondary nature might be called highly conventional instead of highly passionate.

Nevertheless, the primary pattern obtains a limited degree of expression in her great love for her employer, which was strongly developed at the age of twenty-two. So much so that she allows him to do what he pleases with her. But when it comes to sexuality, her resistances to the primary pattern in this field are too strongly developed. They have gone over to the idea of, shall we say, "leprosy." We might say therefore that her love leads her into this sort of trap, and, psychologically speaking, she gets "leprosy" in the course of the intimacy. This she hates in the same way as she has grown to hate her own primitive passionate tendencies.

Hate means destruction. She therefore wishes to destroy that part of herself which would lead her to "leprosy," and, projecting this, she would naturally wish to destroy the instrument or person which inflicts it upon her.

If it is so bad to have her elbow touched "suggestively," how bad must it be to be touched, soiled, or damaged in this more intimate way! The energy responsible for her symptom would normally obtain its relief by the natural processes leading to orgasm. This normal path is frustrated by the resistances above mentioned. This energy, still undischarged, is the main dynamic contribution to symptom formations. The symptoms are compounded of the energy of these undischarged impulses together with the energy of the opposition against their discharge. This opposition was earlier seen in her horror of anything sexual, or even of being touched.

Similarly, at a more superficial plane, it will be remembered that the violence done to her resistances, and to her whole conventional nature, by reason of the love she had for this man, is not improved by the fact that she cannot conventionally justify her conduct by marriage, nor can she satisfy the more organized needs of her passionate nature by the production of children. In practice she has found that she cannot even go so far as to satisfy the less organized needs of her passionate nature by complete satisfaction or emotional relief. The energy of the resulting conflict has at last found its outlet in the form of the symptoms which interfered with her ego, and with her concept of herself. To maintain this concept, she has long tried to repress these conflicting forces. The method has proved unsuccessful, and her breakdown may be regarded as a return of the repressed.

Bringing all these matters to consciousness by means of her own free association of thought, she has succeeded in sorting them out, readjusting her mind to them, modifying her attitude towards the entire position in which she has placed herself, and, above all, in freeing her emotional life from the hampering inhibitions which deprived her of all normal relief of tension.

These symptoms have lost the very source of their energy, and have faded out of the picture of her life, almost, but not quite, as mysteriously as they entered it. This has detracted nothing from the vigour and efficiency which she puts into sublimated ego activities; on the contrary, it has freed these from the interference she so bitterly resented, and of which she almost angrily complained.

She no longer has a compulsion to stab her lover in the back. She no longer has a fear of him, of her own natural tendencies, nor of "leprosy." She is no longer violently resisting either her nature or him. On the contrary, the energy of these stabbing impulses is being expended in a normal relief of tension in association with him, rather than in a violent resistance against him or a stabbing of him.

The psychopathology of such impulses and phobias will be made clearer in the case which follows.

# KNIFE PHOBIA

THIS case of a knife phobia in a pleasant and apparently healthy young woman is here used to illustrate some of the fundamental mental processes which go to form the visible and manifest symptoms of a neurosis.

We all have our phobias more or less, whether they be of knives, of horses, snakes, insects, crowds, heights, train-journeys, thunder, disease, illness, blood, darkness, or mind-analysis. In all cases these phobias have similar origins and are due to similar mechanisms within the mind; therefore the careful study of one case will throw light upon every case. Even in this particular instance it will be shown that the patient was capable of changing the form of the phobia. There were times when she forgot knives and feared physical illness, appendicitis or mental breakdown, or even merely the death of a friend.

There is a popular tendency to concentrate attention upon what is visible in a malady—namely the symptoms.

Deeper study teaches us that these, though of popular interest and, of course, of some scientific interest, should not be over-stressed. Symptoms are only the form which the illness takes. They are not the essence of the illness.

If our attention is, like that of the patient, limited to them, we are liable to miss an understanding of the situation.

The essence is the *source* from which the symptoms spring and the mental mechanisms whereby they reach the form in which they present themselves.

The source is always instinct—dynamically striving towards relief of tension. And this source, at least as a source of the symptoms of which the patient complains, is unconscious.

Thus we get to the important concept of the *unconscious mind*—perhaps the most important concept for medical pyschology.

Some portions of the mind are opposed to certain unwelcome ideas and emotions breaking through into consciousness. In this way we obtain the concept of *resistance*.

Resistance can take many forms, and we may detect at least one of its forms in operation during almost any session with a patient. Resistance leads to a *repression* of unwelcome ideas or feelings so that they can live only in the deeper or unconscious levels of the mind, unknown to consciousness, unless they break through to form symptoms.

This process of something trying to rise to consciousness, and being opposed or resisted, is called *conflict*.

There can be conflict between one instinct and another, as well as between emotions and ideas on the one hand and conscience or consciousness on the other. Conflict is perhaps one of the most important concepts for the explanation of psychological illness.

Conflict, or resistance to certain ideas reaching consciousness, commonly leads to what is called in psychology—*displacement of affect*. That is to say, the emotion which is wrapped up with the idea and which is the dynamic part of the idea—the only part that matters to the instincts—breaks through in spite of the opposition while, at the same time, the idea to which it originally belonged is successfully repressed into the unconscious.

When an affect, or emotion, such as excitement or fear, breaks through, there seems to be a tendency in the mind immediately to unite it with any idea which presents itself or which it can, as it were, lay its hands on.

If there is a free floating fear within the mind, any sudden happening may provide an idea to which the fear can become attached. A car back-firing may easily suggest gunfire and invasion of the country by enemy forces.

Any case of phobia provides opportunity to illustrate this important mechanism of displacement of affect and how psychological symptoms arise.

Unfortunately, the reader may in some cases discover that he is himself inclined to resist certain types of emotional material. These may be merely instances of the same familiar process at work.

It is natural for us all to hate the unconscious; otherwise, perhaps, it would not be unconscious. Some people deal with this resistance by pretending that there is no such thing as the unconscious. We are familiar with this phenomenon at certain stages of the analytical treatment of patients.

In analysis, the psychologist endeavours to *learn* from, and not to teach the patient, unless it be to teach him courage to think and speak freely.

Therefore, in the paper we shall begin by observing the patient and by listening to what she has to say. We will then consider what we can learn from her words and from her behaviour.

This case concerns a simple neurosis in a very simple young woman.

She is a publican's wife, aged twenty-five, married a few years, no children. She herself was an only child (*and still is*).

Her appearance is that of a very normal person. She is neatly dressed, clean and healthy; she is plump, jolly, and vivacious. She laughs a great deal, and sings—even in the analytical hour. Her complaint is a fear of knives.

She says: "People don't believe that I suffer from my nerves; they laugh at me because I am fat and well. I seem to thrive on it. I do not know how it started.

"It may be that I read about somebody who had a fear of razors, and then I got this fear of knives (fear of self-injury). . . . I don't suppose I should really (cut herself) . . . it's the feeling. The feeling is something terrible. I keep on imagining how it would feel if I cut myself."

"How would it feel?"

"The feeling is like a wave going all over me, up my inside—a sort of wave comes up. All my body will get stiff and paralysed with fear. My face gets set, my legs tremble a bit. I feel sick all over. It comes up even into my mouth, and I gulp. Even seeing a sharp blade may make me come over like this.

"I don't understand why I suffer from this idiotic feeling—why I am so afraid of knives. It is all so silly."

I would like to pause here to point out that there are certain things of which the patient is very much aware, and certain things of which she claims to be totally ignorant. She says she is conscious of these extraordinary feelings and also of certain ideas—knives; but she does not know why. That is to say, she does not know the source of these feelings and ideas.

It is reasonable to assume that the source of these feelings and ideas is within her mind—and yet she does not know it. She is *unconscious* of the source of these feelings and ideas. Hence, from this alone, we may postulate the existence of an unconscious level of the mind.

We now ask *why* the source of these feelings is, and remains, unconscious. Possibly we may find the answer in some of the following material:

"I used to get terribly excited about things when I was a little girl. I believe I was only four or five when I fell in love with a boy and wished I were older.

"Later, before I was ten, I had a repulsion against all men. I used to say, 'No! I am going to marry daddy.'

"My first real love affair was when I was fifteen years old, and it was soon after that that I began to get nerves and dreadful feelings.

I fell in love with a boy of sixteen. It lasted eighteen months, then we quarrelled.

"I would not let anyone know how much I wanted to make it up—I was too proud. I used to pretend it didn't matter to me, but I used to think and dream of him all night, and long to make it up.

"It was nine months later, when I was sitting at a ledger, I began to get these feelings for the first time. The other girls didn't realize it was because I was depressed on account of this distress.

"I know it was all about that time because, when soon after I went out with another young man, I immediately developed a fear of assault by him. I became afraid to turn up and afraid not to turn up. I think he was really quite harmless; it was just my feeling. Since then I have been getting worse."

She proceeds to talk about her present "love affair"—her husband.

"He is all right, you know, doctor. A dry old stick—most reliable. Perhaps I shouldn't have married a man so much older than myself. I wouldn't be without him for anything. He is like a father to me. I never did really *love* him. (Oh, aren't I wicked!) The fact is I have been worse ever since I got married.

"Do you know what the trouble is, doctor? It's this—that I don't thrill with my husband. He doesn't thrill me. He is not at all romantic. I have never been passionately fond of him, never thrilled with him. I am bored to death there. *It seems that I get all my emotional kick when I think of a knife or a sharp blade.*"

These remarks did not seem to impress her very much at the time when she made them. But three days later she came to me with great news. She had discovered that there was some relationship between the absence of excitement with her husband and the presence of excitement in connection with knives.

She had been so struck with this discovery that she had not been able to wait for the next session with me but had hastened to her family doctor and told him. She said that she had discovered something that convinced her she was well on the road to recovery. This hope proved to be exaggerated. She was, however, on the road to some other discoveries.

Now we will get back to the question we left unanswered: *"What is the source of these feelings, and why is it unconscious?"*

We may be ready to agree that its source must be a reservoir of emotions or potential passionate feelings, from which sexuality may also have its origin. Why, then, does not her emotional tension obtain its relief or outlet along the normal paths? Why is she not normal in her love life instead of producing these very uncomfortable and distressing exhibitions of emotion?

There has throughout her life been a *tendency* for emotional outlet to find the normal or usual channel. We notice that, at the age of fifteen, her love was tending to attach itself to a young man about her own age. While that was going on she was apparently quite well. It was only when this love affair failed, and after considerable feelings of disappointment and distress, that symptoms began to arise.

We find now that the patient exhibits considerable resistance to normal love—at least, towards its passionate side. She shows resistance towards passion's *aim*, namely relief of tension by orgasm.

If we follow her through one of her analytical sessions, we can observe a similar resistance at work throughout the session as regards this sort of material. In fact, we shall observe an unusual degree of resistance against every aspect of her unconscious mind, amounting to a resistance against analysis.

Her behaviour and remarks tend to be all on a superficial or social plane, and one has to wait an extraordinarily long time for her to get down to the business of the session.

Here is a typical early session. She comes puffing and smiling into the room, beams on me and shakes hands gushingly:

"How are you, doctor? Isn't it cold?"

She starts warming her hands at the fire. Presently she says:

"Oh, I had a terrible dream last night! You don't mind my warming my hands, do you?"

To cut a long story short, she takes about ten minutes to divest herself of hat and coat and to arrange her hair. Finally, she warms her hands again:

"Must I go over there and lie down?"

I say simply, "Yes."

She sighs, and presently lies down.

After a few moments silence, she says:

"Oh! that nightmare the other night! Wherever I went there were pools and pools of blood. I woke up, went to sleep again and dreamt the same thing again."

Silence.

"I have still got this terrible fear of knives."

Silence.

"What about the dream?"

"Wherever I walked I couldn't get away from blood. There was something about a little girl aged four."

Silence.

She breaks silence with the remark: "Excuse me, doctor, are you Spanish?"

"Why do you ask?"

"Oh, nothing, I just thought of you at the moment."

"Perhaps we will come back to that, but, in the meantime, what about this blood?"

The patient ejaculates, "Oh bloody!" then hurriedly apologises: "I am so sorry." She lapses again into silence. Presently she says: "I know what you are thinking about."

"What am I thinking about?"

"I had another dream about blood on the same night. I dreamt I was walking home and there were two policemen struggling in a front garden. I couldn't see who it was. Something terrible had been going on."

Silence.

Presently she says: "I don't like telling you about this dream."

"Why not?"

She bursts into violent vituperation against medical psychologists in general and against psychoanalysts in particular. She says:

"You people put everything down to one thing—sex. I am quite sure my troubles have nothing whatever to do with sex; but I will tell you why I dreamt that dream. I was dancing with a stranger at a party that evening and he made suggestions that made me so indignant that I left him. But I will tell you nothing more about it. I will tell you another dream I had that night.

"I was walking along the Heath, and was very nervous, and a man was following me and I was afraid he would snatch my handbag; and then I saw these policemen and I couldn't tell them.

"You think I should tell you I was afraid of being assaulted. But I wasn't—it was my handbag—my handbag I tell you." Silence.

She suddenly bursts into loud laughter and says: "You've got a very vivid imagination, but it was nothing of the sort. It was my valuables."

This session gives us a vivid illustration of resistance at work. Resistance shows itself in her initial hesitation to lie down and begin the work of free association of thought. It is to be seen in her constant interruptions, in silences and switching off on to another subject.

This sort of thing occurs whenever a "danger point" becomes visible. Her sudden and uncalled-for attack upon what she supposes to be the theory of psychoanalysts, might be called an example of defence-resistance taken to a point of counter-attack. *Nobody had mentioned sex except herself.*

Further, she goes on to confirm with regard to the "stranger" incident, that her own thoughts were undoubtedly sexual. At the same time as she is playing with exciting thoughts and feelings, she is revealing fear of them and resistance against them.

This whole session, like her neurotic symptom itself, brings us to the important concept of *conflict*. There is conflict in the mind between the emotional drives on one side and fear and resistance on the other side. This is evident even in the safe and artificial situation of analytical free association of thought.

We may detect in the emotions she displays or experiences during even this one session, some elements of the emotions she feels in connection with her phobia of knives. As a result of the resistance and conflict it will be observed that, in spite of an hour on the settee, the dream that she first proposed to tell me in the end remained untold.

Later on there came to·light that this dream was the clue to an important sexual trauma of infancy. Although the memory had, up till that time, been successfully repressed, even the dream—as a pointer towards it—was too strongly resisted to be told to me at that stage of the treatment.

To be more specific: this patient's associations of thought to "blood" in this dream, and in many others, included, besides ideas of sexual assault, injury, murder and butcher's shops and knives, such concepts as love-making, courtship and the bridal-night. She herself had never been assaulted as a child but she had been enormously impressed by the story of such an assault and had no doubt identified herself with the victim.

Her own aggressive instincts, strongly developed in infancy, had led her to envisage passion as an assault. Her knife phobia had its origin in a sado-masochistic conception of coitus. Infants, on account of their emotional immaturity, are apt to *feel* that sexuality or passion is a sort of murderous struggle, and conversely, that murder —especially if done with a knife—has an orgastic sexual kick in it. Many adults have not entirely outgrown these early emotional patterns. Much of the horror commonly associated with sexuality has its source in these infantile concepts. Similarly much of the thrill which we feel in reading about murders arises from our repressed sexual tensions.

This patient before the age of five lived near a farm. She was told that the squealings she heard were the cries of the pigs being slaughtered. She can still remember that the conception she then formed of the slaughter was that the knife was thrust in between the hind legs and drawn upwards to slit open the belly.

At that early age she would lie in bed, a mass of conflicting emotions of excitement and fear, listening to the squeals and feeling sensations between her legs and up her inside, identical with the sensations she described in connection with her knife phobia.

Here we have the infant's sado-masochistic conception of sexuality. The knife is a symbol of her own aggression and of what she conceived to be the instrument of masculine sexuality. She reacted emotionally to a knife much as the average young woman would react to exhibitionism or threatened assault.

With the repression of sexuality we get the conflict of instinct on one side and the resistance due to fear on the other side. The symptom is a compromise between these two, embodying within itself elements from both.

That these two feelings, excitement and fear, can attach themselves to such a curious idea as knives, is due to the mechanism of displacement of affect. Therefore, to focus our attention upon the mere idea or symbol "knife" is to emphasize an inessential element in the situation.

A verbatim report of one of her other sessions may render this clear, showing that the affect or emotion can be, and commonly is, displaced on to a large variety of symbolical ideas. She says:

"My eyes are giving trouble, doctor. Do you think I shall go blind? When I had asthma attacks—and I did suffer very much from asthma at one time—my cousin laughed at me because I was struggling for breath. It was just after that, that my eyes began to give trouble.

"Then later I got this fear of appendicitis. For years I was terrified at the thought. It was after that, that it became knives.

"Now I feel it is going to my eyes again. I won't go to a hospital about them. I am terrified of an operation; it's the anæsthetic I couldn't bear. Do you think I am a bit insane?

"There was a long time when I had one fear only, and that was a fear of losing my reason. I used to worry and worry that I might go mad. Then there is the fear of losing my parents.

"I remember now another fear I had as a child—it was a fear about my foot. I used to think my foot was going to pieces."

There is no need to labour this ability of the affect to displace itself upon a variety of ideas. Yet this patient came for treatment complaining only of the one symptom—a fear of knives. This had apparently taken the place of all the others, and it was only a considerable time afterwards that she mentioned the long history of displacement of affect. I may add that the mechanism of displacement occurs at the instigation of resistance.

If "A" is an affect, and "B" the original emotional, sexual or infantile idea relevant to it, resistance, by refusing admission of this idea into consciousness, demands that the affect should express itself in terms of some other (more respectable) idea.

This is the sort of mechanism by which practically all neurotic symptoms, such as phobias, are constructed.

In the course of treatment the emotions began again to change the idea to which they had become fixed for some years. The phobias, as it were, retraced their history and, finally, with the revival in memory of many of her infantile anxieties and worries, she became more normally adjusted to her married life.

Perhaps the reason why this patient did not look worn and haggard was because, even throughout her illness, she was leading a pretty vigorous, if peculiar and abnormal, emotional life even within her symptoms.

Marital relations, though becoming satisfactory, did not give her everything she desired emotionally in her life. Her excitement tended to be social as well as marital.

Finally her interests extended to theatrical work, where she has achieved considerable success.

# REPRESSED SADISM
## AND THE COMPULSION TO PUNISH

A TALL, pale, serious young man comes into my consulting-room and stammers out what he feels to be a series of shameful confessions.

The worst of them all is that several years ago he had secretly put on the trousers of a boy friend and experimented with the sensation of caning himself through them.

"When I was on my way to see you," he says, "I suddenly thought of this incident, and the idea of having to tell you about it nearly caused me to rush back home. Fortunately the train came in just at that moment, and I found myself in it; otherwise I should not be here now."

"What did you think I should do about it?"

"I imagined that you would become livid with anger, that you would be horrified, that you would rise from your chair and order me out of your consulting-room."

This man called himself a homosexual, but the truth is that he would be better described as an asexual or an antisexual, for throughout his life of thirty years he had never performed any sort of sexual act with another person. He proved to be a *repressed* sadist.

We shall see that what goes on in his mind is in the case of bolder spirits projected into the outside world in the form of acts. Action seems to preclude the possibility of mind analysis. It is as though the mental tension is relieved in the execution of the act and then there is little or nothing left within the mind to analyse. That is why we insist upon our patient at analysis remaining inactive on the settee. That is why we find the world around us reflecting in its activities, its customs, its culture, its laws and its wars that same conflicting world which we are seeing daily within the minds of our patients.

Now this was a particularly "good" young man—good because all tendencies to relief of his primitive nature had been severely repressed and dammed up within his mind. This created the inner mental tension which was responsible for his "nerves." This created an inner world which was more accessible to the process of mind analysis.

He had repressed his potential tendencies to normal sexuality, and up to the time of coming for treatment he had in a sense never noticed that such a thing as a woman existed in this world. He was still busily engaged in the repression, or suppression, of any little tendencies to excitement. He avoided any sight or sound that might stimulate his instincts and thus render his task of repression more difficult. One such sight was the back view of young men, particularly in flannel trousers. This precluded him from attending cricket matches, a pastime which he had previously much enjoyed.

Another thing to avoid was the sight of a cane. London apparently contains more canes in shop windows than we realize, for this poor fellow had often to make long detours of the streets to avoid them.

Another sight that particularly alarmed him and occasioned frequent excursions into side streets was the dreadful apparition of a man with a whip riding behind a horse.

Now the point about this was that the man might at any moment strike the horse with his whip.

*In that event my patient felt he would be unable to resist the impulse to fly at that man and lash him to death.*

No punishment could be too severe for the man who beats the horse. One lash would be quite enough to precipitate the direst punishment, the extreme penalty. Our patient feared he would not be able to restrain himself from carrying this out on the spot.

What is the explanation of this compulsion? How comes it that this man—the mildest, kindest, and perhaps most frightened of men —is aroused to such a pitch of righteous indignation and becomes such a flaming avenger if he should witness such an act?

And then an interesting fact emerges: *Once upon a time, in childhood, this patient beat and beat a horse until he had exhausted himself and lamed the animal.*

He does not now beat horses. In fact, when he first came for treatment he had forgotten that he had ever done so. He does not even do it in imagination.

You will remember that we referred to an incident where he had beaten himself. He has therefore combined his sadistic impulse with retributive punishment of himself for it—in the same act. To beat oneself is *to beat* and at the same time *to be beaten* for it.

Nevertheless, the process again tends to be projected outwards in so far as fear and opportunity will permit. His favourite pleasure-giving phantasy is that of beating the posterior of a young man. This is of course a projection of his own.

But the only way in which this is permitted to take place, even in phantasy, is rather complicated. First of all it is essential that the young man should have performed a criminal act, for to beat or punish an innocent person would be to place oneself in the wrong.

So it is essential that the young man should be guilty. The crime allotted to him is, of course, that of having beaten a horse (as our patient did when he was young). Even then the responsibility for the punishment is transferred to a magistrate or judge.

It is essential that the cloak of legal justice should cover the libidinal nature of the act about to take place. In an atmosphere of high moral indignation it becomes incumbent upon our patient to perform the act. Thus is the impulse satisfied as a highly virtuous instead of as a diabolical act.

I would emphasize that it is nevertheless the *same* impulse. Also in this case it is even the same *act*, even although by this ingenious device it has become "justice" instead of "crime."

This case is interesting because, in our insistence on punishment, we are all doing similar things, with similar elaborate safeguards against detection.

A long analysis revealed the origins of this elaborately "civilized" (or diseased) structure. For simplicity and brevity three stages will be described.

1. We discover the infant with his aggressive instincts becoming prematurely libidinized. That is to say, he was in earliest infancy obtaining considerable *pleasure* in the exercise of his destructive and aggressive impulses.

These feelings became in his mind associated with his mother, or rather with a part of his mother. This part-object later became displaced and identified with an animal—a horse.

The horse then came to symbolize that part of his mother towards which his infantile aggressive sexuality (sadism) had originally been directed. In this guise he presently gave expression to the original impulse when he indulged in the orgy of beating the horse.

He later gives mental expression to it when he indulges in phantasies of inflicting legal punishment for the crime.

2. Interlacing with the first stage is the stage of repression. The earliest influence of this prohibiting force is to stop the phantasies in so far as they were originally directed towards a part of his mother's body, and so to occasion their transfer on to a non-mother object, namely the horse.

Repression did its work so well that up to the time of coming for analysis he had never looked with desire upon any woman. She was in the shape of the mother, and therefore totally prohibited from thought.

In connection with horses these sadistic impulses did obtain their expression for a brief interval. The forces of repression were not satisfied, however. If they had been, the man would have developed into an ordinary horse-beating sadist. And we, by the agency of our laws, would have dealt with him much in the same way as he dealt with himself.

But the same psychology and mechanisms embodied in our laws were already developing in his mind. Within his own mind violence was met with violence.

The aggressive elements of his sadistic impulse, with all their dynamic energy, are transferred to his super-ego (conscience) in order to destroy these destroyers. A savage super-ego is formed to oppose the savagery of his primitive impulses.

It is as though the strangler's rope had been taken over by the Lord Chief Justice. I would stress that it is still strangling that is being done with it.

This poor patient, through the agency of his savage super-ego, had strangled practically all his pleasure-seeking nature and well-nigh destroyed the very springs of his life in the process. Nevertheless, he was still under the cloud of its threatening severity. He was still going through a miserable prison-like life in fear and trembling.

I may mention that his father, who incidentally was a jurist, encouraged the severity and form of this morbid process by subjecting him, when a child, to periodic formal canings. This cane was only too readily taken up by our patient's super-ego, both as a mode of pleasure outlet and as a punishment for it. He has ever since been beating himself, both metaphorically and literally.

In this repressive stage we see the dynamic energy of the instincts transferred to their opposite number, the super-ego, and used against themselves. Their excessive strength caused not only the normal suppression of the infant's pleasure feelings towards his mother, but included in that taboo the whole of womankind.

In turn, the horse, as an object for the sadistic impulse, was repressed to the extent that he would have to kill the person (that is, himself) who beat it. We see him coming for treatment when he has reached the pass of not being able to go to a cricket match, to see the back view of a young man, or to pass a shop where canes are displayed.

Nevertheless, in spite of all the efforts of repression—or perhaps because of them—we discover that caning is still going on in the unconscious levels of his mind.

*Lying on the analytical settee he finds that he is not relaxing, but is instead holding his back muscles in a state of tense rigidity. He comes to his sessions as though he were coming to be caned, and all the time he lies there with rigid muscles as though I were actually caning him.*

The old experiences are being repeated in his symptoms and in his unconscious phantasy.

3. The third stage is one in which some measure of relief is obtained. The patient had never attained it since childhood except to a very limited extent in phantasy.

He discovers that somebody else is performing the very act which he wants to do but must not. Now these impulses, so long restrained, will be denied no longer. At last he can let fly at this culprit, and so obtain his relief.

The permissibility of punishment, provided guilt is proved, solves the problem, relieves the deadlock. The sadistic act is done at last, relief and health are achieved.

When out for satisfaction the tendency is not to stint oneself; no punishment can be too bad for the culprit. Thus we get the extreme violence with which our patient (in phantasy) attacks the man who beats the horse.

Punishment, father-inflicted or self-inflicted, never healed this patient. On the contrary, there is evidence to show that this was the morbid process responsible for his injured psyche.

This person was mended to a very large extent.

Curious as it may seem, he was throughout his analysis never in any danger of giving expression to sadistic urges. On the contrary, his interests became progressively more normal.

Finally, in spite of my expressed misgivings he concluded analysis and left me to get married.

## GLASS OF WATER

THE cases recently described have been distinguished by some striking symptom or some vivid characteristic. It would be a mistake to give the impression that *all* neurosis implies the presence of some colourful peculiarity.

We are not all outstanding personalities, leaders or dictators: there are also the common herd who blindly follow, and some of whom may seem to possess no individuality. These form the vast majority of mankind and among these may be the vast majority of neurotics.

In contradistinction to those previously described, this case presents a study in colourlessness. Nevertheless there may be a place for colourlessness if only as a background for more striking and vivid personalities. The leading lady would not appear so striking were it not that the chorus are all dressed alike—and surely the majority of human beings belong to the chorus.

Incidentally we shall discover that the absence of the normal self-assertive drives of life is more apparent than real. Repression has taken the place of expression. We shall discover how such a person comes into being. We shall discover that a strict and "perfect" upbringing is apt to stifle the normal development of personality.

No amount of training, with or without rules and punishments, can make a human being; nature or God alone can make that.

We all have something in common with this patient. We all have had our natural impulses more or less curtailed by authority in order to fit into the rigid social structure. And we in our turn continue as parents, teachers, etc., to impose the same process on the rising generation. Up to a point this may be good; but I am sometimes reminded of those tales of the beggar-class in India who have been said to fit a permanent metal cap over the head of an infant so that natural expansion of the skull was impossible. The child grows up an imbecile.

All we can do with excessive discipline is to make an automaton; and if we make it of flesh instead of steel it will usually be a marred and miserable piece of work.

I realize that I am attempting a difficult task in essaying a study of a negative personality.

Nevertheless, it will be discerned that in spite of the marring effect of her upbringing, in this case the hand of nature can still be detected as a sort of sweetness permeating this patient's otherwise insipid soul.

If we have had a happy day's outing walking through the sunlit fields and somebody asks us what we enjoyed so much, it is difficult to explain. There were no adventures; nothing happened. Perhaps the best thing to do is to take the inquirer by the hand and lead him along the same path.

We will ask this colourless patient so to lead us.

She is a very ordinary-looking woman of forty who has for many years been a nurse at a small infirmary. Her first session is characterized by an extraordinary degree of hesitation; in fact it takes several minutes to get the first hint why she is consulting me at all. I am afraid, therefore, that her early remarks will be somewhat halting and jerky.

She makes the following staccato statements:

"I feel I am not getting all I should out of life, I never feel that I am like other people. I do not seem to make friends. I was never brought up like other people.

"We weren't allowed to do anything. We weren't allowed to play the games we wanted to play. We had a very close upbringing under a very strict nurse. We are all a bit queer, my sister and my two brothers. One of them showed that he did not want to live. I am not sure that I want to live."

"What do you want? What do you feel would improve the situation?"

"I want somebody to want me. If you're single nobody seems to want you. I think I spend all my life trying to get people to like me and I don't succeed. Nobody seems to like me. I only get contempt and rudeness in return for my pains.

"At the age of twenty I had a breakdown. I used to stay in bed all the time. It happened when my cousin got married. He was twice my age but I had fallen in love with him, secretly, at the age of sixteen. I had not told anybody—not even him. I think I just had my dreams about him. Then he got married and I had my breakdown. I had no wish to live or anything."

"What do you think is missing in your life?"

"I think everything is missing. I have no reason for living. You see I am not gifted in any way. I feel I have failed in life. Somehow I have failed to find life. I am just half alive, if that."

A pathetic story. These further early remarks will help to show how her earliest sessions repeated the depressive phase of her life and gave us some hint of its equivalent in childhood:

"As children we had a nurse who was very domineering. She never let us do anything on our own initiative. She treated us like dolls. This nurse used to look after the family. I was in her charge from birth up to the age of fifteen or sixteen.

"Everything we did was most closely supervised by her. She was quite a character. She would not let us wear the school uniform; we had to wear queer frocks.

"We were never allowed to play in the garden. When we went to the seaside we weren't allowed to go near the wet sand or the water. We were told exactly what we could do and what we couldn't do on a certain part of the beach.

"My parents were funny people. They thought they had solved the problem of their family by putting us into the hands of this nurse whom they considered most excellent.

"Mother was a dreamer. We were never brought up to a career. Mother used to think we would just get married, but we never went anywhere and never met anybody.

"Nurse used to make us very self-conscious. She'd dress us up with curled hair, when all the other girls had plaits. She even kept our parents from us. She has trained me so well that, after all these years, I cannot find anything of myself.

"The world I lived in was the nursery, and even there one had to sit quietly and never do anything unless one was told. There was the daily walk; we were dressed up and taken down the garden passage at the side of the house. There the baby would be put in its pram.

"I would hold the pram on one side and my elder sister would walk on the other side and off we would set in a solemn procession —always the same route, along the same pavements and along the same streets, and back to the house and back to the nursery.

"She even slept in our nursery with us. Borstal could not have been worse. If we had been brought up in the gutter it would have been far better.

"This is all I learned in my childhood: not to do anything myself but always to wait until I was told, only to do the things I was told to do. When I found myself grown up I felt all at sea. The result was that although I had been left a private income I sought for someone to be in charge of me.

"And I have found someone: a white-robed sister or matron dressed exactly like our childhood nurse (she always wore this uniform), so that I still work under orders all the time. Unless somebody is ordering me about, I don't know what to do."

At a subsequent session the patient said:

"I know now why I work in a hospital. It is because I had to have the old situation of a nurse in charge of me giving me orders. I was brought up in a prison-like life and I had to find a jailer similar to my nurse. I never knew what I ought to do or what I wanted to do.

"When my prison doors were opened and they thought I was grown up, all I did was to walk back into another prison. I went from one jailer to another, from my Nanny to the Sister in the hospital. They are both very much alike, and they dress the same.

"Convict 99—that's what I am! I fit in there, in this life of discipline and I do not fit anywhere else. Perhaps it suits me. Everything works to time, like machinery. We work to time and we have our meals to time and there is always somebody to tell me what to do."

It is very difficult to clarify the subsequent remarks of this patient. All attempts to classify will have to be incomplete, because her moods dovetail into one another.

In her analysis then, we first get the present-day depression, and soon after we get a re-enacting of the forgotten earliest years of happiness and hopeful anticipation of greater happiness. We trace the succeeding disappointment and the hopelessness and depression which followed it and permeated her whole life.

It seems that her life has been a succession of repetitions of this sequence. Her nature has blossomed forth hopefully in the expectation of love and happiness only to meet the same disappointment; withdrawal from hope has followed and then the subsequent resignation to nothingness.

The same thing happens in her analysis, but this time we are able to trace its original pattern. Reliving and *remembering* these original experiences frees her from the compulsion to repeat the pattern. Particularly it frees her from the compulsion to resign herself to the doldrums of her repressed childhood.

We began with her first interviews and a recital of her complaints, but now in order to follow the sequence of her emotional development and its vicissitudes I shall proceed to those early sessions of her analysis when life became much brighter and happier.

She says: "When I first came here I was interested in you because you were a man and I thought I would be a woman. Now you have made me go back and be a small girl."

Apparently she is discovering that she has never grown up, she is still a small girl emotionally.

"It seems now that you are saying that I have to go to school and go to bed early. Grown-ups have the best things of life; they sit up late at night, while we children go to bed in the daylight with the traffic passing outside.

"We were shut out. We had a sort of part in the family life for a few minutes of the day and then we were put in a drawer, shelved like dolls. We were certainly not the essential thing in the house as modern children are. I felt it rather shameful to be a child, a thing that was *endured*.

"Shameful things happened all the time. Everything we did was wrong'; we were marionettes, nurse pulled the string and we did what we were told. When father came along another string was pulled—like little specimens that you picked up with forceps."

The following more advanced session reveals the early stages of what is called in analysis the "transference." As it progresses it gradually shows a hidden part of the patient's nature and a previously forgotten part of her life. It brings to light the happy years of love—before the age of 3½—when she was "the only pebble on the beach."

Later it transpires that she somehow nursed the expectation that love relationships with her father would become increasingly enjoyable. Though she is overtly talking to her analyst, it must be remembered that he is consistently an unknown figure to her. He is merely the blank slate on which she is writing the love story of her forgotten infancy. This is what she says:

"I am like a child at the crossroads and I am waiting for you, to see which road you will take, then I'll follow you like a dog. But you only sit on a gate and smoke a pipe and I am getting impatient of playing around waiting for you.

"Don't you see that every child needs *guidance*? Children only play in their spare time. They need an adult to follow. I have been brought up to be only an animal or a dog."

"What do *you* want to do; where do *you* want to go?"

"I only want you to let me go with you and spend my time admiring you. You'd just allow me to admire you, and you'd have your own interests."

"What are *your* interests?"

"I'd like you to go for a walk because *you* wanted to, so long as I could go with you and you didn't mind my following you wherever you went. I wouldn't even wish for a show of affection on your part. I'll do all the hero worship; you'd be self-centred.

"You would be better if you were my parent because then you couldn't get away. I'd have a right to call on you to be taken about. I don't want to be bothered with anyone else's life or listen to their troubles.

"I dreamed I was a little girl in bed and I was holding your hand; and then we were going for a walk and I had on a little bonnet and coat. . . . I suppose all this is to do with the time my father was interested in me before the baby brother was born.

"I want someone to centre my love on; all one wants is to unload one's affection on to another and to be allowed to do it."

If she cannot be a complete woman—complete with male—it seems that she must be a child, an appendage to somebody. She says:

"You ought to give me some guidance. You ought to tell me what I ought to do and what I ought to feel. I'd like it best if I didn't have to think for myself at all, if you gave me exact instructions, exact orders, so that every action of mine, every thought and every feeling were directed and ordered by you. I don't get anything solid from you. You are like a jelly; you are no use to me.

"What is the use of asking me what I think and what I feel? I don't know what I ought to feel; I don't know what I ought to think. I don't know what I want. I don't know what sort of person I am."

At another session she says:

"I have got over my excitement at seeing you, but still I like you as a background, a part of the whole, a part of the world. But still I do not want any friends, I do not want to talk to other people because I feel that while I am talking to them you will escape.

"Now I feel I'd like to go and play in the garden. You must sit here in a set place. It is very frightening if there is no one in the house and all is dark. You cannot enjoy playing in the garden if the house is empty, so I must have you sitting here all the time."

As the treatment progresses, coming to see the analyst becomes the crux of this patient's emotional life. All her phantasies, all her emotions are connected with these daily visits. She feels that something new has come to brighten her existence. Some days she is almost in a fever of excitement to get to her interview.

At the same time, she has dreams of a very pleasurable nature in which she is the mother of a succession of babies. She has apparently entered a phantasy world of marital bliss.

During this happy phase of analysis she remembers a period of her life which she had completely forgotten, her earliest years when she received a certain amount of affectionate attention from her parents and nurse.

Before many weeks have passed all this fades away and her earlier depression and boredom with life return. When she was $3\frac{1}{2}$ her brother was born; this was the turning point. Immediately everybody's attention was diverted from her on to the new arrival.

He was a fine, healthy baby boy and the delicate little girl felt that the universe had completely changed. For a few weeks she could not understand what had happened. It was a catastrophe in her life from which she never recovered. The unseeing adults had apparently no appreciation of what they had done to her.

She says: "I still feel that if anybody else is around, especially one who is nice or attractive, I have to fade out or take a back place. I can remember now that, after my baby brother was born, I did not know what to do to get back into favour. No matter how good I was, nobody noticed me. Eventually, after some weeks I found something to do which attracted a little attention—*I took to rocking baby's cradle.*

"It seems that I spent hours rocking this cradle, and it was always with one object in mind—to get back into favour. I used to sit for hours looking after the child, and I can still remember that it succeeded to some extent, for people used to say how good I was, and I seem to remember the phrase, 'Just look at that marvellous child.'

"Now I can remember a dream I had only the other night; it had something to do with injuring a baby in a pram. I believe I dropped a dog on top of the baby.

"The other day I got a thought that when I see a baby in a pram, for two pins I'd hit it; suppose I went mad, I'd go round smashing up children. I felt a violent hatred for babies.

"I never knew before that I felt like that towards that baby brother. Anyhow, it was all crushed, I was much more concerned to win back people's love."

Space will not permit us to trace this patient's development through the subsequent stages of release from the thraldom of her nurse and succession of nurse surrogates to the acquisition of a normal degree of independence.

But at last her repressed drives were relatively released and she came to know what she herself wanted and how she could best adjust her environment and herself. The successive stages of emotional experience through which she passed during the course of her analysis may be roughly divided into six.

The first stage, which arose soon after the beginning of treatment, might be called that of a hopeful expectation. For a few weeks she came to her sessions like a girl going to meet her lover.

She was light on her feet, always chose a road through the park and noticed all the flowers which she had never previously noticed. The world was a most cheerful and exhilarating place. It was as though the sun had arisen for the first time in her life; her dreams, too, were the pleasurable dreams of a bride-to-be.

During this stage she remembered the happiness of her earliest years when her father used to take notice of her. A typical dream of this stage of her analysis is as follows:

"I was standing in the entrance of a garden of pink roses and masses of flowers. I had on a large picture hat. It was a hat that I wore at a wedding a few years ago, but in the dream my clothes were those of a child."

At a later stage of analysis she dreams the same dream again, but this time it has an unhappy ending, in keeping with the unhappiness that brought her to analysis.

". . . I looked very nice and fresh and young. *Then I went out into the rain.*"

She comments on this: "It has been raining ever since. Happy bride indeed! All the rest of my life the rain has carried on."

Gradually, but most distinctly, the first stage has given place to a second one of painful disappointment. She suffers the emotions which are normal to a broken engagement. After all this anticipation she began to realize that absolutely nothing was forthcoming. She felt that I was no longer interested in her; that nobody was interested in her; that nothing pleasurable was going to happen to her in this life.

*The excitement of her previous hopes was the measure of her present distress.* This corresponds to the stage when her infantile happiness had come to a close at the birth of her brother.

As an infant she had had similar fantastic hopes of Daddy's eternal love, only to find that the situation, instead of being progressive, had gone the other way and she was no longer noticed.

A dream symbolizing her abandonment of hope and her retreat from love is a miserable one of being in a nunnery with females only around her. In the last analysis it is seen to hark back to the disappointment she felt when her father's love turned from her to her baby brother.

Her subsequent love failures are shown to be unconscious repetitions on her part of this original event. She lives the "love affair" in her dreams, and in the meantime the real man escapes her. Eventually there comes the rude awakening and her habitual retreat into hopelessness and depression—"the nunnery."

The third stage of her analysis might be described as the stage when all desires or feelings are nipped in the bud. Having once experienced the distress of disappointment she was loth to be so hurt again. She therefore suppressed or repressed any natural tendency towards hope, happiness, pleasurable feelings and phantasies.

The fourth stage is even more serious. The process of repression extends from the repression of erotic feelings and phantasies to the repression of every day-dream, every impulse and every desire.

This is the stage of *nothingness*, when she dare not have feelings or a soul of her own, but must resign herself to being an automaton, taking her orders from authority. This stage was so protracted in her early life (it included all her nursery days, from the age of three and a half to fifteen) that it is not surprising that it occupied the greater part of her analytical experience.

It is only after reliving these stages of her early life that she came to realize in a fifth stage that the prison doors had now been opened, that there was no need to subject all her potential urges and desires to the dictates of a harsh authority. Nor was there any need to repeat indefinitely the only escape from a drab world that she had been able to find in her childhood, namely that of indulging in day-dreams and phantasies, without any attempt at making them come true.

She found at last that not only were the prison doors open, but that she had provision for herself in the world outside the prison. This was stage six. Realization of freedom provoked action.

For the first time in her life she tackled her elder sister to whom, in keeping with her character, she had entrusted all her legacy from her father. It appeared that she had been unable to ask this sister for her own money because she "felt her sister would be hurt." This and similar difficulties no longer hindered her.

Her relatives were considerably annoyed at her changing character, and it took some weeks of pressing before they surrendered her rights to her.

Thereupon she resigned her minor position at the infirmary and went abroad to Africa for a long holiday. From a card I received it seems that the poetry of her dreams is finding some equivalent in her reality experiences.

She was unfortunate merely in her subdued disposition, but not unfortunate in the material things of life. At last she is in a position to use these for her own happiness, and it seems likely that with this change in character she will find a way of leading a fuller and happier life.

# GOD VERSUS DEVIL

*When I was about* 19, *the following thought came into my mind: I imagined God on His throne. I shook my fist at Him and said in imagination that I would prefer to go to the Devil.*

*Now, I certainly did not wish to go to the Devil, and why this thought should come bursting into my mind I do not know. I recalled it some weeks later and began to feel very guilty. In fact I thought I had committed an enormous crime against God, and I feared that I was damned. I could not get it out of my mind, and it has caused me agonies, day and night, ever since.*

*I might mention that, at that time (I was* 19 *years of age) I was very much in love with a girl. But, strangely enough, I was scared of her . . . too scared to give her any indication of my feelings.*

*Although I am now* 36, *I do not think I have made any progress since that time. I am still just as scared of women, and the feeling of guilt for the insult to God still keeps recurring in my mind.*

WHEN I received the above letter, it seemed to me impossible to help such a man by correspondence, and I therefore asked him to come and see me.

At the interview he said:

"My trouble has come to a head. I am again in love with a girl, and am too scared to give her any indication of it. I have a married friend about the same age as myself, and I have fallen in love with his daughter of 17.

"When they were on a holiday, I went all the way to Scotland, determined to declare my love. I spent a week with them, but found I could never bring myself to say a word. I got back, terribly disappointed with myself. I developed strange ideas that I was impotent. I have never had any experience, so I don't know if I am or not.

"What I have been brooding about is my inability to express what I felt so keenly. I am not particularly afraid of people in a group, or at parties, but I am scared stiff of a woman in any intimate relationship. Whenever I feel amorous towards a girl, I just seem to fall down, and can't do a thing.

"At 19, I was in love with a girl. That is when I got my obsession that has worried me ever since. The love petered out: the obsession has persisted. I had no interest in women for the next ten years or more, and then I fell in love with the present girl, when she was just a child of 14.

"Not only is there this fear of being in an intimate relationship with a woman, but I am also obsessed with the fear concerning that blasphemous thought. The reason for this seems to be that I had sold myself to the devil, merely by thinking this thought to myself. It is a fear of being possessed by the devil. I know it is rather absurd and based on the old theology. The devil seems to represent all that is evil or bad.

"The fear of selling myself to the devil takes my thoughts back to a dream I had at the age of 5 or 6 years. I was sleeping with my mother at the time. I woke up trembling very violently. I thought I saw a phantom fly across the room. It was like a flame, and yet it was like an imp grinning at me. It flew across the room and out of the window. I was scared to death."

*Analyst:* "What is the flame you would get if you were sleeping with your mother?"

*Patient:* "Love of my mother, I suppose."

*Analyst:* "What is the flame you would get if you were sleeping with a young lady?"

*Patient:* "Passion."

*Analyst:* "Would you?"

*Patient:* "No, I expect I should be scared to death, and trembling violently, like I was in the dream."

(*Silence*)

*Analyst:* "What are you thinking?"

*Patient:* "I was thinking to ask you what are the effects of masturbation. I started masturbating at the age of 10. At 15 or 16 I thought it was very wrong and sinful. Is this guilty fear of mine a matter of a bad conscience? I tell myself that the devil is merely a symbol, but there is a childish fear as though he were real, and a fear that I have committed myself to him. I often wonder why the thought ever occurred to me. Has it anything to do with the fact that I was at that time keen on this girl and too scared to do anything about it? I might have regarded the whole of sex as wrong. Perhaps I was saying this to God: 'If God forbids any expression of sex, I will have none of God, I will have the devil, that is Sex.'

"And then I got the reaction, and have since felt that any feelings of the kind had better be repressed.

"My parents were both rather tyrannical about the whole thing. Now my main concern is this idea or obsession that I am possessed by the devil."

*Analyst:* "Suppose you are?"

*Patient:* "That would mean that one would lose control of one's will."

*Analyst:* "What is natural?"

*Patient:* "Do you mean that what I am afraid of is my own natural urge to live a normal natural life, and that that would include a natural expression towards a woman, and enjoyment of my work, and to have a number of friends around me?"

*Analyst:* "What for?"

*Patient:* "I naturally like people and company."

*Analyst:* "What for?"

*Patient:* "Well, I'd feel terribly nervous if I were left with one girl; I should not know what to say or do. I might feel the urge to tell her that I liked her, and on the other hand I'd be too scared to do anything about it."

*Analyst:* "Devils are not so scared."

*Patient:* "If it is the devil I am afraid of, would he lead to natural, normal love? If I were possessed of the devil I suppose I'd make love to her."

*Analyst:* "Is that what the devil would do?"

*Patient:* "I don't follow the trend of the argument."

*Analyst:* "Perhaps you did when you were 5 or 6, when you were sleeping with your mother, and saw the little devil fly across the room."

\*　　\*　　\*　　\*

Here the session ended, but the patient was determined to come back next day to continue it. He was given an afternoon appointment. But a few hours after he had left he telephoned, begging to come back that same evening. As I could not see him then he wished for an early appointment next morning. That, too, had to be refused. Finally, when he arrived at the appointed hour, he was still full of excitement and ideas.

He said: "I am better. I see it now. My fear of the devil that I have had since I was 19, or perhaps since I was 5, is nothing more or less than a fear of my sexual nature. The thoughts I have been having roused all sorts of spectres in my mind."

*Analyst:* "For example?"

*Patient:* "I have been wondering if my fear is due to a fear that I might be cruel to the girl, or do her some physical injury . . . commit some crime.

"A few days ago I read of such a crime in the paper. A man killed his wife. Such crimes, particularly sexual crimes, have always filled me with a sense of most utter repugnance and dread. Is that because there is something like that in me? Perhaps I am scared of a girl because I am terrified that my sexual feelings might run away with me, and I might not act rationally."

*Analyst:* "What might you do?"

*Patient:* "I might love her too much."

*Analyst:* "What would that lead to?"

*Patient:* "My desire would be to put my arms round her, and tell her I love her. But I was scared."

*Analyst:* "Does that seem so terrifying?"

*Patient:* "Well, I might lose control, and go too far."

*Analyst:* "How far might you go?"

*Patient:* "Well, I might have sexual intercourse with her: that would be going too far."

*Analyst:* "Would it?"

*Patient:* "Well, perhaps not as far as sexual intercourse. If that is the devil, perhaps he is quite a harmless devil. Perhaps the sooner I went to the devil the better."

*Analyst:* "If that is all there is to it, why is there all this scare?"

*Patient:* "Apparently all this time I have been afraid of being possessed by my own nature. The thing I want more than anything else is to lead a normal natural life. Since coming to you I have understood that this fear of being sold to the devil is nothing more or less than fear of my own nature on the one hand, and on the other hand a preference for it, which I have thought was a preference for the devil.

"The whole amazing thing has become quite plain to me. It is amazing how the obsession left me last night after that talk with you.

"I had been fearing that having said to God that I would go to the devil, there was no turning back. Now I see that it was just two opposite parts of my own nature in conflict with each other. Part of my mind was synonymous with God, and it would allow no sexual expression at all. On the other hand, the devil was synonymous with sexual expression.

"At the time when I was in love with this girl at 19, I wanted sexual expression, and thus I turned to God and said, 'I will prefer the devil.' But immediately I thought that, I was frightened. I felt I was sold to the devil. I was so frightened that I have striven ever since to run away from the devil. And I am still afraid of girls.

"I have not yet told you that the real reason I came to you was a feeling I had last week—a feeling of fear that I might commit suicide. It is not that I have a desire to do so, but a fear that I might do it against my will."

*Analyst:* "What is it you were afraid you might do against your will?"

*Patient:* "The only thing I can think of, except suicide in my present state of mind, is a fear that I might get hold of some girl and have sexual intercourse with her."

*Analyst:* "What happens then?"

*Patient:* "Sexual intercourse must terminate when once desire is satisfied."

*Analyst:* "What happens when it is satisfied?"

*Patient:* "It is dead. It has led to its own suicide."

*Analyst:* "Is that anything to be afraid of?"

*Patient:* "No, I see it now.

"I tried to ignore all these things. At 19 I was so infatuated with the girl, yet so scared, that I could not approach her. The feeling was so strong that it seemed to bottle itself up. Thus it was all or nothing with me. So far it has been nothing. With the present girl, when I feel so strongly about her, I feel I must do *something* about it. I do nothing. I am afraid of that devil."

*Analyst:* "It does not look as though you have sold yourself to that devil after all."

*Patient:* "If it broke out, I would go wild."

*Analyst:* "And that is?"

*Patient:* "Possibly I might hurt the girl in some way. The thought occurs to me that in this frenzy I might kill the girl."

*Analyst:* "How would you kill her?"

*Patient:* "I might strangle her, with my hands round her neck."

*Analyst:* "What is it that you are strangling?"

*Patient:* "I am strangling my own feelings—my own feelings of a great desire for sexual intercourse with her."

*Analyst:* "So the girl stands for your desire which you are so afraid of, just as the devil stood for it. In this phantasy of strangling the girl you are dramatizing the struggle that is within your own mind. What might you do with the girl instead of strangling her?"

*Patient:* "Nothing—except sexual intercourse in the normal manner. But, surely, I would not have been so scared of that all my life. Can it be that I have been so scared because I am a sex maniac?"

*Analyst:* "Or an anti-sex maniac?"

*Patient:* "Last night . . . you will appreciate that I was rather stirred up after my conversation with you. . . . I had an extra-ordinary attack of nasal catarrh."

*Analyst:* "What is nasal catarrh?"

F

*Patient:* "Congestion . . . mental indigestion . . . feelings which cannot obtain expression. . . ."

*Analyst:* "Expression of what?"

*Patient:* "Expression of nature . . . expression of my sexual nature. Nasal catarrh is also an emission of fluid. Is that a manifestation of congested sexual feelings?"

*Analyst:* "If so, they were rather at the wrong end, weren't they? Like the strangling."

*Patient:* "Are these the things the devil is doing to me? I have often had the crazy fear that one of these days I might come home and find him sitting in the chair waiting for me."

*Analyst:* "What does he look like?"

*Patient:* "Like the picture of Mephistopheles—a long, hooked nose, pointed chin, pointed ears, slit eyes, and a reddish face. In fact, the usual stage figure."

*Analyst:* "Thinking of that vision vaguely, what is the thought that comes into your mind?"

*Patient:* "I have got it! I told you, didn't I, that I used to masturbate from about 10 years of age to about 16? Then I stopped the habit with difficulty. It was after that, when I was in love with the girl that I said to God, 'I prefer the devil.' I suppose the same devil as I had given up. I had the idea that it had done me harm physically."

\*        \*        \*        \*

The letter which I wrote to this patient before I had ever seen him, in reply to his original letter, was as follows:

"The symptoms of which you complain such as 'Shaking your fist at God,' clearly reveal a conflict between two opposing sides of your personality. While you are trying to support the 'good' side, your 'lower nature' naturally feels unduly oppressed, and it is this which shakes its fist, as it were, at its oppressor, the other side of you.

"The measure of this oppression of one side of yourself may be revealed in your fear of the girl (i.e. the natural side of yourself—because this is what the girl stands for in your psychology).

"In other words, the measure of the repression of your nature can be gauged from the fact that you are 36, and still unmarried, and still with these conflicts about yourself."

The material which the patient provided in his three interviews only amplifies and confirms the conclusions cryptically put forward in my reply to his letter.

\*        \*        \*        \*

This case is chosen on account of the simple and clear conflict between the patient's sexual instincts on the one hand and his ego ideal on the other.

His life has evidently been an unusually successful attempt to mobilize his instinct energy on the side of his ego ideal, and against his sexual instincts. These latter he has identified with the concept of the devil.

It seems that only once did he wilfully and consciously lean towards the latter, and the worry of this choice has obsessed him ever since. The reason why this obsession has persisted is because the energy of his sexual instincts has also persisted.

He succeeded in keeping sexual conduct at bay, by this persistent obsessional preoccupation of keeping the devil at bay. Thus his obsessional activity has been a substitute for a normal sexual life.

The morbid factor in the situation has been the unusual degree of anxiety or scare of these instinct forces. This fear has transferred itself on to the natural object of this instinct (the girl), and thus he has always been scared of any intimate situation with a woman.

On account of the abnormally strong defences against normal sexuality, the instinct "to do something to the woman" has been prevented from taking a normal conscious form, but has nevertheless been too strong to remain permanently repressed, and has therefore emerged, but in an altered or displaced fashion.

In fact, it is the familiar mechanism of displacement upwards which causes him in phantasy to do something with his hands, the upper part of him, to her neck, the upper part of her.

This abnormal travesty of the sexual act is then used as a rationalization for his fear of what his impulses will do to the woman, and, as it were, a justification for his continued repression of his instinct.

Helped by real insight into these mechanisms, a good deal of the morbid structure is already breaking down, even after a few interviews. With a further lessening of his anxiety it is a foregone conclusion that this patient will find a more healthy and happy method of releasing his natural energies than by maintaining his obsessional preoccupations.

## COMPULSION TO CONFESS

A YOUNG woman came to me at a hospital with a problem that has a basic element common among many other cases that, to the non-specialist, appear to be of widely different kinds.

The same element is present in cases of over-conscientiousness, over-scrupulousness, shyness, shame, discontent, introspection, fussiness, unsociableness, worry, doubting, indecision, compulsive thinking and compulsive acting of every variety. The hospital has not the best atmosphere for a careful analysis—nor indeed is there generally the requisite time for it—but here is what took place:

"What do you complain of?"

"*I cannot stop worrying.* All the time my mind seems to be in a constant state of worrying, examining and thinking about everything I have done and every thought I have thought."

"What do you worry about?"

"That's the silly part of it, doctor. I can't think what it is about! Sometimes I've thought it was about losing my job and a few weeks ago the worry grew so great that I *resigned* my job. But I worry just as much now as I did then. It's about anything—or nothing."

"What else can you say about it?"

"I have no control over it. All my efforts to stop it are useless. In my struggle to stop it I have lost all my will-power. And that's a further source of worry. Sometimes I feel it will kill me."

"Do you keep it all to yourself or do you talk about it?"

"Talk about it! That's another instance of my loss of will-power. I try to keep it to myself but I simply cannot. I have a mad desire to tell my mother *everything* that passes through my mind. I battle with this impulse but it's no good. I'm afraid I shall drive poor mother silly."

"Give me an instance."

"Well, last Sunday I was out with my young man. All we did was to visit some relatives. But as soon as I got home I had to tell my mother every single thing we did and every single word we said. Not content with that I was uneasy lest I had *thought* anything which I had not told her. I spent a good deal of the night examining my mind to discover if there were any thought that I had not told my mother."

"Is it as though you had to confess?"

"Yes. Especially if I'm going out to enjoy myself and want to be free and happy."

"How long have you suffered like this?"

"It's been worse for the past year or so."

"When did you notice the first sign of this trouble?"

"When I was fifteen years old."

"What was the first sign of it then?"

"Well, I'm afraid that at that time it was all sexual. It's not that now. It started with my getting sexual imaginings. Pictures or visions of a sexual nature kept appearing before me."

"What did you do about that?"

"They became so frequent and persistent that I got alarmed and tried to shut them out. The more I struggled the more insistent they seemed to be. I found I was powerless to stop them. I felt I was losing my will-power."

"Surely this had the same power of compulsion as your present symptom?"

"Yes. I suppose it was the same in that respect."

"In that *essential* respect. For it isn't the *form* your worry takes but the *compulsion* to worry that makes it so distressing."

"That is so."

"Why did you *have* to strive to banish these thoughts and images from your mind?"

"They were such horrible things."

"Horrible things? You mean one particular image?

"Yes."

"And at the age of fifteen you had this picture in your mind. How was that?"

"I suppose the misfortune of actually seeing something like that in real life happens to many a girl. At least I have been told so. And I am not altogether a fool. But why should it affect me to such an extraordinary extent?"

"Why at fifteen must you struggle so hard to banish it? Why must you break yourself rather than permit the image?"

"Because it was so horrible."

"Horrible? But something in you kept conjuring it up again. Do you think perhaps that *something* in you—something which you were not willing to recognize as part of yourself, even as your lower self—was *attracted* by this image and would not part with it?"

"I thought it horrible."

"Yes, *you* did; but this *part* of you kept on."

"That wasn't *me*."

"You hoped not. But why on no account must this be a part of you?"

"It was too shocking. Besides, whatever *would* mother have said!"

"So you ran and told mother?"

"I told her everything about it."

"Just as you now insist on telling her all you do and say and think?"

"Yes, exactly the same. I *have* to tell her."

"What was mother's reaction?"

"I think she was upset."

"And you were upset?"

"Yes. I was in great distress."

"That was at the age of fifteen?"

"Yes."

"But you hadn't told her before?"

"No."

"Why didn't you tell her *at the time*?"

"Goodness knows! I suppose I felt guilty for some unearthly reason. Just as though *I* had done something. Anyhow at that time I felt I mustn't tell anybody."

"When was 'that time'?"

"Well, there was an occasion at the age of twelve."

"And so for years you kept what you had seen to yourself. For years and years you bottled up your guilty feeling of concealment from your mother. It grew. And *now* you cannot do enough 'confession' to make amends for the years of concealment. Moreover, you are *punishing* yourself by suspecting guilt in your every thought and act, and also by this compulsion to confess.

"Unfortunately, however, your confessions are irrelevant, for despite their morbidly exacting nature, they concern themselves only with the innocent matters of to-day. Would you like to 'confess' to me the 'guilty' thoughts and feelings which you had as a little girl of twelve—or earlier?"

"It is only to my mother that I have the compulsion to confess."

"As though you suspected yourself of sinning against her?"

"Yes. I suppose that is it."

"How could you have sinned against your mother?"

"Well, I suppose I did conceal those sexual things from her for many years."

"Why?"

"I felt guilty."

"And frightened?"

"Yes."

"Why guilty? Guilty of what?"

"Goodness knows!"

"I'll tell you: Guilty of sexuality. Guilty of being sexual."

"I suppose it must be so, though I don't remember it."

"Do you remember being frightened?"

"Yes."

"Afraid to tell mother?"

"Yes."

"You thought she'd punish you?"

"I thought she'd kill me."

"And a little while ago you told me you sometimes thought your worry would kill you. So the punishment and the killing are still going on."

"I wish they'd get it over."

"But you've shifted the scene of battle away from the relevant events of the past on to the irrelevant (innocent) events of the present day. Otherwise it is the identical battle—the fight with a compulsion (originally a sexual compulsion) which is going on to-day. One factor that remains the same is mother, evidently the equivalent of your conscience, to whom you must confess."

"I'll have to go home and tell mother everything that we've said to each other."

"Just as though we had been doing something guilty together?"

"Yes. Isn't it absurd?"

"So if mother stands for your conscience, what do I stand for?"

"I don't know. But you're a man."

"Perhaps you identify mother with one half of you and you identify me with the opposite half. In that way you can bring your old conflict, the struggle between your 'good' side and your 'bad' side right up to date."

"I seem to be the wretched battle-ground."

"But it is an old battle—continued on new and innocent ground. You can only deal with it if we go back and unearth the old guilt-feelings of your child life.

"Judging by the severity of your illness I don't suppose you have any causes for guilt-feelings or self-reproach in your current daily life?"

"If you mean sex, you are right. I have no use for it. I think it is quite unnecessary. I have an affectionate disposition, and I would like to show affection, but I have no desire to go any further than one sees people go on the films."

"Perhaps mother would not approve?"

"*I* would not approve."

"Didn't I say that mother and your conscience were the same? It seems that your sex-life was stopped in its development somewhere about puberty; nipped in the bud as it were by a surging up of guilt-feelings. You promptly rushed back to mother, strove to content yourself with the child-parent level of affectionate feelings and the residue of sexuality was converted by guilt and fear into this new form of compulsion—not to *do* sexual acts or even to have sexual thoughts—but to confess every thought as though it might be guilty. Again it became bound to mother as though it were only an intimate relationship to her that she would permit."

That is roughly how our conversation went on.

There is much more in this case of a severe obsessional neurosis, but the foregoing preliminary discussion reveals, I think, some interesting and typical mental mechanisms. Now let us look into it psychologically.

To reconstruct the psychopathology of a neurosis it is necessary to reverse the order of investigation.

In an interview such as the above, the symptom we observe *is an end-product* having an origin, a history and a mechanism.

We are in the position of a detective who sees only the end results of a crime and from the clues thus presented must reconstruct everything that took place, verifying his findings at each step of the investigation.

In this case, we may begin with the observation that the essential characteristic of this, as of every other case of obsessional neurosis, is its *compulsive* character. In fact the illness is sometimes called "compulsion neurosis."

Reason and will-power are in all cases ineffective against the compulsive force of the symptom, whether the latter is that of thinking or acting.

This patient exhibits both—the compulsion to examine her deeds and thoughts (compulsive thinking) and the compulsion to detail them all to her mother (a variety of compulsive act).

We then ask what may be the origin in the psyche of such a dynamic force that can so consistently and repeatedly override the power of the reason and the will.

Surely we should not be surprised if we find that it originates from a law of nature, a great biological force, against which the more recently constructed laws of man, of reason and of conscious will-power, are comparatively puny and unavailing?

Let us then search among the instincts, those innate drives of our life-force, individual and biological, to discover which of these it may be that gives rise to these curious compulsions.

In this particular case we have apparently not far to seek, for the patient tells us quite frankly that this compulsion arose by her being obsessed at the age of fifteen (at puberty) with sexual imagery. In the face of her conscious will to banish them, these images assumed compulsive force.

Is not this a characteristic of the sexual impulse in general, particularly at the age of puberty when such a compromise as that of matrimony is out of the question?

However, it takes two to make a quarrel, and similarly it takes two opposing forces in conflict to make a neurosis.

The inherited biological instincts are on one side and on the other, arranged against them, we have the forces not so much of reality (though these would have to be dealt with sooner or later) but of another mental force, namely a very exacting morality absorbed from the specialized social reality created by the moral precepts of parents and state.

In the symptoms of obsessional neurosis the marks of this latter protagonist are particularly evident. Over-scrupulousness for instance and such obsessional acts as compulsive handwashing (in our patient's case "mind-washing" by confession) clearly bear the mark of this latter defensive command or prohibition.

Is it then that these unfortunate sufferers are those who at puberty were cursed with a superabundance of animal lusts against which the opposing forces of social (or parental) reality had to engage (*with only partial success*) in a particularly fierce battle?

According to Freud the answer is both "yes" and "no." "No" to the extent that these persons are often not particularly sexual in the ordinary sense. In fact, they often seem to have lost, as it were by the wayside, a part or almost all of their adult sexual potentiality.

For instance, the case we have just considered truthfully says she has no use for sex.

Perhaps the social or "moral" opponents of sexuality have won the battle in this field or to this extent?

What then has become of her sexual instinct? Freud tells us it lives as the dynamic force behind her symptoms, converted as it were into this form because its normal path of development into the ordinary adult form was successfully opposed by the moral forces arranged against it.

In fact a considerable portion of the instinctual force never reached an adult form at all.

But why was this? And what was the call for so strong a battle against it?

This is the part of the answer where we say "yes" to the question previously asked. Yes, this person was cursed with a superabundance of animal lusts. So much so that they developed prematurely, according to Freud in infancy, when they included a disproportionate amount of the component instincts of aggression and sadism and when they were bound in their object relationship to the child's own parents.

"Without exception these are children who even in early life betray very intense aggressiveness." Later on they betray intense scrupulousness or defensive acts and ceremonial. Thus, we had at that early age over-intense animal instincts consequently and necessarily opposed by an equivalently overstrong morality borrowed from the parents and developing out of the relationship of these impulses towards the parents.

A hint of this element may be gathered in the case of our patient from the relationship of her symptom to her mother.

To clarify the picture then, and to cut a long story short, we may reconstruct the psychopathology of such an illness as follows:

*First,* there is a stage of over-development of the animal instincts, particularly of the instincts of aggression and sadism.

*Second,* the moral forces instilled by parents, etc., are accepted by the developing mind and arranged in conflict against these primitive instincts and lead to a state of self-reproach.

*Third,* the symptom of shame or scrupulousness may emerge.

This is as it were the result of overdoing it. Such a symptom is called a reaction formation. On the other hand, the conflict may be repressed from consciousness and the sufferer may seem apparently well.

This may have been largely our patient's condition before the age of puberty when she says the symptoms first appeared. Her infantile sexuality hitherto repressed successfully may have suffered a rude awakening by the experiences at the age of twelve or earlier. The arrival of puberty with its physical contributions finally tipped the balance and the battle began anew.

The *fourth stage* is that of the emergence of the illness.

It should be explained that every memory, every idea or thought, carries with it a certain emotional tone. This emotional tone is called the "affect." Now the affect is the dynamic energy and is much more difficult to *keep down* (repress) than is the idea or meaning to which it was originally attached.

The result is that the affect commonly bursts into consciousness *without* the memories, thoughts and experiences which originally gave rise to it.

Thus in this case we get the unpleasant affect of "worry" which accompanied the early infantile struggles bursting through into consciousness, but separated from any *memories* of the original struggles with which it was first associated.

We see in the clinical history a replica of this process, for the patient confesses that her struggle at puberty was concerned with sex or sexual images whereas the same affect, the distress of conflict and compulsion, is now tormenting her with totally different ("innocent") ideas accompanying it.

What then has happened to the original *ideas*? They have been so successfully repressed and over-repressed that she cannot bear sexuality. In this "phobia" we detect a symptom produced from these sexual ideas in the form of a reaction formation against them—going to the opposite extreme for protection.

One of the characteristics of obsessional neurosis is this tendency to substitute new and harmless ideas for the previously "guilty" ones, and to attach the affects.

It is as if the mind said: "If I can't get rid of the emotion or affect I can at least get rid of the idea or thought, and attach the feelings to some less 'horrible' thoughts."

But throughout, the quality of compulsion inherent in the original dynamic instinct is present in all these changeable substitutes. Also the struggle for mastery of the compulsion continues unabated although it has been diverted to symbols and the will is now grappling only with these shadows.

The associated distress of the original struggle persists whether the symptom is constructed out of substitutes for the original impulses or, as is more common, out of the acts against those impulses or out of the two combined.

The special mode of defence in this illness is *substitution* of the original ideas. Something in the actual present-day life (e.g. the Sunday's outing with her boy friend) is put in place of the early "guilty" experiences or thoughts; something non-sexual or innocent (e.g. her present-day thoughts) is put in place of the sexual or guilty phantasies.

Nevertheless the original feelings of guilt, or rather her reaction formations against "sin," are betrayed in many ways: her need to "confess," her constant self-examination, the "punishment" she suffers or inflicts upon herself in worry, etc., and most of all by her repudiation of all pleasure, particularly the pleasure of any sexual love-life.

How can we free her from this everlasting torment?

*Not* by an exposition of its psychopathology as revealed in this article and particularly not by any hint of a sexual element in it.

The slightest reference to sexuality as a factor, particularly infantile sexuality, even in a case where the patient has herself openly referred to it, is liable to be met with denial, repudiation, and anger—even greater than it encounters in normal persons. For the battle against it has in the obsessional been even stronger, and the victory, if such it can be called, won at an even dearer price.

The patient can be cured only by getting her mind itself to go back to the origin of her struggles and sufferings—by bringing back to memory, the experiences and phantasies and particularly the early modes of defence (reaction formations) adopted against them.

It is only when she has become conscious of these, the real or original protagonists of her struggle, that she will be in a position to grapple with the substance instead of the shadow of her compulsive illness.

Then only will she be in a position to reconstruct the past and finally to divert the dynamic energy of the compulsion to the instinctive level to which it belongs.

## INFERIORITY FEELINGS (I)

IN deference to public demand, I have agreed to write a case sheet or two about inferiority feeling. But I must confess at the outset that I have failed to find it a clinical entity.

My experience forces me to regard it as merely one of the commonest and perhaps most superficial manifestations of nervous conflicts and anxieties, accompanied in every case by a crop of collateral, and often more serious, symptoms.

I have never had a patient whose trouble could be diagnosed simply as inferiority complex. So in order to deal with this subject, I have preferred to choose excerpts from a succession of cases where inferiority feelings figured as one of the most prominent symptoms.

Thus a patient at his first interview makes the following remarks:

"My chief complaint, Doctor, is a lack of confidence in myself; I cannot make myself feel at home in any environment.

"When I am with people I am not at ease; there is a general nervousness, an unsettled feeling. Am I inferior to other people, and if not, why do I behave as if I am?"

From another patient: "I don't seem to be able to take on any responsibility. I feel I can never carry on by myself. I always need someone to fall back upon; I couldn't bear to be anywhere alone. There must be somebody about or else I feel helpless and lost. This has been since I left my mother eight years ago.

"At the same time a sexual habit began to worry me—perhaps as a sort of consolation. I feel it would be more 'natural' to direct my thoughts into more suitable channels—something more creative, something that would be of benefit to me in time to come. The men at the office insinuate that I am a baby.

"Oh, yes, I have girl friends. At the tennis club I usually find myself among the girls. *In fact, I think they treat me as one of them.*

"Oh, yes, I have kissed them sometimes, *but only just to say goodnight or goodbye.* But that doesn't worry me; what worries me is a fear of losing mother and a dissatisfaction with myself because I do not seem to have any confidence or ability, and because of my bad habit."

Again from a third patient: "What I complain of is a lack of self-reliance, and nervousness in company. I have never been able to tell a funny story convincingly. I have a hesitating way of talking and sometimes break into a stammer. My powers of self-expression go wrong."

Remarks such as these, here recorded verbatim, could be multiplied *ad nauseam* by turning up almost any page of a medical psychologist's case notes.

In their most general aspect they indicate an individual's dissatisfaction with himself, specifically with his character, a feeling or opinion that he is not all he should be, that he has failed to satisfy his own requirements regarding himself.

He has fallen below the standard which he has set himself. This may be due to the standard being too high, or at least beyond the capabilities with which nature has endowed him.

In psychological terms one would call it a disparity between the ego ideal and the real ego.

This is, however, a rather too superficial aspect of the matter. We must ask *what* is dissatisfied with *what*, and *why* it is dissatisfied?

We will find ourselves in a muddle unless we immediately divide the mind into those three topographical divisions which psychoanalysis has to postulate to clarify most of its concepts: the *super-ego* (with its ego ideal), the *ego*, and the *Id*.

There are only three of these terms, and you will find that they simplify rather than complicate the explanation of the nature and source of inferiority feelings.

A brief definition of each will be necessary, and then everything will be clear.

*The super-ego* is that part of the mind which criticizes the ego. It includes more than conscience, for a portion of it is unconscious. It includes also a standard of perfection for the individual which is called the *ego ideal*.

*The ego* is that part of the mind with which the individual identifies himself. It is conscious and in touch with reality.

*The Id* is the reservoir of the blind instincts and impulses. It accumulates tension and strives to relieve it. It is thus the source or origin of dynamic energy, although itself unconscious.

Now we can see clearly that this dissatisfaction and inferiority feeling is a feeling that comes from the super-ego blaming the ego for not having come up to a standard of its ego ideal.

Is this just a complicated way of saying that the individual is dissatisfied with himself? Is it necessary to introduce these special terms?

I think we will find that it is necessary when we come to consider that the super-ego can do more than blame; it can actually punish. It can punish in a variety of ways besides dissatisfaction, inferiority feelings, and remorse; there can be the most severe depression—even melancholia. There can be illnesses, accidents, and worse.

An outraged super-ego can even enforce self-destruction.

If we ask why the super-ego is dissatisfied, why it blames the ego, we will discover some most interesting answers. In the first place it appears most generally that it is blaming the ego for having accepted impulses emanating from the Id. It is as though mother smacked the child for being a naughty boy—a very severe mother and a very naughty child.

The intrapsychic situation is, however, a very serious one. The individual may be troubled with most uncomfortable guilt-feelings. Even Freud, so expert at detecting minutest differences, expressed doubt as to whether feelings of inferiority can truly be separated from feelings of guilt.

Read the following and judge for yourself:

"I used to be continually blushing. I am a religious man and it seems to me that I ought to be better than I am. I ought to give up something and start something better, but I don't get started with any of my good resolutions.

"Ought I to give up the struggle? But in that case I would never be satisfied with myself. I would not want to live. It seems I must struggle to be *perfect*. It's an all or nothing business with me. Am I fighting for an ideal that I cannot achieve, which I am too weak to achieve? What is the good of me?

"I am extremely sensitive to any remarks or criticism. I am always wondering if I am doing right. I have this weakness, this secret vice, which I have been unable to overcome. I have read that one should sublimate it into a religious interest. I feel that only in that way would I cease to be troubled by it—but I have never succeeded. It is no good the other way either because I cannot express myself.

"I saw a girl daily for six months and never had the courage to speak to her. I am shy and somehow I feel terribly guilty about it all."

And again from another patient: "What I complain of is a lack of self-reliance, and nervousness in company. The latter is most marked with the opposite sex, especially before engaging in conversation. I am continually blushing; I get terribly self-conscious. Sometimes I break into perspiration, which is most uncomfortable.

"I started blushing at fifteen. I was shy even as a small boy, especially when I was being fitted for clothes; it had something to do with my body. I despised myself for a bad habit that I was trying to give up.

"Now after all this emotional strain, I have lost confidence in myself and I keep on blushing as though I were guilty of something.

"I am one mass of fears and repressions and inferiority feelings—and yet I have been trying to get flying instruction to become an aviator. Can you make that out, Doctor? In spite of my lack of confidence and self-reliance! Is it an attempt to compensate for something I feel to be lacking?

"And also, though I feel so embarrassed and inferior in company, I keep looking at myself in the glass. I think I am becoming very vain, yet it does not get rid of the acute inferiority feelings I have about my eyes."

Again from another patient: "Has the blushing something to do with my habit? I have been told that that is common enough, much more common than blushing. Is it because I feel uncommonly guilty about it that I blush?

"I get embarrassed if somebody even mentions a girl's name."

*Analyst:* "For instance?"

"If someone says: 'Have you seen Gladys lately?' I may get no reaction; but if once I get this blushing reaction I get it every time her name is mentioned."

*Analyst:* "Have you seen Gladys lately?"

"If I say, no I haven't seen her, the feeling is that the other person probably thinks I have seen her and that I am concealing something."

*Analyst:* "What are you concealing?"

"The absurd thought comes to me as though I had been up to some mischief with her. It is absurd because I have never even flirted with the girl. Admittedly she is very attractive, and I'd like to have . . .

"I remember now. I have had phantasies about her, sexual phantasies and imaginary acts in connection with my habit, but it is absurd that this should make me afraid or shy to have lunch with my friends. Can it be that I feel inferior on account of things like that?"

Whether or not inferiority feelings are inextricably wrapped up with guilt-feelings, the question remains as to why one individual should be cursed with them out of all proportion to the facts of inferiority or guilt, and why another individual, perhaps far more inferior or guilty, should be relatively free from this mental distress.

It is notorious that the very good man—the saint—is for ever beating his chest and calling upon God to forgive him for being a sinner, whereas those who have perpetrated the greatest crimes against their fellow-men, those who have bathed the world in blood—the Attilas, the Cæsars, the Napoleons, the Mussolinis, the Hitlers—are conspicuously lacking both in feelings of guilt and inferiority.

Hence it seems that these feelings do not arise from any factual evidence, from the ego which is appreciative of reality values. Whence do they arise?

The evidence of medical psychology points to their origin from two opposite sources—the super-ego and the Id. To understand how this comes about we must study the nature and trace the development of each of these components of the mind.

The super-ego develops in infancy and early childhood and is influenced and modified, if not actually brought about, by parents and monitors. Demands are made upon the infant to forgo or to control his instinctual pleasures and his natural tendencies to relief of tension.

A standard is set him which he is compelled to try and live up to. The penalty for even trivial failures is not, necessarily, so much punishment, as the withdrawal of parental love. This love is very necessary for him; indeed he feels that he would be lost or perish without it.

We mentioned that if the super-ego does not love the ego the individual feels inferior, and if the super-ego blames the ego the individual feels guilty.

The predecessor, or rather, the progenitor of the super-ego is the parents and monitors, and sooner or later we find that patients with inferiority feelings, rightly or wrongly, consider that their parents did not love them adequately, or that they were guilty in the eyes of their parents.

Two examples are given:

"My parents didn't bother about me much when I was a child. They certainly gave me no attention after my younger brother was born. I spent my time fruitlessly trying to get back into favour. Perhaps it was then that my inferiority feelings started. I thought I was of no value.

"Father was a queer sort of man, all business and hoarding money; he did not notice the children. Whenever he came into the nursery it was only to cut down some luxury for economy's sake. With him it was always 'take away,' never 'give.' Mother was just a dreamer; the *real* children did not concern her."

Again from another patient (this time from a late stage of analysis):

"As a little boy, even as a baby, I remember that I used to feel very guilty because of what the nursemaid was doing to me. They [his parents] seemed to think I was all nice and worth loving; but

G

if they knew this! Once they found this out they'd know I was just nasty and they'd throw me away.

"I'd awake from sleep thinking they knew it all and that I was finished, and then I'd see my mother's face bending over me and smiling, actually smiling, as though she loved me, and I could hardly believe it. It seemed amazing that they should love a horrible creature. It could only be because they didn't know.

"I lived in terror of their finding out . . . and then I got infantile paralysis (at 2½) and nearly died. I knew this was punishment. It was their love that brought me back to life, but I knew that I was really unworthy although mother and father did not know it."

Thus we may conclude that whether it be the parents in early life or the super-ego in later life which does not love the individual or which (he thinks) adjudges him guilty, the result is the same feeling of inferiority, unworthiness or guilt.

It was mentioned that feelings of inferiority can arise from an apparently opposite source to the super-ego, namely the Id, the sort of body-mind foundation of all mental processes.

The explanation of this seemingly absurd contradiction lies in the fact that all functional illness arises from *conflict*. Conflict implies a battle between two incompatible or opposite forces. As a result of this battle one or other of the contestants can be wounded, injured or destroyed.

In the contest between super-ego and Id, if the super-ego is destroyed or partially destroyed, we may get a murderer or a conqueror. The Id can only be destroyed, together with its ego, by the act of suicide.

It seems, however, that the Id can be injured to a variable degree and yet life continue, though with some mark of mental, psycho-sexual, or physical ill health.

Thus, in many patients we may detect on deeper analysis some apparent foundation for their feelings of inferiority in a deep-seated mental or physical symptom or disability.

The question may arise as to whether such an inferiority is real or imaginary. May they not even have inherited some mental or physical disability which gives them a real foundation, a real cause for feeling inferior?

Let us here pay our respects to Alfred Adler, who is said to have invented the term "inferiority feeling." (The popular term "inferiority complex" may be regarded as a misnomer since feelings of inferiority do not necessarily, as does a complex, arise from repression.)

This term has been used by some authors to cover the entire gamut of psychogenic disorders.

Thus, one Adlerian writer says:

"Symptoms of the inferiority complex include (besides feelings of inferiority, social maladjustment, blushings, sweatings, nervousness) headaches, migraine, nervous indigestion, asthma, palpitation of the heart; the vague fatigue, loss of appetite and general malaise, which used to be called neurasthenia and psychasthenia.

"Impotence and premature ejaculation in men; frigidity, painful menstruation and painful intercourse in women; vomiting, tics, grimaces, bed-wetting, and night terrors in children; insomnia, 'nerves' and panic, the fear of old age, death, cancer, tuberculosis, or syphilis, together with the profession of 'being healthy' or 'being sick' are additional symptoms of the inferiority complex in adults."

Small wonder that such volumes can be written on the subject if under the heading of a subjective and superficial sensation we include every manifestation of psychogenic illness!

Would it not be a less distorted concept if we regarded all these symptoms together with inferiority feelings as being collateral branches of a growth which has its roots in deep-seated unconscious disorder?

And if we are to systematize our terminology, would it not be better to include the lesser under the greater, the part under the whole—instead of vice versa?

Accordingly I would prefer to classify inferiority feelings as a special manifestation of anxiety rather than include anxiety, together with its various other manifestations, under the term "inferiority complex," or to say, as does the author here quoted: "What is commonly known as 'nervousness' is another expression of the inferiority complex."

If psychology is to remain a science it seems it must look to its terminology.

Adler wrote much about organ inferiority. His thesis was that the individual was afflicted (by inheritance or otherwise) by some inferior organ or function from which arose his inferiority feeling which led him to compensate or over-compensate for this defect by striving to develop strength in lieu of weakness.

It is intriguing to consider the possibility that every one of our patients who complains of inferiority feelings possesses some organ inferiority. The patient himself, even unasked, will do his level best to aid and abet this theory. He will parade before our eyes all his minor physical and functional defects, real and imaginary.

Take the following two cases for example:

"I have always wondered why some people have more brains than others. I want a decent brain. I do not think I have one, it hasn't developed. I have a receding forehead, and I think that means a lack of brains. I was told by a psychologist that I had an outsize inferiority complex.

"I am scared that my girl will notice that I have a defect in my eyes; they are slightly divergent. Then she will throw me up."

Significantly enough, he goes straight on to say: "Masturbation has troubled me a lot; it is a constant worry. Twenty-four hours after it I start worrying about the eyes. Five years ago it was none of these things, it was only my shortcomings, my inferiority, that I worried about.

"I do funny things. For instance I often go to switch off electric lights during the day when they are not on. I tried to give up meat because I wanted to go on to a fruit diet. I tried to give up masturbation and all sexual thoughts and feelings; but I never stick to anything, I never succeed in anything that I try to do."

From another case: "I am awfully squeamish about passing a butcher's shop, especially if I see any animals skinned or cut open.

"Some time ago I decided that what was wrong with me was my nose. If you look carefully you can see that it is not quite straight. I went to a surgeon who said I had a deflected septum and that he would do the operation and put my nose straight at the same time.

"I decided to have it done and for weeks I banked all my hopes of complete recovery on this, and could think and talk of nothing else. Finally my elder brother said that if I went on with it he would kick me round the room until I had some real defect to worry about."

Our difficulty in assessing Adler's theory is twofold: the most careful examination of a person complaining of inferiority feelings usually fails to reveal any defect over and above those shared by the majority of normal persons. Moreover, the inferiority he feels is usually quite unrelated to any minor defects he may possess.

On the other hand, many persons with pronounced physical defect or severe organic disease are no more than normally afflicted with inferiority feelings. Indeed, in spite of a natural bias in favour of Adler's view, with the exception of cases of dementia praecox, I have failed to find it more than an intriguing hypothesis.

However much we wish really to justify and substantiate our symptomatic findings, it seems that the feelings of inferiority—like those of guilt—are usually antithetical to facts and must therefore be regarded as products of the mind. This makes them no less real to the sufferer.

What, then, *is* the deep-seated mental or physical disability that gives rise to feelings of inferiority? And how in its turn does it arise?

Those versed in psycho-analysis, or those rare individuals with an exceptional facility for reading symbols, will already have found the answer in the case notes which I have quoted.

It is not for nothing that the word "*impotence*" has two meanings; one designating psycho-sexual impotence and the other any and every variety of impotence, disability or inferiority. Analytical experience teaches us that it is right to use the one term for them all.

It appears that impotence in the ego is only, as it were, a reflection of the deeper impotence of a frustrated id. Inferiority feelings sometimes have this much basis.

We can hardly expect such strongly censored ideas to present themselves to consciousness in their naked form. Even in dreams it is usual for some symbol other than the sex organ itself to be employed.

For instance, a patient of mine with pronounced inferiority feelings and, until recently, totally psycho-sexually impotent, dreams that he is: "*Taking his fishing tackle to a shop at Shepherd's Bush to have it repaired.*"

He says he has never possessed fishing tackle and the only "fishing" he has ever done is fishing for a lady's favours. He was so engaged the day before the dream, but found he was getting only anxiety and no pleasure out of the situation.

It must not be concluded that all individuals with inferiority feelings are equally severely afflicted. In the conflict between super-ego and Id, the super-ego may not be so completely victorious nor the Id so completely defeated. Even some degree of external frustration to the Id impulses, in so far as it is effective, may produce a considerable degree of inferiority feeling emanating from the Id.

However, for this to reach any pronounced degree it may be necessary for the individual himself to be co-operating in the frustration, that is to say, inhibiting his own impulses. Thus, for instance, we may see in the case of a potentially normal man with an undue degree of devotion to his mother, living with her and endeavouring against his instinctual nature to live up to the ideals set by her and by his mode of life, a certain degree of inferiority feeling emanating from a frustrated, inhibited, and therefore temporarily injured or impotent Id.

To sum up: inferiority feelings arise from the conflict between super-ego and Id with the ego as a sort of buffer in between—a buffer that gets punches from both sides and feels damaged or inferior in consequence.

If the ego has leaned too much to the side of the Id, the super-ego refuses to love it and the individual feels dissatisfied or inferior.

If the "crime" of the ego has exceeded the tolerance of the super-ego, the latter chastises it with a severity proportionate to the disparity between the ego's Id-tolerance and the super-ego's ego ideal.

Guilt-feelings arise and may result in any degree of mental depression and suffering. Even physical ills may ensue.

If, on the other hand, the Id has been unduly denied self-expression, a deep-seated discontent emanating from a sick or damaged Id, may be responsible for inferiority feelings breaking through into consciousness.

In psycho-analysis this is called the "castration complex." The inferiority feeling may *be pinned on to*, or *symbolized* by any "damaged" organ or concept, such as, for instance, in the cases we have mentioned: defective eyes, crooked nose, fishing tackle that needs repair, receding forehead, a deficient brain, a weak character, or *a general feeling of inferiority*.

It should be emphasized that according to psycho-analysis the castration complex is common to all. Certainly feelings of inferiority are more the rule than the exception. It is only when possessed in a very severe degree that they deserve the name of symptom.

Even here it should be remembered that many great men have been afflicted with an undue proportion of them. Indeed those most conspicuously immune, or totally incapable of inferiority feelings, are pronounced psychotics with delusions of grandeur.

## INFERIORITY FEELINGS (II)

*or*

## WHAT IS THE USE OF ME?

A HIGHLY educated woman, not yet thirty, a university lecturer, comes for treatment on account of a feeling of inferiority and inaptitude in life in general and in her work in particular. She says:

"You may be inclined to assume because of my degrees and university standing that I am intelligent, capable and successful in life. The exact contrary is the case. I an utterly dull and stupid, quite incapable of doing my job, and nobody has been such a complete and impossible failure as I am.

"All I have succeeded in doing so far is to conceal the falsity of my position from the authorities, but it is impossible that I can have successfully concealed it. They must know I am getting my salary on false pretences. What I cannot understand is why they have not dismissed me already.

"However, it cannot be long before I am sacked. When it comes it will be a relief, for I couldn't be any more miserable and hopeless than I am at present."

*Analyst:* "What is the matter?"

"Everything is the matter; I cannot do my work efficiently; nobody is interested; I am not interested. I am dull and stupid; my mind is no good; I am no good. Why, I cannot even make a success of my life outside my working hours.

"I have no friends, no social life. The reason is not only that I am stupid but that I feel awkward and embarrassed in company. People do not want me, they want to get away from me, and I want to get away from them because I feel uncomfortable.

"Oh, yes, I have tried. I try to say polite things, the correct things. But it falls flat. I am frightened they will see what an awkward fool I am. I am full of stupid embarrassments and have a completely empty head. I can't even think when I am in company. Surely the other lecturers and the Dean must have noticed it! I can't think why they put up with me. I'll be thrown out before long and then what on earth shall I do for a living?

"There is only one good thing about me. I am physically fit—like a horse or a cow. But I don't suppose anybody would employ me even for physical work, because I am so unattractive and ugly. Whatever is the use of me? I am utterly dissatisfied with myself, and I can't understand why I go on living except that I haven't the courage to take my own life."

The inferiority feelings are plain enough, also the depression. She is far from satisfied with herself. Let us see if she reveals the various factors which we have found commonly associated with feelings of inferiority: guilt-feelings, impressions of being unloved, particularly by her mother in infancy, and the most fundamental and specific of all, *organ inferiority*.

Will she tell us which organ is felt to be inferior, or rather, from which unconscious phantasy of organ inferiority there springs her general feeling of inferiority?

In this particular patient, the more superficial elements, namely the feelings of guilt and the feelings of withdrawal of love, are not so marked as in some cases, but there is enough material to substantiate their existence and to assess their rôle in contributing to general feelings of inferiority.

For example:

"Do you think I should resign my position? Can't you see that it is very wrong of me to go on accepting my salary when I know I am not doing the work efficiently? It's obtaining money under false pretences. I have been a fool all my life, a fool to take up an academic life, a fool to let my father spend all his money on my training when I might have known that I was incompetent and not worth it.

"How can I resign now and let him down? Whichever way I turn I shall be doing wrong. If I try and stick to my job I am defrauding the university authorities; if I resign I am letting my father down after all the money he has spent on me.

"Do you know, I sometimes feel a terrible sinner, though I can't think what sin I have committed unless it is the worst sin of all, that of being perfectly useless to everybody."

*Analyst:* "Does nobody love you?"

"Oh, yes, my father loves me, I suppose—that is why I cannot let him down—but it is only because he doesn't know how hopeless I am. He is just a dreamer, he doesn't know me. Besides, I rarely see him, as he is up north and I live in lodgings.

"No *man* loves me, if that is what you mean. Why should he? The idea is too absurd. I have no sex appeal—unattractive—ugly.

"Yes, I know even ugly women get married, but they must have something that I haven't got. I am terrified of meeting people socially; I am awkward, stiff and ungainly. There is no charm about me. I am hopeless. No wonder that I am un-wanted."

The next session belongs to the more advanced transference period of her treatment, but it may be regarded as a continuation of the last session in that it brings up guilt feelings and shows us the feelings of inferiority and being unwanted that arose in her infancy and childhood.

The "transference" means that she is unconsciously living this early part of her life with me and this is what opens the door to these early, forgotten memories:

"Have you been telling the Dean of my college that I come here?"

*Analyst:* "Why do you ask?"

"There's no reason; it is just an idea I got. She'd know then that I was there under false pretences, that I was hiding something all the time."

*Analyst:* "What are you hiding?"

"Hiding that I like coming here. Hiding that I am afraid of something. Am I doing something guilty by coming here? Should I give it up? I am much better; ought I to stop coming now?"

*Analyst:* "Do you want to?"

"Good Lord, no! It is the one thing that keeps me well. I don't seem to care so much now whether I lose the job or not. I feel all right. But have you told the Dean; do you think she'll dismiss me?"

*Analyst:* "What is guilty about coming here?"

"Because I like it. Everything I liked was always guilty. I was taught by my mother and father that duty was the only right thing to do, and duty was always something one did not like doing. If one liked doing a thing it showed that it was not duty; it was self-indulgence and must be stopped."

*Analyst:* "What did father tell mother about you?"

"I don't know what he told her, but I do not think she liked him being kind to me when I was a child. Anyhow, it was not often, because he was usually miles away or dreaming. I was left with nannie and my mother. They didn't like me; at least they didn't like me much.

"That was quite natural because my brother (three and a half years younger) was much nicer. Sometimes I felt hostile to my mother and to nannie because they made such a fuss of my brother and seemed to ignore me. But in the end I came to the conclusion that they were quite right.

"You see, he was a boy, a fine, handsome boy, and I was evidently pretty useless, a poor specimen. How could I expect them to want me?"

Perhaps enough has been given to show that this patient's inferiority feelings were connected with some suggestion of guilt-feelings, with feelings of being unloved and therefore worthless, and with ideas of the withdrawal of mother-love in infancy.

We come now to the most difficult task in this paper, the "organ inferiority" of which Adler makes so much, and which Freud insists boils down to one particular organ. The others Freud regards as all symbols representing the one.

This may not seem so one-sided if we bear in mind that this organ itself is, in its anatomical presentation, also merely a symbol, albeit a symbol of particularly strong affect (emotion).

The measure of the strength of this affect may be gauged by the strength of the censoring and repressing force arrayed against it. Herein we have the essential ingredients of *conflict*. It is from conflict that symptoms arise.

To uncover this deeper material I will give two short dreams, one representing father prohibition or rejection (rejection by the male) and the other mother deprecation and rejection (rejection by the female). As a result of this unconscious material of infancy the patient has, all her life, felt rejected by men and women. She has accepted her mother's (really her own) undervaluation and has felt herself to be inferior and worthless. The first dream is as follows:

"I came into the dining-room to talk to my father while he was having supper. I was sitting there playing with my cat. The cat was asking for a long finger biscuit, which she likes. I was going to give it to her but my father said she mustn't have it as it was not good for her.

"I said 'very well' and put the tin away. The cat was annoyed, and it bit my shoe and scratched me. My father had finished his meal. I went upstairs to a bed that was much too high for me to be comfortable in. I felt very depressed."

In the course of her associations of thought, she says:

"Father would not let me wear pretty clothes and go to parties when I was a girl. He seemed to have forgotten that girls get married. Career was everything to him; I had to do exams all the time. There was never any love making, nor indeed any pleasure, in my young life. The bed that was too high is my job which is too exalted and uncomfortable for me." Thus her father rejects and refuses her sexual life (the desires of the pussy) while gratifying his own (he finished his meal). Conflict and injury results (the cat bit and scratched her). She ignores this and goes to a high uncomfortable bed (her academic career) and feels depressed (and inferior).

The other dream is very short. She says:

"There is a senior lecturer at the college whom I rather like and recently I have wanted her to take notice of me. *In the dream I invited her to come and have tea with me in my apartments. She replied, 'I won't do that because I don't like second-hand cake.'* I felt humiliated, confused and guilty as though I had done the wrong thing."

Her associations to "second-hand cake" are most illuminating. She says:

"When I was an undergraduate at Oxford and I had to return an invitation to tea, I would get a cake that had already been used at somebody else's tea party. You see, I was a scholarship girl and had very little money. Usually I got quite a good cake, the only thing was that it had had a section cut out of it. There was always a big chunk missing."

The dream is allowed to remain incomprehensible, but her free associations throughout the session continue to be illuminating. She says:

"As a child, even when only four or five years of age, I was always wishing that I could be a boy. I saw what a fuss was made of my young brother just because he was a boy, whereas I was no good, because I was only a girl.

"I do not think my mother wanted me. That senior lecturer in the dream reminds me of my mother. But what on earth has second-hand cake to do with it? I felt that mother didn't want me because I was a girl—she rejected me like that woman in the dream.

"I have been brought up on the inferiority of women. Perhaps all my life I have been trying to be a male by pursuing an academic career. I believe that intellectual plain women like me really are inferior. I feel as though I am an inferior sort of male.

"What have I got? Just a bit of education aping the male without being able to be a real male. I do not seem to have what even stupid women have, good looks, etc., and certainly I haven't got a husband or family.

"Women like me are neither one thing nor the other; there is something lacking, something missing. It feels to me as if it is everything that matters. . . .

"Who on earth would want to have tea with me? Why should they? Why should anyone want me? Is that piece missing out of the cake something missing out of me? I certainly feel lacking."

The symbolism of the cake is well known to psycho-analysts. There is an unconscious association between food and femininity, perhaps dating back to the original association of the child to his mother as the milk giver. This rôle of the female is maintained throughout life by her domestic function as preparer and server of the meals.

Cake, however, appears to have a special symbolical significance, a significance which reaches its high-water mark in the ritual of the wedding cake—the pride of cake makers.

At the wedding this cake is symbolically cut by the bride (i.e. at her volition) using the bridegroom's sword, if he be a military man. The bridegroom always assists at the operation.

Subsequently the cake is divided into small pieces and dispatched to the bride's various friends and acquaintances. Thus is the passing of maidenhood symbolically enacted.

The patient under review is a spinster and a virgin. The defective cake with the piece missing can refer in her case only to her feelings of damage or inferiority through being a girl instead of the boy (like her brother) that she longed to be.

She felt inferior; she felt that, as a girl, she was inferior to her brother because he was a boy. She felt from infancy that she was not so good, owing to this deficiency, that mother rightly regarded her as valueless and refused to partake in love (tea party) with her.

The organ inferiority, here symbolized by a cake with a chunk missing, in this case at least, is seen to hark back to infantile feelings of inferiority of sexual difference.

Is this the sort of organ inferiority to which Adler unconsciously alludes? Does Adler, like most patients, reveal it not by cake or fishing tackle (see last paper), but by a variety of other organs used as symbols for it? It would appear that in this case at least Freud's contention is right.

We now pass on to consider what, if anything, can be done to enable the individual to gain some relief from the distress of inferiority feelings.

One of the advantages  the practising psychologist has over the speculative (or introspective) psychologist is that the former can observe the changes actually taking place in his patient during the treatment. Nevertheless it is not always possible for him to be quite sure why or how these changes came about. Even he may find a certain amount of speculation inevitable.

The patient whose case we have just been reviewing gradually lost her feelings of inferiority. At the same time the "muddle" in her head disappeared and she regained her nervous health.

She herself attributed these changes largely to having found some-one, the psychologist, to whom she could freely unburden her very soul, and who accepted her as she really was without once betraying the slightest contempt or condemnation, but, on the contrary, always treated her with kindness, understanding and respect. In consequence, she readjusted her own attitude towards herself.

An important element here was that she had unconsciously placed this father-confessor in a very exalted rôle in her phantasy. He stood for a sort of super-parent—almost a god.

If father and mother (to the infant) or "god" (to the adult) could know everything about her, all her inner workings and weak-nesses, and yet respect and value her, then surely there was no further need for her to feel ashamed and inferior. She was, as it were, reinstated to a position of equality among her fellow men.

There was, however, a deeper and less conscious process at work which did much to mitigate her inferiority or inadequacy. She had found the long-lost good parent of her infancy. She was, as it were, now no longer an "orphan"; she was attached to, *a sort of appendage to*, a "bigger," "wiser" and "exalted" personage; she felt herself to be a part of him and, as such, unassailable by these lesser persons, "brothers and sisters," with whom she associated in her work and recreation.

The difference in feeling was perhaps the difference between the feelings of a lost, forlorn child afraid of the other children's jeers and cruelties, and the feelings of a child secure in the knowledge that it had good and powerful parents who valued it and of whom it formed a part.

A dream she had during her analysis may help to show the sort of changes taking place in her unconscious and their relationship to her inferiority feelings:

She dreamt she was having dinner with the Duke of Windsor. "I sat opposite him at table. I felt proud at the exalted company, but he did not seem to take much notice of me and so I felt, also, a little humiliated.

"Then I was walking down a dingy, dirty little street; there was a slum house at the side, and I knew it was the house where I had been born. It makes me think of all the inferiority feelings I had as a child, and since. Then I emerged from the slum, and again met the Duke, who had been looking on. I felt terribly ashamed, but he smiled and shook hands with me and I felt much better."

The Duke in her dream is, of course, her elevated concept of her analyst.

The process of transference relationship to the analyst had passed through several vicissitudes before it reached the stage that proved so helpful to her. Three stages may be described.

In the earliest stage her anxiety grew less and her confidence increased; she was more and more freely pouring out her free associations of thought.

In the second stage, with this increasing relaxation, this diminsihing anxiety, feelings arose which she had previously (at least since the onset of her illness) not dared to admit into consciousness. These were sexual feelings and desires. They were naturally directed towards the new-found confidant. She was never made to feel ashamed of these and yet it was gradually borne home to her that she could never hope for their practical expression in their personal relationship.

The third stage, which we have described above, came about as a result. She accepted herself, including the sexual side of her nature, and accepted also that the father-figure in whom she confided was not to be a partner in her sexual life. He thus became an exalted "parent," and she too felt less inferior through having found herself and through having found strength and self-esteem in her relationship to him.

The situation brought about is emotionally and fundamentally a reinstatement into the family life of her "parents." She is now, as it were, a successfully adjusted "child" feeling adequate to the task of facing her fellow "children" and so no longer inferior in their presence. The "child," like the branch of a tree, gets its strength from its relationship to the "parent" trunk.

Her relationship to the analyst did not remain a complete expression of her developing life, and it is possible that her inferiority feelings would not have been entirely and permanently removed had it not been for the fact that, soon after, she acquired a husband and perhaps the prospect of a family.

Her femininity was too strongly ingrained for the masculine compensation of academic achievement to satisfy her completely. I fancy she will only feel a completely adequate human being, with hardly a vestige of inferiority feelings, when she has achieved the birth of a son.

Thus we see in this case a lady, with her emotions repressed through fear, shame and guilt-feelings, overburdened with feelings of inferiority.

We see her becoming unrepressed, finding herself, with the progressive disappearance of guilt-feelings and of inferiority.

Eventually she acquires first an "exalted parent," and subsequently a husband also, and perhaps in due course a son. Inferiority feelings disappear progressively with each and every stage of her natural emotional development.

Possibly a chrysalis that remained confined within its case and never became a butterfly would naturally feel inferior!

In practice it seems that if an individual has friends and is enjoying an adequate social life with persons of his own social and intellectual calibre, he is unlikely to suffer unduly from inferiority feelings. He feels himself to be one with his contemporaries, he feels himself to be a member of a large and solid family. He is in possession of much of what this patient acquired in her "parent-figure" analyst.

The fallacy, however, in advising those overburdened with inferiority feelings to join clubs and to make friends, etc., is that such persons are lacking in these social advantages just because their intense guilt feelings, shyness, or inferiority cause them to feel embarrassment, or even agony, in all social contacts, and in consequence they tend to avoid their fellow beings.

Some little help is usually necessary before the initial steps can be taken; the child must feel it has a parent before it can confidently and happily play in the playground with the other children.

Have I told the reader how to gain some relief from the distress of his inferiority feelings? Well, I have told a true story as a parable, and we must each have the intelligence to apply parables to our particular case.

## WHO AM I?

A YOUNG lady of 19 was brought to me on account of "strange feelings in her head."

She had been attending the mental out-patients' department of a hospital on and off for several years, but, nevertheless, during the last few months her condition had become considerably worse, and she was now unable to continue at her work (shorthand-typist), and moreover was unable to venture out of the house unaccompanied. Her parents rightly felt that they could not tolerate the thought of her being permanently invalided at this youthful age, and that something more intensive than sporadic attendance at a mental out-patient department was necessary. Accordingly, it was arranged that she should attend for psycho-therapeutic treatment three times weekly.

I saw a healthy-looking, plump girl, very neatly dressed, almost circumspect in her appearance and deportment.

What struck me most at the first attendance was the very careful way in which she walked, as though she were picking her steps. It appeared subsequently that not only her movements, but also her every thought was carefully picked. There was a purpose behind this over-carefulness.

At this, and at all her subsequent sessions, she arranged herself precisely and complacently on the settee, and adopted a general demeanour of calm and contentment.

It was difficult to break through her calm, or to persuade her to abandon this over-carefulness, in action, speech or, it transpired, even in thought. When she can be persuaded to speak she says always the same thing.

"All that is in my mind is what I have already said to you before. There is nothing but the same feelings and the same thoughts."

*Analyst:* "Well, if you have nothing else to say, you must say that, even if you have said it before."

She says:

"The feeling is that I don't know who I am. My thoughts consist only of one thing all the time: a condition of puzzlement, as though I did not know who or what I am—as though I did not recognize myself, and cannot remember anything. My mind seems to consist of one thing only, and that is just a sort of feeling as though I am only just alive. That is all, and that I don't know anything else, except that I am just alive, and I am not always sure about that, but the feeling is with me all the time. It is as though it seems to put a sort of *stop* to all other thoughts and feelings. If I say a thing, or do a thing, I just can't imagine that I have done it. It does not seem to be me. There seems to be no connection between what I have done and me. It's as though I had no memory for anything that has happened, even if it is something I have done only a moment ago. My mind seems to be occupied only with these strange feelings, and even these I seem to be holding carefully in check. But in spite of this they sometimes are inclined to reach a pitch, and then I feel at the moment that something terrible is going to happen. I feel that something is going to burst or explode in my head. I think that is the feeling I am trying to stop, and in consequence I have this feeling of something that stops me, that is always present in my head. If, in spite of this feeling to stop, I do get right up to this pitch, then it seems it cannot go any further, and I get awfully hot and confused. After that it goes back to the ordinary feelings again, the feelings of not knowing who I am, and of something stopping me. That is all."

These are the sort of statements that this patient makes over and over again, in part or in whole, after the first few minutes of silence, at the beginning of every one of her sessions. For some few weeks it seems that we shall never get any farther. The task of curing her, or even of making the slightest progress, seems hopeless. That stop, or full stop, in her mind appears to be stopping every therapeutic endeavour.

The question arises in the mind of the analyst, what is that stop stopping?

She herself has provided a partial clue when she says:

"I feel that something is going to burst or explode in my head."

That is, it would seem that she is stopping an accentuation of her feelings. She is stopping something from reaching a heightened intensity or climax.

In due course attempts are made to pass beyond a mere repetition of all these current mental experiences and feelings by pressing her with various questions. She is asked when she first experienced the condition which she complains of, and how it came about. She says:

"It suddenly came upon me, this feeling that I don't know who I am, at the age of 15, when I was looking at myself in the glass, and it has never left me since."

*Analyst:* "What had you been doing or feeling just prior to the event?"

H

"I can't remember. In fact, with these feelings in my head I have no memory at all for anything. Before that happened, I was perfectly well and happy. I wish I could get back to that state. I don't seem to be able to realize that I am the same person that I was before that happened. I was alive before that, and now I don't recognize myself."

*Analyst:* "Tell me about that liveliness. Did it feel nice to be alive?"

"I can't remember it; I can't remember what it felt like. There seems to be this stop in my mind which prevents me from knowing anything, from knowing what I was like, or what I felt, and even from recognizing who I am."

There can hardly be a more vivid account of the operation of repression within the mind than that which this patient is giving us. What is she repressing, and can we get her ever to give us an account of the conflict or fight with herself which led to such extreme measures as this, and to the persistent holding to these symptoms, rather than that she should revive the struggles and experiences which she has evidently been at such pains to forget? That these experiences against which she had struggled were very important to the feeling life of the psyche is beyond question from the fact that, with their successful repression, has gone a recognition of her own personality and the memory of everything that could be of importance to her feeling life. In place of it we have this new feeling life that is confined to the symptoms of which she complains.

One can only reply to her, as I did at one of her sessions:

"You do not recognize yourself, because it is not you. What has happened to the 'you' that lived before you were 15, when you were perfectly well and happy? Why can't you be the person you were then? The feelings that that person had, what was there about these feelings that you have been at such pains to forget, to put a full stop to—a stop which has ever since remained in your head? Evidently you prefer your present condition to the happy condition you had before you were 15, and against which you have fought so hard. At present you are clinging on to these symptoms lest you remember, and lest the mental experiences of that previous happy time come back to you and are remembered and re-experienced. What a fight you must have had against them!"

Nevertheless, the patient begins each session just as though it were again the first session. She enunciates the current feelings which comprise her illness, and claims that there is nothing else in her mind.

She continues:

"While I lie here and tell you about it the room seems to go round and round. It seems to make me giddy, as if there was something pressing on my brain the whole time. It seems to make me so dull."

*Analyst:* "Is it as though there is something you won't let your mind think about?"

(*Silence*)

*Patient:* "I can remember that when I was at school, and even up to quite recently, if ever anything was spoken about sex I used to get nervous. It used to make me terribly hot in my head, and my feet and legs would go cold. I wondered if others got the feeling. I thought it might injure my inside in some way. I used to worry about that. It seemed to push all the blood into my head, and then I could not think clear, and my mind would be dull."

*Analyst:* "That is the same as the feelings that you complain of now. And you say this was when you were in school. What age are you referring to?"

*Patient:* "I can't really remember. I think I used to imagine a lot of sexy things. I can't remember very well, but that seemed to be the beginning of it."

*Analyst:* "Tell me the sexy things you used to imagine."

*Patient:* "Did I say 'sexy'? I don't know why I said 'sexy.' It was, I think, just when I felt nervous. I think it was just worry that something would do me some harm. Anyhow, my legs and feet would go cold and my head hot. I seemed all nervy at the time. And there would be this feeling of something hot rushing up to my head. I must have been only ten years of age when it started. There seems to be something that I used to like, but I can't remember what it was. All that I can remember is that it used to worry me. I had a queer feeling that some feeling I used to get would do me harm, would injure my inside. I knew that used to worry me a lot. Even then I felt somehow that it would affect me when I got married.

"I had some curious feeling that pushed the blood up into my head, and I know now that I felt that the blood that went to my head stayed there. I believe that it is from that that all these present feelings have developed. It does not seem clear up there at all. And now it has all died, and it is as though everything was stopped, except when things begin to reach that pitch, and then it stops them again. I have to stop things happening whether I want to or not. I don't really know what would happen to me if I were to relax. I feel that somehow I should completely lose my memory."

*Analyst:* "What is it that you are striving so hard *not* to remember? What have you tried to forget?"

*Patient:* "I don't know."
*Analyst:* "What would it be very unwelcome to remember?"
"Nothing. . . ."

*(Silence)*

"Except. . . ."

*(Silence)*

"The feelings I used to get at school. It used to worry me very much at the time. I believe it first happened when I was nervous or worried about something. I can't remember what used to happen to make me get these feelings, but I used to like it, and then I would worry in case it was injuring me. I used to think it was not right."

*Analyst:* "What are these feelings you refer to and never describe?"
"An irritation in my tummy that made the blood rush into my head and my feet go cold."

*Analyst:* "Where was the irritation?"
"In my tummy." But she puts her hand over her pubes to show the position.

*Analyst:* "What did you do about this irritation?"
"Nothing at all."

At the same time as she says this she unconsciously crosses her legs one over the other. This is the first movement of her legs which she has made during the sessions.

*(Silence)*

*Analyst:* "What made you cross your legs just now?"
"I don't know."

*Analyst:* "Put them back as they were, and keep still."

*(Silence)*

"I remember now. I used to make the feelings come. I always liked it, but I used to think it was wrong and that it might injure my inside. And it seems to me that while I was doing that that the blood rushed into my head and has stayed there ever since. I did it most if I was worried about anything, if I could not get my work done. My face used to get terribly hot.

"I'd cross my legs and work one on the other to work up the feeling. I used to think I worked it too far. I used to stop for a few minutes, and then do it again. It was like a magnet. It seemed to draw me to it. If there was any relief from it, it was not any good to me, because I used to think it was so wrong and unnatural, and yet, in spite of all that, I would do it again.

"In the end I would manage to stop it. Then my head would feel as if it were going to explode.

"I wish something would happen, but that is what I am afraid of, and that is what I am stopping. But I don't want to carry on like this, because now I am always at this final pitch.

"I suppose I did manage to stop it, for I have not done it for a year. But it is this past year that I have got this breakdown properly. It is true this past year I have been at this final pitch all the time, with this stopping all the time, and not being able to get on with my work or anything, feeling I have no memory, and unable to go out alone.

"It is only this last six months that it has been at its very worst, and I have had to give up my work and everything.

"I don't see how it can have anything to do with my boy friend. I have known him for about eight months, and it got worse after we had become engaged—six months ago. But he left me three weeks ago to join the army, and the feelings have not gone."

*Analyst:* "Where are the feelings?"

"In my head."

*Analyst:* "And what use is the boy friend to those feelings?"

"Well, I do have other feelings when I am with him—sexual feelings. But I like being with him, and I can't say that I like these feelings in my head. The feelings in my head go on all the time since I stopped the leg-swinging."

*Analyst:* "In fact, it seems that the 'leg-swinging' is going on all the time inside your head, but with the worry predominant. You have just transferred it into your mind, but it goes back to its original position occasionally, while you are with your boy friend.

"Nevertheless, it gets no relief, and it returns to your mind with redoubled violence, when your boy is no longer with you. It seems that it is this extra stimulus during the past eight months which has made your condition more acute, so that you are incapacitated from work and ordinary mental activities.

"Your feelings are never fully relieved. They merely reach a high pitch of intensity, which you describe as blood rushing to your head. The point is that you hold it there unrelieved, and put all your remaining energy into the attempt to stop it from getting relieved. Thus you get the feeling of things having reached a pitch and also the feeling of stoppage.

"The attempt to stop the orgasm brings all hands to the pumps, and the effort is so successful that it stops everything else as well. This is the condition in which you have held yourself, and which you maintain all the time. It is the antithesis of the normal sexual cycle. In short, it is sexuality, constantly present, constantly being striven against, and displaced into your head to keep it more 'safely' from relief."

At a later session this patient behaved as follows:

She lay silent for several minutes, while her hand wandered unconsciously round the armholes of her sleeve, and then along her shoulders and neck. Finally, she said, "I have nothing to say to you to-day."

*Analyst:* "What is your hand saying to me?"

"Nothing."

She continued the movements.

*Analyst:* "Put your hands at your sides and keep them still, but put your feelings and thoughts into words for me."

"I don't know what to say, except the usual thing. I feel that I don't know myself."

(*Silence*)

Her hands again begin to wander, and her attention is drawn to it, and she is again asked to keep them still.

Presently, she says:

"Yesterday I had a great urge to do the leg-crossing, and this time I did it again, for the first time in twelve months. The old feelings came back, except that I didn't worry about it afterwards."

*Analyst:* "Tell me everything you thought and felt in the greatest detail."

"I have told you all I can remember."

(*Silence*)

"I did the same thing this morning, before coming here."

*Analyst:* "Why did you tell me only about yesterday? Why did you not mention to-day?"

"I thought telling you about yesterday would be sufficient. I can't remember anything about what I thought and felt yesterday. But I can remember about to-day's. To-day when the urge came I thought it might make my feeling in my head worse. Then I thought it could not be worse, and so I didn't worry so much about whether it happened. Still, I was going to get up and try and do something else instead, in order to stop it. But then I remembered that what I had been telling you suggests that it was stopping it that brought on this illness. And then I was really very pleased to think that I had an excuse to do it. Because I really wanted to do it very badly. So I worried no more about it, and I got a much better relief than ever before. Instead of making the feelings in my head worse, as I had expected, it made them better than they have been for a long time—at least for a little while afterwards. Although I cannot say it relieved them altogether."

*Analyst:* "It is easy to understand why you did the leg-swingings —but tell me why you *stopped* doing it?"

"I just thought I should not do it any more after a few minutes."

*Analyst:* "Why did you stop it after a few minutes?"

"I wanted to post a letter, and I thought afterwards I would not catch the 1.30 collection. I wanted to get the letter off to my young man."

*Analyst:* "When did you write the letter?"

"Just before doing the leg-swinging."

She smiles:

"I keep thinking you are thinking that writing to him made me want to do it."

*Analyst:* "What do you think?"

"I think I liked it. At the time, even when I was doing it, I was thinking that probably it wasn't right to do it. I wish in a way that I did not have to do it."

*Analyst:* "You wished in a way that you had your boy friend making love to you instead. But, after all, in his absence this might be the best you could do. Thinking of him. Although it wasn't completely satisfactory, because you were alone, you had the urge to get satisfaction at least on a physical plane. Did you get it?"

"Yes. I did to-day, though not yesterday; that is why I told you about yesterday and not to-day. Since then I have not thought about this illness so much, and I haven't had those feelings in my head nearly so much as usual."

## PSYCHOPATHOLOGY

This is a case of Anxiety Neurosis, built upon a foundation of early sexual conflict.

The precipitating factor, which proved to be the last straw, was the additional sexual stimulation entailed in her courtship. This had the disadvantage of stirring up sexual tension without ever providing for its relief. In consequence, the opposition (the full stop within her mind which opposed the feelings reaching the pitch at which they would cause orgasm) was in turn reinforced from the super-ego as a whole, and was much intensified, absorbing any remaining available mental energy and resulting in exclusion from all ordinary forms of activity.

The fundamental cause of her condition, as distinguished from the precipitating and exacerbating factors of the last eight months, was the conflict which preoccupied her in her school days from the age of ten to fifteen.

The conflict began with the precocious development of the sexual urge, which she called "irritation in my tummy," and which she quite naturally relieved by the device of crossing and swinging her legs.

The fact that she adopted this rather indirect method of relief suggests that she was already inhibited from putting her hand to a prohibited region.

But the success of this method was only temporary, for the forces which prohibited the use of her hand soon became too active to permit even this mode of relief without making their voices heard. Thus, she suffered from feelings of guilt and its twin brother, morbid anxiety. In consequence, she conceived the idea that she was harming herself, and injuring her inside. It is interesting to note that, even at that immature age, she associated the idea of injury with the idea of marriage.

In due course the voices of opposition became stronger as the sexual urge itself became more insistent. By the time she reached the age of fifteen, the general opposition and worry associated with her mode of self-relief overbalanced at least the executive elements in the process of instinct relief. The leg-swinging was more often stopped than enjoyed. Nevertheless, the instinct itself was not thereby deprived of its dynamic energy. Already as a result of this opposition the conflict was being displaced from a sexual region to a disembodied or non-sexual locus. In other words, its head accompaniments were being felt as if no such thing as a sex-organ, or even the body, existed at all.

Thus she came to have sensations in her head, and so gradually became aware that they had nothing to do with the sex organs.

It was about this time that she looked in the glass and thought to herself: "Who am I?" She was already failing to recognize her sexual feelings, or in fact herself, as she had previously done. It is almost as though she were denying that she was the person who had felt sex feelings existed or ever had existed.

The advantage of this manœuvre was that she could thereby free herself from the worry, guilt, anxiety and general distress of the conflict which was ever recurring in connection with her sexual instinct, and its demands for relief. One can gauge the suffering caused by the conflict from the fact that the head symptoms which displaced it were thereafter clung to with all the energy she could muster. In spite of their obvious disadvantages, they evidently had for her a great advantage in avoidance of distress over the previous condition from which she had fled, and to which she was reluctant to return.

It was only by the relief or partial relief of her guilt-feelings that she was prevailed upon at last to revive the old conflict, and perhaps to re-fight it this time with more tolerant appreciation of the needs of her nature, and less morbid stressing of the ideas of guilt, and the phantasies of punishment and injury.

Auto-erotic satisfaction had no real danger for her, for it could never be fully satisfactory, as it was not ego-syntonic. That is to say, it was at variance with her ego-instincts, and her social or heterosexual tendencies. She would always prefer normal love-making to such modes of relief, and when she became in a position to provide herself with these latter the habit, otherwise unavoidable save at the expense of her mental symptoms, would automatically give place to normal married life.

## FEELINGS OF UNREALITY

THIS is a case of a single woman in the early thirties who, rather characteristically, was brought to me by her mother.

Having ascertained that the patient could speak for herself, I insisted upon seeing her alone.

She complained of a curious vague symptom. The indescribability of this symptom will remind us that the *form* that the symptom takes is a most inessential feature of an illness. Listening to this patient's account of attacks of a strange *feeling of unreality*, her reference to the "agonizing misery" and even "acute panic" which accompanied them reminded me, of all apparently different symptoms, of a patient who had once consulted me for attacks of acute trigeminal neuralgia.

Why should my mind link up such utterly. different symptoms— panic feelings of unreality and acute facial neuralgia?

In both cases the patient had been at a loss to account for what precipitated the "attacks." In both cases the patient had groped vaguely after such theories as strain and stress and boredom and fatigue as precipitating factors. In both cases the attacks had been intensely dreaded, and the first threat of an attack was liable to throw the patient into a panic. Each patient had assured me that life was not worth living unless there could be some hope of relief from the affliction.

In the neuralgia case the attacks had mysteriously disappeared after a long analysis in which much deep-seated conflict had been revealed and resolved. At her first interview the new patient says:

"It is very difficult to describe these extraordinary feelings. All I can say is that they come in attacks, often when I am least expecting them. It is a feeling as though I am not here at all. Everything seems to go dim or black. I struggle against it without effect, and then the feeling works up into a sort of panic.

"It is as though it were something that I must fight or I would be overwhelmed. But my fighting is of no avail; I feel myself getting more and more lost, and then the panic gets worse and worse. I get an attack of these feelings almost every day; they have become more frequent and severe. They make the whole of my life utterly miserable."

*Analyst:* "Is your life in general satisfactory and happy?"

"Yes, I think so, apart from these feelings. I live at home with my mother. It is not frightfully exciting, of course. We do not always agree. She is difficult and I feel she is watching me all the time. But recently I have decided to accept the situation as it is. For years I'd have done anything to have left home, but that is rather impracticable, and so recently I have decided to settle down to it."

Later on in the session she tells a curious dream she had: "I dreamt there was somebody in Holloway Gaol whom I had to go and visit. I knew that if I went I would be arrested and yet I felt I must go. I talked to the woman personally, and someone came up and arrested me. I thought to myself, 'well, I did this with my eyes open so I have just got to put up with it and stay here.' It was a most depressing dream."

*Analyst:* "What thoughts pass through your mind if you think of this dream and the depressing feelings it provoked?"

"Well, I did not think of it before, but now the thought comes to me that I have accepted the unsatisfactory situation at home and decided that I have just got to stay there. It is similarly depressing. Mother watches me all the time like a jailer, and I suppose I do feel as if I am in a prison."

As we found in subsequent sessions, this patient usually dreams of herself as two persons. Often they each symbolize one half of her conflict. The person already in jail is her dutiful self which has throughout accepted mother-domination. The visiting self is the part of her which would rather have been free and live her own life, but which decides that it must join the other half in "jail."

She says these unreality feelings first started when she was thirteen; but at another session she remembers that she occasionally had "far-away" feelings at a much younger age.

"I can remember now sitting in a cinema at about the age of eleven. I got this feeling of unreality only it had quite a different effect upon me then. *I found it rather exciting and pleasant.* I used to give myself up to it and enjoy it. And then as a young child I used to get a very pleasant thrill when in bed. I couldn't have been more than seven. Since I grew up I have had the same thrill in connection with a woman [older than herself] with whom I was infatuated. In this connection I found that it was sexual, though of course I did not recognize it as that when I was seven.

"As a child I simply adored my mother and was terrified of anything happening to her. Then it was love of mother and it was a pleasure; now my devotion to her is purely duty and it is the forgoing of all pleasure. It is a misery."

These last remarks should remind us that, to the infant, mother is *the* source of gratification, including especially sensuous gratification. Originally, pleasure is at the oral (mouth) level during the period of suckling; but later with the development of maturity mother comes to stand for the opposite of gratification (frustration), for the sensuous pleasure-giving zone has shifted from the oral to the genital region and mother is an obstacle to the natural fulfilment of this urge.

That this reversal of our patient's feelings towards her mother has deep-seated emotional causes is revealed by the following dream. Incidentally, it shows also the marked, if totally unconscious, homosexual streak in her make-up. Homosexuality, like all other relationships of persons, has its source in the original infant-parent relationship.

She dreams: "I was looking for a particular, most fascinating woman, older than myself, whom I had heard about and whom I wanted to make love to. Then suddenly I got terribly frightened at the thought of meeting her. I rushed away in a panic and found myself all alone in a big open space with this terrible far-away feeling."

Free association of thought to this dream reminds her of a recent emotional scene with her mother when, after quarrelling, they both wept passionately, her mother putting her arms around her and beginning to kiss her with so much emotion that suddenly the patient got an acute revulsion. She felt somehow that her mother was becoming sexual towards her. She felt utter disgust and horror.

It transpired, too, that her life with her mother consisted largely in her assuming a defensive wariness, seemingly against the possibility of her mother's attentions to her.

Thus the older woman in the dream is the mother. The child is now more mature and its love requirements, however much they may originally have been directed towards the mother, are now sexually genital: the idea of the mother in this connection is felt to be disgusting. Nevertheless, the mother is still regarded as the opponent of her sexual life.

It is noteworthy that in the course of repression of infantile sexuality, the original object or recipient of it, namely the parent, is evermore most strongly repressed or forgotten. The following material is perhaps even more significant:

"As a very little girl I was always fussing round my father, climbing on his knee and trying to get close to him. I could never have enough of him. Then suddenly, at some period of my life, a feeling of great awkwardness arose with him, something like the awkwardness I have felt with you, but it was much worse with him.

"I think it occurred from the time my elder brother took me into the garden and did something to me. He must have aroused some feelings in me. I know I felt awfully guilty and very self-conscious after that. I not only felt awkward with my father, until he died a few years later, but I went on feeling awkward with my brother until I was twenty.

"Shortly after this feeling of awkwardness first arose—I know it was as early as the age of thirteen—I began to get worried feelings, feelings that everything in life was futile. There seemed to be something I wanted to do but I could not think what it was. It occurs to me now that perhaps what I wanted to do was something sexual, only I did not know it. But that seems absurd at thirteen! On the contrary, I decided, shortly afterwards, that what I wanted was to be very, very good indeed.

"In addition to feeling awkward with my father and brother I became very devoted to my mother from a sense of duty. I have stuck to that duty ever since, though I have felt most miserable in it.

"It was about the same time that the far-away feelings which had previously been only rare, and always pleasant, now became very frequent and most terribly unpleasant. They were accompanied by dull misery. Sometimes they were agony, and when I couldn't stop them I would get into a panic.

"In early days I had plenty of respite from them; now they are much worse and much more frequent I think. I must have begun at thirteen a strenuous campaign against relaxing for fear I should get forbidden feelings that were not in keeping with my high ideals of perfection and my duty to my mother. But in spite of the stress and strain, or perhaps because of it, I could not prevent these terrible far-away feelings from getting into my daily life."

Later on it transpires: "They come most particularly when I make myself do tasks which are against my inclination. For instance, if I pick up and read the paper because I want to know the news I do not get an attack, but I can bring on the feeling by setting myself to read something in which I am not interested.

"You see, I have always had the idea that I ought to read serious things and fill up every moment of my time. I started that idea about the same time as I started these bad feelings. I do not think I have ever really relaxed from that day to this."

At another session she says: "You see I *had* to do something of this sort because if ever I did anything I *wanted* to do, I was always unhappy afterwards as if I had done wrong. Was it because I really wanted to do wrong?

"There are two very wrong things I have done in my life and I have been too ashamed to tell you, although after I had told you that dream the other day, I guessed the meaning of it, and I guessed, too, that you knew . . . and yet I couldn't tell you.

"When in the dream my brother told me that I need not tell you about the money I had picked up in the garden, but that I ought to tell you about the raspberries, I did tell you about his touching me in the garden, but I did not tell you about my touching myself.

"But even that is not so difficult as telling you that once I stole money from my mother, and went on stealing it for some time. It had to do with the touching somehow. I think I had some vague feeling that mother was herself getting away with similar things. I felt she was getting all the nice things and watching me and preventing me from getting anything nice. So I took her money *and* touched myself.

"I got a terrible reaction shortly afterwards: I thought, 'Good God! I'm a thief.' And then it was that I suppressed all my tendencies and became such a dutiful, devoted daughter."

The reference here to the psychology of stealing is of particular interest. I have discovered from previous cases that the usual sequence of events is as follows:

First the child loses its mother as a source of satisfaction. Fundamentally, this would be the equivalent of losing the nipple as a pleasure-organ. If we skip such intermediate steps as thumb-sucking, we arrive at the second stage. This is the stage at which he discovers his own sex organs as an alternative source of self-consolation. Eventually, this is repressed with the general repression of sensuality, and in the course of a process analogous to sublimation, he looks for cultural substitutes with which to console himself. At this third stage the impulse, still very compulsive, becomes one of seizing pleasure in the shape of goods or money. It is not without significance when these are robbed from the rival parent.

Perhaps these further remarks of the patient will help to elucidate the superficial aspects of her illness.

"Almost throughout my life, at least from the age of thirteen, I have always felt pulled in two opposite directions. On the one hand I have felt I wanted to let myself go, defy my mother, clear out and do as I liked. I've felt I did not want these stupid restrictions. The impulse has been very strong to go to the opposite extreme. Then there is the other part of me which will not allow the slightest concession to the bad half of me. It can only be satisfied with 100 per cent spiritual life.

"This is the half of me which has made me cling most dutifully to my mother all these years. If I ever yielded in the slightest degree to the other half, I have only been all the more unhappy after it. Therefore, the only course for me is to resign myself to living with mother and being all good—even if it does feel like jail all the time. It is only by the success of my ideals that I can be happy. That is why the spiritual side of me always wins in the conflict between conscience and sex."

*Analyst:* "What is it that wins when you get the unreality feeling?"
Silence.

"Is that sex? Or is it something which is not me? It cannot be not me; it must be some part of me which I will not admit as a part of myself. When I find I cannot stop it or conquer it in spite of all my effort, then I get this miserable panic, as though something stronger than me, stronger than my will, were going to take possession of me.

"Is all my trouble due to trying to ignore absolutely something which cannot be ignored? Is it due to my conscience being too uncompromising and my passionate impulses or instincts being too strong to be subdued? Is it as though something which I have slammed the front door on forces itself back through a side door unannounced, and in spite of all my opposition?"

At a more advanced session the patient says:

"I feel very awkward and uncomfortable here with you, like I used to feel with my father at the age of fifteen. He was awkward, too. We could not bear to be alone together.

"When I first lay down here I began to feel sexual, then my panic feeling came, and now I have the horrible dead feeling."

*Analyst:* "What stopped the sexual feeling?"

"Mother's face. Mother's face when I came in from the garden after my brother had touched me. I felt she knew. I felt she was going to pounce on me, and cut my inside out. I have gone dead to stop it. I have gone dead in anticipation."

At a later session she says:

"No sooner do I lie down on this settee than I go completely dead. It is agony. I only get it here. And yet when I'm away from here I have intense anxiety lest something, for instance an air raid, will stop me from coming to you. It isn't the air raid that I'm frightened of, not a bit, it's being prevented from getting to you. Away from here it is all pleasurable anticipation of coming to you and no sooner do I get here but I go dead all over, and simply want to get away at once.

"I do not want to be sexual with you. On the contrary, I dislike you. I feel intense hostility towards you.

"I would like to go into a convent. I suppose I will have to resign myself to living with mother and getting these bad feelings all my life."

The interpretation of the above material is that father watches her starve (for him) and does nothing to relieve her agony. Would not any starving child feel hostility towards such a parent?

Mother, on the other hand—mother, who would destroy her for incest—offers her the consolation of martyrdom. She embraces her cross (the bad feelings) and becomes mother's good girl.

Incidentally, the patient went home and wrote a successful article on the Crucifixion. It appears that she had chosen Crucifixion in place of father.

Although this case is essentially one of hysteria, it has a streak of obsessional neurosis mixed with it. The source of hysteria is conflict at the genital level, in the course of which the anti-sexual (or anti-incestuous) opposition succeeds in displacing genital effects to any and every non-genital locus, at the same time forcing them to change their emotional tone.

The "locus" here, unlike that in most cases of hysteria, was principally away from the *reality of bodily feeling*. This attempt to escape from sexuality (more specifically from "incest") was not altogether successful. For although the patient occasionally succeeded in "going dead," more frequently she achieved only a feeling of unreality which was accompanied by all the agony of the conflict. More accurately this agony should be regarded as having its source in sexual feeling whose feeling-tone has been *altered* by the opposition.

It only remains to be added that the psychopathology of the obsessional element in her neurosis goes deeper than the genital level of sexual conflict. The patient is still working out her conflict in terms of genital sexuality and conscience, but it would be a mistake to suppose that some such solution as marriage would cure all her troubles.

The infantile super-ego (conscience acquired in infancy and still unconsciously active) would not be placated by such a superficial and reasonable solution, although admittedly marriage might help after analysis had been carried to a deeper level.

Although in obsessional cases the conflict is commonly *expressed* in terms of genital sexual impulses versus conscience, nevertheless, its real origin lies in infancy at an even earlier level than the development of genital sexuality. Deeper analysis will reveal that this same conflict had its roots at a very early age when aggressive impulses tended to have their phantasied expression in connection with pleasurable excretory activities.

In all such cases there is precocity in the development of particularly strong passionate urges, coupled with an equal and opposite over-strong resistance. This resistance is built up by the extraordinary energy of the aggressive impulse itself going over, as it were, to the opposite side and becoming equally aggressive towards the impulse itself.

Thus it is that an unrelenting conscience is brought into being. The fight is a particularly strong one between particularly strong opponents and it can absorb a considerable proportion of the mental energy, thus rendering the ego (or reality principle) relatively impoverished. Unreality feelings are the sequel to this impoverishment. The panic is largely the fear of losing touch with reality or, in other words, of going mad. This "madness" which is so feared may prove, as it did in this case, to be nothing more than the momentary "madness" which occurs normally during orgasm.

If the deadlock (between the instincts on the one hand and the opposing conscience on the other) can be overcome, some of the mental energy absorbed in this struggle will be available for the use of the ego.

In such cases as the above it is only by a long and patient process of analysis, carefully conducted, that real benefit is achieved.

## THE LORRY DRIVER

A LORRY driver of thirty, a stupid but honest and sincere man, complains of a sense of "confusion in the head" so that he is afraid to drive his lorry or, indeed, even to travel alone.

He says: "It seems that my head is not working with my body. I don't think I am really frightened of the traffic. I am frightened of myself in the van. I am afraid of a far-away sensation in my head. The war doesn't worry me at all.

"It all started with an operation I had eighteen months ago. I seemed to get all right, and then I was going to visit a young lady who had corresponded with me when I was in hospital. I found I could not travel to go and visit her. This feeling in my head came on, and has recurred ever since.

"At the hospital the doctor says there is nothing the matter, that it is all just lack of confidence. He has told me to take no notice of it, and to drive my van.

"When I make myself do this in spite of my feelings, something comes over me—a feeling of horrors—and the outlook seems completely black.

"When I have succeeded in driving even a little way, I find that all my muscles are aching for days afterwards.

"At the same time that these troubles came on I began to sleep badly, and to have many disturbing dreams."

*Analyst:* "Can you tell me one of these dreams?"

*Patient:* "Only the other night I dreamt that I was driving my van, and I came to a wood, through which the road passed. Somebody, a policeman I think, told me not to drive on, not to go in there, because somebody had been murdered in that wood.

"At this point the dream changed completely. A lady came into it, and her face was very familiar.

"I don't remember the rest of this dream, but I awoke to find I had had one of those discharges.

"I may tell you, Doctor, that this sort of experience has worried me a great deal. I have been told by the chaps that if I was not careful it would go to my head, that it would lead to paralysis and all sorts of troubles. It was on this account that I broke off a bad habit I had had. That was just before I went to hospital; it is only since that and the operation that I have suffered from this sleeplessness and bad dreams, and of course all these nervous breakdown troubles.

"I have always wanted to get a girl and be friendly with her. I like the company of women, but at the same time I don't feel that I have anything to offer women. I can't picture myself married and carrying on like that (sexually) with her. I don't think I had thought much about it before I went to hospital. Up to that time it was only my mother I ever thought of taking out anywhere."

This patient's treatment has not begun. In any case it is doubtful if he has the requisite amount of intelligence to be a favourable case for analytical treatment.

Nevertheless, the small amount of material he has given at this first interview is sufficient to give the analyst a pretty deep knowledge of the psychopathology of his illness.

It will be observed:

1. That he had been in the habit of masturbating.
2. That, on account of fear of its consequences, he abruptly ceased this practice.
3. That at that time he underwent an operation.
4. That he first observed the nervous symptoms when he was about to visit a lady with whom he wished to make friends.
5. That the only woman in whom he had previously been interested was his mother.
6. That the dream and his unconscious associations to it (i.e. the thought material he produced immediately after relating the dream) included a wood with the road running through it, a warning that it is dangerous and somebody has been murdered in it, a lady whom he fails to recognize and a pollution.
7. Also his reference to his previous sexual practice, with the anxiety dependent upon it, reveals his fear, not only of the sexual practice, but also of a wife, and intimate relations with a woman.

Putting all this material together, it is evident to the analyst that the wood symbolizes the female, and the lorry which he dared not drive along the road into it, either in his dream or in reality, symbolizes himself or his vital urges. His anxiety in connection with everything sexual is represented in his dream by the warning from the policeman (a father-symbol) that in this wood a man was murdered and, presumably, that he himself will be murdered if he enters it.

It will be remembered that one of his unconscious associations following the dream was that he could not imagine himself having intimate relations with a wife. Neither can he, even in his waking life, drive his motor lorry.

If it should be assumed by the inexperienced that the interpretation of this basis of the dream is unfounded and far-fetched, we have from the dreamer's own lips the second portion of the dream to confirm it. It is the analyst's frequent experience that the second part of a dream, or a subsequent dream, is an attempt on the part of the mind to clarify (by a second edition, as it were) the symbols unduly disguised and inadequately expressed in the first part.

Here the disguise is largely dropped, and the form of a woman appears. Apparently the "motor lorry" enters the "wood," for the patient awakens with the appropriate physiological experience. Moreover, he tells us:

"It worries me when I get these discharges. I have been told that if I was not careful it would go to my head."

In other words, the policeman apparently has warned him in real life, but evidently, notwithstanding this warning, he feels as though he has entered the wood *and been murdered*. That is why he feels such a sick man, suffering from a nervous breakdown, not only unable to drive his lorry through the wood, but unable to drive it anywhere.

Analysis would ultimately reveal that the wood symbolizes the forbidden part of the mother; also the unrecognized but familiar lady would prove to be the mother.

The guilty feelings accompanying masturbation and commonly leading to a breaking off of the practice are shown by psychoanalysis to be due to the unconscious Œdipus Complex with its incestuous guilt and its fear of the parent of the same sex (the policeman (father-symbol) warns him not to drive his lorry into the wood, where murder (castration) will take place).

On the sexual level this man has stopped sexuality: on the reality level he has stopped driving a lorry. The absence of sexual detumescence is coincident with feelings of congestion or tumescence in the head.

He has been afraid to travel along that road into the wood. In real life he is afraid to travel anywhere without somebody in the rôle of a parent escorting him.

It is commonly the analyst's experience that what happens on the plane of sexuality happens also on the plane of actuality. The impression is conveyed that from a psychological or medical point of view the latter is merely, as it were, an extension and elaboration of the former, perhaps in the same way as the living adult is merely an extension and elaboration of the egg from which he grew.

One might also say that that egg is still within him and is the nucleus of his being, and when its works go wrong or its life is stopped the activity of the entire organism also goes wrong and its health is stopped.

Those not actually engaged in the work of psychotherapy can hardly be expected to give credence to the constancy with which this phenomenon is met.

Although all these matters may be so clear to the analyst, curing the patient will prove a very different story from merely understanding his psychopathology. To attempt to explain it to him, even if successful, will not achieve therapeutic results. One has to choose which procedure is most likely to do this, according to the nature of the individual and his circumstances.

The ideal would be a course of analysis, in which a person of average intelligence would gradually come to realize the nature of the phantasy or dream which he is playing out in real life, would come to recognize its inappropriateness and would cease to be the victim of its illusions. To achieve this result one would require a great deal of patience and many hours of relaxation on the analytical settee.

In this particular case one is badly handicapped by the low-grade intelligence of this lorry driver. Nevertheless, a considerable degree of improvement would undoubtedly result, even without much intellectual understanding.

## CONVERSION HYSTERIA

FOR many years I have made it my practice to see the *patient* first—in spite of the eagerness of relatives and friends to thrust themselves into the foreground.

Imagine my surprise, therefore, when on this occasion I found myself completely outwitted. The mother came to explain. She had arranged for her husband to bring their daughter in an hour's time, when I would have an opportunity of seeing the patient herself and of conducting my physical examination.

Mother said the patient was their only child and had always been rather nervous, but there was nothing that required medical advice until she reached adolescence. She had been becoming increasingly jumpy, and at that time—about the age of sixteen—she suffered from a "fainting attack." This has been connected with menstruation, which was always exceedingly painful.

There followed intermittently a succession of distressing symptoms. She would get attacks of cramp in her hands and legs. Later she complained that her legs would "go dead," and there was a period of her life when she had not been able to walk. This had given place to alarming attacks resembling fits.

These and similar symptoms seemed to increase in frequency and in severity, but in spite of them she had been able to carry on her work as a clerk in an office until three or four years ago, when all these symptoms had given place to *abdominal pain*. This had completely invalided her. Now, at twenty-three she was quite helpless.

The history of this abdominal pain was itself of interest. For two years her local doctor had paid little attention to it. But her intermittent attendances at her office finally ceased altogether as this pain became the centre of her life.

"We all went down to see the doctor about her," the mother went on. "Finally, when we had each badgered him in turn, he consented to get a surgeon's opinion.

"I have got very sharp ears, and I heard the surgeon say to him in the next room: 'My boy, you have been cooking a grumbling appendix for two years.' But my daughter would not change her doctor.

"The operation took most of our savings and seemed for the time to have effected a cure. At the nursing home she looked happier than I have ever seen her before. Everybody remarked how brave she was.

"When all her pains returned exactly as before, the doctor said that at the operation (at which he had assisted) the surgeon exposed a perfectly normal appendix. So convinced was the eminent man that there must be something physically wrong inside the abdomen that he enlarged the wound and thoroughly examined every internal organ in turn. Everything was found to be perfectly healthy.

"Finally he removed the normal appendix to avoid subsequent possibilities, and expressed himself baffled.

"We took her to another doctor, but she went back to her own doctor, and he has sent us to you."

By this time the patient herself had arrived. The story alone was almost sufficient to convince me that this was a case of conversion hysteria, and I had expected to encounter what might be described psychologically as a "blank wall."

The somewhat pale young woman was soon at her ease but, unlike her mother, chose to talk only about her abdominal symptoms. The subject never varied.

It struck me: Why was not this fairly attractive girl of twenty-three talking about her social life and her contacts, her future, and even her past? What was she talking about? *Her body!*

I realized that *some* physical examination would be expected of me. I asked her to recline in the chair on which she was sitting, and without so much as removing her coat I carefully touched the offending abdomen.

*The effect was electric.* It is not for nothing the Greeks called this illness "hysteria," sometimes translated as a "wandering womb."

Undoubtedly acute appendicitis, peritonitis, and many other acute abdominal conditions will cause a similar hypersensitiveness to pressure. But there is an almost indescribable difference in hysterical conversion.

In this case the condition was long standing, not acute. Only the hypersensitiveness, *the feeling*, was acute. Again we often find in such cases that the "electric" reaction may occur when the hand merely approaches, before it has actually established contact, or at least before any degree of pressure has been applied.

But why this violent defensive tightening of all muscles?

At a second interview the patient was induced to describe her earlier symptoms. But one noticed that she omitted any mention of the relationship of the faintings to dysmenorrhœa (painful menstruation).

She said the chokings began in her early schooldays. They were particularly troublesome when she had to read aloud in class, and also if anyone spoke sharply to her. In her early business years they had made life almost impossible for her. "Every time I got windy, particularly if my boss wanted to talk with me, I'd get this terrible feeling in my inside, and at the same time I seemed to swallow my voice so that I couldn't speak at all. I'd feel as if I were choking.

"In my early years I used to get on fairly well *provided there was nothing special, nothing that mattered very much*, provided I was not called upon to deal with anything important. If I were given a special job, if I had to speak to the boss even on the telephone, or if somebody told me to speak up because it was important, then I would swallow my voice altogether and I'd be completely helpless— everything would stop. I could never do anything important in life."

*Doctor:* "What is it that you have stopped in life? Is it the *important* thing?"

"I don't know what you mean, doctor. Of course my illness has stopped me from carrying on my work and everything else in my life. The hysterical fit I had at business upset my pride very much. You know how I jumped when you were going to touch me; well, I was so jumpy at that time that I couldn't help jumping when anybody even spoke to me.

"There was a lot of noise at the office—I had a rush job to do, then a bell rang. I found the figures all going blurred in front of me, and I suppose I fainted. I came to with pins-and-needles all over. I couldn't breathe; my hands and legs were pulled up. I asked the girls to rub my hands for me because they were all stiff and dead except for the pins-and-needles. I felt exhausted after it all, and I had a splitting headache."

For want of space we shall have to cut a long story short. I asked her about her emotional life. I drew practically a blank. It seems that in describing her symptoms she had told me *all* about it. She had had a girl friend—rather a formal contact. There had been a man at the office who had been "very kind to her." "On one occasion he actually kissed me. I was surprised; I hated it; he never tried it again."

"Yes, perhaps I was more fond of my doctor than of any other man. But I did not regard him as a man; he was more like a father to me. Of course he used to examine me when I complained of pains. And he used to take my blood pressure, and so on."

Silence.

*Doctor:* "What are you thinking of?"

"I was thinking, if you must know, that he did much more thorough examinations than you did."

On the subject of religion the material was far richer and more abundant.

"I am an Anglo-Catholic. Yes, I say my prayers every night. I go to Mass every Sunday and to Confession each quarter. For me it is a grand feeling that Mass should be there every Sunday. The feeling is that it is so grand and one is so small.

"You have asked me about my emotional life. Well, I suppose religion is the biggest emotion I have ever felt?"

*Doctor:* "Where do you feel it?"

"In church mostly."

*Doctor:* "I mean whereabouts in your person?"

"Oh, I had not thought of that. I suppose I do feel it in my body. The feeling often comes up into my chest at the Mass—not always. Sometimes I have noticed that my hands are clenched together and that I am kneeling with one foot crossed over the other. I have had a choking sensation in my throat and an intense desire to swallow, and sometimes I have felt as though these sensations reached a sort of climax. Anyhow, I don't think these experiences have occurred much since I got really ill with my abdominal pains. It was much more marked before I got so ill."

Silence.

*Doctor:* "What are you thinking about?"

"I was thinking of that hysterical attack that you have made me recall to memory, when my fingers went so stiff and so full of pins-and-needles that I had to get the girls to rub them. Now I come to think of it, it was that kind man at the office who rubbed them for me."

*Doctor:* "Did the rubbing make them better?"

"Oh, yes, I was soon all right except for the headache."

*Doctor:* Your legs went stiff too?"

"Yes."

*Doctor:* "Would you have liked anyone to rub those?"

"Certainly not."

*Doctor:* "Why not?"

"I couldn't bear that; besides, it would not have been proper."

*Doctor:* "I see. Nobody has ever suggested massaging your stomach?"

"No. My doctor has examined it sometimes."

*Doctor:* "And the surgeon cut it open. Do you think these medical advisers have been almost as repressed as you are?"

"Repressed! What does that mean?"

*Doctor:* "You have described sensations, acute sensations, in almost every part of your body. Is there any part of your body in which you never feel any sensations?"

"Well, there may be, but it doesn't occur to me at the moment."

*Doctor:* "Is there any part of your body where you could not bear the rubbing that relieved the pins-and-needles in your hands?"

"I don't think I could bear to have my stomach rubbed or even touched."

*Doctor:* "And you told me a little while ago that you could not have borne to have your legs rubbed. Perhaps you will think over our conversations and tell me your reflections next time we meet."

At the next session surprising material accumulates. She says:

"You remember that last time I told you that it was always when there was anything specially important to do that I completely lost my voice and was quite helpless? Well, it has occurred to me that this was because I found it particularly exciting, emotional or thrilling. This led me to remember that before I first got ill, at fifteen years old or so, I was particularly fond of swimming, especially diving.

"Then something curious happened to me, something similar to what I think nearly happened to me at the last session. I think I was becoming aware that I was a woman, or something. Anyhow, the effect was that when I went diving I couldn't quite let myself go freely. What I had formerly enjoyed was sliding straight into the water. I now found that in the process of approaching the water I had a tendency to resist it, to roll up. I came away with my thighs terribly bruised.

"After that I couldn't dive at all, and I soon gave up swimming altogether. I feel this was an instance of a special pleasure which I had brought to a standstill. Later I brought all special or exciting jobs to a standstill—and you suggested that I had brought my whole life to a standstill.

"When I choke I have stopped my voice. Is it that I am stopping my natural instincts?

"What I have been thinking about most since our last meeting is my wanting my hands rubbed when they went stiff, and there have been a lot of thoughts and feelings associated with it.

"I have had feelings which I hardly like to mention to you. And I seem to remember having had such feelings years and years ago. I suppressed them, and they went into this tight, painful feeling in my stomach—like a ball rolled up tightly inside my stomach. I have had these feelings—I suppose you would call them sexual feelings —and I have been thinking about them and thought much less about feelings in my stomach. In fact, my stomach seems to have relaxed quite a lot."

Perhaps in hysteria more than in any other illness a reversal of the defence may be achieved as if miraculously. The patient who is repressed and even sexually anæsthetic may suddenly become the reverse.

The psychotherapist, unless he is himself analysed and experienced enough to interpret the phenomena, may well find himself in an awkward position as the target of all the patient's passionate love, hate, and recriminations. This may not matter; on the contrary it may be a necessary stage in the process of cure—provided the therapist is competent to interpret it and thereby expose the very source of the illness.

At the next session she says: "When you ask me to relax I try to do it, and then when you ask me what I am thinking about I remain silent. I will tell you why that is. When I relax I am aware only of one thing, and that is that my pulses are throbbing. My pulses throb more and more, and I become aware of a desire *not* to relax."

*Doctor:* "What are you afraid of?"

"I am afraid that if I relaxed not only would the screwed-up feeling in my stomach disappear, but something worse would happen to me."

*Doctor:* "Try it. Let it happen."

"Something terrible would happen. I feel my pulses going very fast."

*Doctor:* "What is going to happen if you relax fully?"

"I couldn't. Sex feelings would come up."

*Doctor:* "So you have spent all your life trying to stop sexual feelings, and you have succeeded so well that you have stopped everything. You have been left merely with a screwed-up feeling in your stomach."

In this illness there is a fight against nature, a fight which results in an attempt to repress natural impulses—an attempt which is not wholly successful—so that *something* is produced, in the mind (hysteria) or as a symptom in the body (conversion hysteria).

It will have been noticed that the patient does not talk or think of the ordinary interests in life, of love, courtship or marriage. Nor is she concerned with pleasure or consciously worried by sex. She has one concern, and one only, and that is some part or parts of her body and the feelings, usually painful feelings, in them.

The difficulty in diagnosis, if any, may arise from the fact that pain produced by an external agent, or by an internal physical agent, would naturally focus all one's attention upon it and withdraw one's interest from other matters in life.

The difference is that in hysteria, and even more markedly in hypochondria, the process has taken place in the reverse order.

That is to say, interest has been withdrawn from certain directions and has itself produced the symptoms. In other words, the source of the illness is in the mind itself.

Unlike the hypochondriac, the hysteric shows an enormous capacity to be interested in some person (here the doctor) other than herself. Such an interest may temporarily relieve her other symptoms. When it ceases the symptoms return.

All psychogenic symptoms arise from conflict. Intra-psychic conflict, like conflict or war outside the mind, results in damage, injury or destruction.

There are at least two opposing interests in every conflict. "It takes two to make a quarrel"—or a fight. In this case one of the forces is the life force itself: the innate life force which runs through all living things and forces or urges them to behave in a specific manner which serves their biological purpose and perpetuates the species.

Freud has called this force *libido* and has defined it as the energy of the sexual pleasure-seeking instinct.

Now against this force there is arrayed all the opposition of parental training, upbringing, the requirements of propriety, and often social necessity and other reality matters. Nevertheless the average normal person manages to make a tolerably successful adjustment between these two conflicting demands, and thereby to maintain his or her health.

The problem in such a case as that described is what opposition could have arisen within the mind of such a person which could be so strong or so unrelenting as to force her into illness?

It is always found that the conflict assumed its almost unendurable pattern during the emotional life of early infancy. It was when the *libido* was first becoming canalized into what might be called infantile sexuality, or infantile erotic pleasure-seeking, in relation to the infant's parents that it started. There is evidence that at this stage love feelings are inextricably wrapped up with hate feelings towards the same persons at the same time.

If the conflict was then precocious or too strongly stimulated, a seed of illness was left behind which might not grow into definite neurosis until a later date in the person's life.

It is at this infantile stage that certain parts or perhaps all parts of the body are eroticized as though the pleasure feelings were not so strictly localized to sex organs as they are in the adult, but were, relatively speaking, diffused all over the body. It seems that as a result of the later conflict between the sexual pleasure-seeking instinct and its unrelenting opposition the natural urges or feelings become driven from one part of the body into another part which had its erotic or pleasure-giving value during the immature stage referred to.

The struggle is against some prohibited pleasure. In consequence this pleasure is denied or obliterated.

Thus we see in the hysteric very commonly a condition of sexual anæsthesia; that is to say, the sexual organ, normally so sensitive, may be partly or totally unappreciative of any feeling.

This anæsthesia may also, or alternatively, be felt in any other part of the body, acting as it were in lieu of the sex organ. This is a result of a *denial* of the pleasure-feeling.

If the pleasure-feeling is *over*-denied, its opposite may be substituted, namely pain instead of pleasure. Nevertheless the symptom or type of conduct or treatment it leads to may often be unconsciously directed towards the *satisfaction* of each opposing component in the conflict.

Thus in this patient her symptoms led her, after two years of "wooing" of her doctor, to achieve the result of a knife cutting into her abdomen. This, curious as it may sound, was a mental substitute for the sexual act—admittedly at a very primitive or masochistic level, but masochism and sadism are the common expressions of infantile, or insufficiently developed, sexuality.

Our patient, at the same time as she achieved this gratification of her primitive libido, was attempting to satisfy the opposition half of her conflict in that she was achieving a punishment for her desires, and an attempt—shall we say—to cut out the evil.

It seems likely that her conflict was so strong that the impulses contained in it could only achieve a partial gratification, provided the opposition were at the same time equally placated.

It is only when all these matters are brought into consciousness and relived through the patient's obtaining full insight into them, and at the same time readjusting her emotional life, that she can find a better method of satisfying these opposing elements.

The patient here referred to has only just begun treatment, and it is therefore too early to predict results, but already in the light of the material produced the outlook appears hopeful.

## A MYSTERIOUS ILLNESS

THERE are two mysteries with which this article proposes to deal.

One is the mystery of the illness, and the other is the equally important mystery of the failure of the medical profession to understand it.

The patient is a healthy-looking man of 55, with a fresh complexion, greying hair, an upright carriage and distinguished appearance.

He is eminently sane, capable, well read, and an interesting conversationalist.

He appears to be self-possessed, calm, and suave.

He began work as a shop assistant at the age of 15. In the course of thirty to thirty-five years he has established a large business with branches in a dozen towns. Having accomplished this, and reared a now grown-up family, he "collapsed" five years ago, and has, in spite of every medical endeavour, remained incapable of taking part in any sphere of activity—business, social or recreational.

His principal symptom is a condition of fatigue, collapse or utter prostration, often so great that he cannot undress himself, and has to be assisted to bed.

He has found he must avoid all possible sources of stimulation of his interest or emotion—business, social, etc.—because he becomes over-stimulated, over-excited. One thing would lead to another, and he would (and does), gradually find himself working up to a vortex of energy or emotion which he cannot control, and which is inevitably followed by a complete collapse which may last for several days and nights, necessitating bed, doctors, nurses, drugs, etc.

One doctor after another, and one specialist after another, have struggled, with blood-pressure apparatus, blood tests, test meals, X-rays and so on, to diagnose this devastating illness. We need not follow their endeavours, save to mention that amongst the various diagnoses formed have been Addison's disease—which the blood pressure disproved—or some other endocrine disorder, gastric ulcer —disproved by further investigations—migraine, etc.

Occasionally, when no other diagnosis could be maintained, a doctor has labelled the illness "neurasthenia." But the very doctors who have so "settled" the problem have returned at the next consultation with further researches for organic factors, or have fallen back on theories of endocrinology.

I propose to give now, in an itemized or tabulated form, an abbreviated account of what the patient himself, undirected, unquestioned and uninterrupted, told me in the course of one long analytical session lasting two hours.

The patient starts by remarking upon his life: (1) About the age of 15, soon after puberty, he was launched into the commercial world, and began the stressful and exciting task of fighting for a living. This task increased in excitement, stress and anxiety for thirty-five years, seeming always to be heading towards a climax, when excitement and anxiety would become too great to be tolerated. At last the "crisis" came—collapse, prostration and total invalidism for the past five years.

He relates several instances, within this five-year period, of short-lived activity, increasing in energy and followed by collapse and prostration of varying duration.

For instance: (2) After years of invalidism he began to feel the stirrings of some active impulses. He saw some premises where he might open a new and larger branch of his existing business (now under the direction of a deputy). "Business" for him means expansion and enlargement, and the excitement of making money. In the course of a week his activities had reached a pitch that can only be described as hectic. He lay awake at nights plotting and scheming. Before he could reach the conclusion of his venture, collapse came, and he was utterly prostrate for two months.

(3) To escape the stresses of civilization (even that of living as an invalid in his own house) he set off to drive his car into the heart of the country fifty miles away. After seven miles collapse came on. He had to stop and considered that he would have to give up the attempt. After two hours of prostration and rest he thought he'd venture a little farther. This time he did fifteen miles before collapse supervened. Here he lay in a field and slept. On awaking he did the rest of the journey of about thirty miles, and arrived at his camping place full of energy and excitement. The next day he could not walk across the field, and had to spend two days in bed.

(4) On another occasion at home he felt he would do a little gardening, and started slowly to cut the garden hedge. His energy increased so that in half an hour he found himself working furiously. He struggled indoors, collapsed in a chair, and had to be assisted to bed.

(5) On account of his invalidism, he goes upon a voyage. He gets into conversation with a lady. This causes the prostrate invalid to

get into a state of increasing sexual excitement, which, of course, he keeps strictly to himself. He is confined to his cabin in a state of collapse.

(6) While confined in bed in this condition, he awakes the next morning in a state of restlessness which threatens to develop into an uncontrollable tossing and wriggling about of his whole body all over the bed, and even on the floor—a sort of "fit" from which he has suffered on occasions in the presence of a distressed family and family doctor. On this occasion, however, he manages to abort the threatened attack by the simple process of phantasying himself having sexual intercourse with various ladies of his acquaintance.

In consequence a period of restfulness sets in—but he says that a further or extreme degree of this would amount to the prostration with which he is so familiar.

Though his usual state is one of prostration and invalidism, it is not unusual for periods of restlessness, "a sort of suppressed energy," irritability amounting to fits of temper, "suppressed violence," and frequent occasions of strong sexual desire, to alternate with longer periods of prostration.

"I can't think where the vitality can come from, Doctor, when I am in other respects more dead than alive."

(7) At the same session he decides to tell me about the greatest period of stress and distress which disturbed his life. This, he says, was from the age of about 12 to 16.

He took to self-abuse, and for some years indulged in it, at first without self-reproach or conflict, though he kept it secret, and in fact this is the first time he has told a soul about it.

"I don't think, Doctor, that anyone could have practised it as much as I did—as often as three or four times a day. I did not know there was any harm until I learnt better and tried to stop it. Then to my horror I found I could not stop it. The hell I went through is indescribable.

"As a young man I was obsessed with sexual desires. It used to occur to me that how could anybody give his mind to anything if he were obsessed with sexual desires as I was. There was never any real satisfaction. Tiredness always supervened too early for that. Then I went to business and had to live away from home, and immediately the self-abuse stopped.

"I was a bit of an invalid as a youth; either irritable, excited, anxious and over-energetic, or else in a state of fatigue. But nobody knew anything about it."

At this stage I would merely point out to the reader that under each item (1 to 7), whether we consider his life as a whole, or any one of the isolated events related, we may detect that each involves a period of *beginning energy* (stimulated by external factors or not) *increasing in emotional tension and anxiety until a sort of crisis is reached, which coincides with collapse and is followed by a greater or lesser period of prostration.*

Dreams have been described as the royal road to the unconscious, so let us now pass on to the consideration of two dreams and his thought associations to them. The first of these dreams was related at the same (full) session as the other material, and the second dream at the next session.

(8) "I dreamt I was lying in bed listening to —— (a famous politician) preaching. I could see him standing very upright in his pulpit and gesticulating.

"Then the meeting was thrown open for discussion.

"I was lying prostrate and flat in bed, but something stirred me so that I was impelled almost involuntarily. I rose up straight and erect on the bed and began to address the meeting. My sentences were to the point, sharp and acid. 1 could see I'd got the old man's ear. I waxed more and more eloquent until I reached a point where I began to shout. I did shout. Then suddenly my voice was finished. I couldn't go on, couldn't articulate. I collapsed in bed.

"The next morning my wife told me that I had risen up in bed in my sleep and shouted, and then suddenly collapsed back on the bed."

With reference to the dream, he remarks:

"I was robbed of my final triumph, as in self-abuse—collapse—without the success one feels in sexual intercourse."

The erect form of —— gesticulating and exhibiting is associated with his erect penis. His own body rising up from a state of collapse to an erect active posture is again associated with sexual erection. The glowing pleasure of his speech, increasing in volume, is associated with the increasing pleasure and excitement of sexual activity. The shouting is the crisis, and the subsequent collapse the condition of his organ and himself thereafter.

The morning after this dream he awoke in a state of restlessness and achieved quietness by phantasying sexual intercourse.

(9) The second dream (abbreviated) is as follows:

"I was back in the village where I was born. Mother and father were there. I was in the main street (where as a youth I was so self-conscious and embarrassed that I would try to hide myself). It was full of business houses that were all going to have their premises enlarged and extended.

"I was there giving estimates for the expansion, taking their

K

stocks, etc. The expansion of everything seemed to be *my* expansion. Trade was getting better and better. The position I was in seemed to be growing greater and more important. I began to get anxious, but I boasted to mother and father. I felt I was getting overwhelmed. Somebody said, 'What about your health?' Then I knew I'd have to stop because my head was beginning to ache.

"I awoke.

"I slept again and dreamt I was lying in bed, collapsed, with my head on my wife's bottom."

His associations are:

(*a*) His business life has been a similar process of expansion followed in a similar manner by collapse—his present illness— pillowed on his wife.

(*b*) After a moment's silence he says he is not thinking of the dream, but of an attractive lady who talked with him. "Doctor, this treatment does not cure me of my sexual mania. If I were dying I believe I'd be dreaming of seducing women . . . Merely talking to this woman made me feel so expansive and excited. As a matter of fact it was the same feeling as in the dream, and something else was expanding. I collapsed afterwards."

The increasing excitement in the dream is associated with the increasing excitement of sexual activity, and the collapse with its sequel.

(*c*) In the dream it is his aching *head* which he rests on his wife's buttocks, and in association he shamefacedly confesses that he has had sexual dreams of having intercourse with his wife that way (of "resting" the head of his penis there).

The foregoing is merely an excerpt from almost unlimited material extracted from but one or two sessions. All the material serves either as corroborative evidence to the general outline or to fill in innumerable minor and accessory details of the symptom picture.

The main symptom or the general outline is all that is attempted here, and to that end whole masses of equally stimulating psychological material are omitted.

The points of scientific interest that I wish to bring out are these:

1. This is an illness which is real enough to totally incapacitate a formerly very capable and successful man. Therefore it will not do to dismiss it lightly.

2. This is an illness which, regarded in the ordinary way by a consideration of the symptom picture alone, has completely baffled a succession of doctors.

All orthodox methods of investigation have proved utterly irrelevant, and have not led even to the beginning of any sort of understanding.

Where all is darkness, even the faintest ray of light should not be scorned.

3. The faint ray of light which the foregoing investigation may throw upon this puzzling illness may be summarized in the form of the following tentative suggestion:

The patient, now a man of 55, was in his youth a chronic masturbator. Masturbation has its source in psycho-physical processes feeding an innate instinct. With or without stimulation from an external factor this led to a short-lived but very intense sequence of emotional or feeling experience. The sequence consisted of a feeling of well-being increasing in emotional intensity, tension and anxiety until some pinnacle of excitement (crisis) was reached or passed. Then followed a period of sexual collapse accompanied by a general condition of greater or lesser prostration.

The second stage of his life, when he left home and mother, corresponds to the intrusion into his inner world of the real or commercial world. Cultural values have to be adopted at pain of going to the wall in "real" life. His masturbation, which previously he could not of himself discontinue, now stops completely, and the energies at the source of it are now displaced (sublimated) on to activities and emotional excitements of a socially valuable nature. He attacks the real world of business competition. *And now on this new level he repeats a protracted emotional experience similar in its sequence to that epitomized in each former sexual experience.* Excitement reaching a crisis and followed by collapse was the essence of his onanistic acts—and now it is the essence of his sublimated activities.

The parallelism is, of course, completely disregarded or lost sight of by his consciousness, but nevertheless the same conglomeration of emotions, and the same sequence of feelings is faithfully repeated —both in the general outline of his life (Item 1) and in the individual details of shorter duration (Items 2 to 7).

A recognition of the parallelism or "identity" of the shortlived sexual experiences of early life and the protracted experiences of his life in general, and his symptoms in particular, may be a first and perhaps essential step towards understanding the patient's incomprehensible symptom picture.

This recognition is indeed only a *first* step; for to establish or prove to the reader beyond doubt that symptoms are emotionally parallel to the patient's sexual experience is not so much a solution of a mysterious illness as a faint light that shows up the mysteriousness of the illness—increases the mystery of it. It is, however, the only step I propose to take in this short paper.

Case after case reveals to the investigator this unexpected and astonishing relationship between symptom and sex.

We have not solved the problem by equating symptoms with sex. We have only transferred the riddle from symptom to sex. We are then, and then only, in a position to *begin* our investigations.

These investigations carried further show us that sexuality itself is, on its own plane, a highly finished product, having many primitive roots or components. These may occasionally become conspicuous in pre-coital activities, in the perversions, in psychoneurotic symptoms, and in cultural sublimations.

## PART II

It was stated in the first paragraph of this paper that there were *two* mysteries to be dealt with. One was the mystery of the illness and the other the mystery of the failure of the general medical profession to understand it.

Let us now turn our attention more specifically to this second mystery:

It will be appreciated that in propounding the first mystery I have been able to put forward only an inadequate portion of an unlimited amount of material. It will be immediately assumed that the material here given has been especially selected to twist the truth.

I can merely protest that the strength of the theory (like that of the theory of evolution) lies solely in the unlimited extent of the circumstantial evidence. It grows apace with increasing experience.

Nevertheless, whether we are gaining such experience for ourselves in daily clinical (analytical) sessions, or, far more markedly, if we are merely hearing the secondhand testimony of another's investigation, we *cannot* really believe anything quite so "*grotesque*." The investigator must be the victim of some perverse sexual bias.

Evidence of bias on the part of the investigator is abundant enough. I myself have been guilty of it a thousand times. *BUT it is all on the other side*. The mind is biased *against* seeing a sexual parallelism to apparently non-sexual symptoms and sublimations.

Patient after patient forces upon the reluctant attention an exact correspondence or parallelism between symptom, unconscious sexuality and conscious life.

We are all familiar with the patient who progresses merrily with his free associations of thought, and freely with his symbolic expressions (so long as the sexual equivalent of the symbols he is using is unsuspected by him) and repeatedly comes to a dead stop—a protracted silence. Inquiry invariably leads to the reluctant confession or protest that some "irrelevant" sexual thought "that has nothing to do with the matter" has intruded—or, more usually, has been forced into his mind by the insidious evil presence of the analyst.

We are all familiar with the doctor who similarly pooh-poohs sexual theories of the neuroses.

We are all familiar with the doctor who, with riper experience, admits their applicability in *some* cases . . . more or less rarely.

We are all familiar with the operation of our own psychotherapeutic minds, which constantly forget what we have learned from our previous cases, and begin each case anew fortified by our own anti-sexual bias against insight.

We know that the psychotherapist who does not stress the sexual etiology of neuroses, or who denies it, is likely to receive more cases from his medical colleagues.

We remember that Jung wrote to Freud from America that he had discovered a way of making psycho-analysis more acceptable to the public—by ignoring or disguising the sexual etiology. Freud replied that such successes won at the expense of truth were not to be commended. Nevertheless, Jung was accepted and Freud rejected.

We are evidently prepared to enjoy sexual emotion in various forms, primitive or sublimated, but most reluctant to analyse it, and particularly reluctant to recognize it behind its powerful disguises—symptomatic or cultural.

First hand familiarity with clinical material and constant and repetitive insistence of the patients' free associations upon this sexual etiology of symptoms are apt to convince the investigator of two things:

(1) That the sexual etiology is the truth; and

(2) That the doctors, no less than the patients, do not like it —have a bias against it, a bias which causes neurotic illness to remain more or less mysterious.

The resistances of the patient observed clinically, and the incredulity, dislike or hostility of the doctor observed generally, have much in common with each other.

Both are found to have their sources in the struggle between a tendency of the organism to remain on the pleasure principle versus an intrusion of unwelcome reality, painfully demanding recognition.

From this struggle and the partial victory of the reality principle, man (and to a lesser extent other animals), was won from a mere simple biological or sexual purpose to at least a temporary diversion of these primitive energies into substitutive aims. Thus, it seems, there arose culture, civilization, intelligence—including a repudiation of the lowly (biological or sexual) origin of these same sublimations or symptoms.

Thus we see the patient's resistance and the doctor's incredulity as remnants of the old forces which produced the higher levels of the mind from instinct sources, and which remain to safeguard them from the "danger" of regression.

Forty-six years ago, Freud* defined neurasthenia as having certain specific symptoms, namely exhaustion, headache, spinal irritation, dyspepsia and constipation (all of which my patient exhibits in marked degree), *and as having an etiology in excessive masturbation*, or the conflicts connected with it.

The modern investigator, having at long last given in to the repeated impact of clinical experience, is denied the possible compensation of originality. He finds that he is merely repeating an old theory of proved unpopularity—a theory that all who can (through an absence of experience) reject or ignore, have so done, and most others working in the same or adjacent ground have rejected to the greatest degree possible to them under the circumstances of experience which they have been unable to avoid or completely ignore.

Can it be that the doctor's objective clinical science, founded upon a training in the physical sciences, must degenerate into a sexology? Must he accept the perhaps unwelcome company of Freud and the sexologists?

Havelock Ellis is said to have spent a lifetime, and eight large volumes, in describing the world in terms of sexual tumescence and detumescence. Can it be that in order to understand the psychoneuroses, to begin to understand the mystery of the mysterious illness here described, we must perforce embrace this outrageous theory, this theory at which we have laughed throughout the greater part of our life?

Is the only alternative no alternative at all, but merely to form our own theory, based strictly upon our own clinical psychotherapeutic experience, and to find that in essentials it is identical with the foregoing, and not even original?

If we may regard the bias against sexual theory as a symptom of the "normal" mind, we have taken the first step towards recognizing

* Collected Papers, Vol. 1, No. 5

this symptom as a portion of a far larger mental process of repression or suppression of primitive forces which the ego repudiates because it fears it may be overwhelmed by them.

Nevertheless, these primitive forces do obtain admission to the higher levels of the mind, *but only in a modified or altered form*; indeed the higher levels of the mind are composed solely of these primitive forces, *modified beyond danger of recognition*.

Investigation of the psychoneurotic patient shows that not only symptoms, but also *sublimations*, the very conscious and intellectual structure of his mind, has its foundation and source in a more primitive mechanism closely related to sexuality. It shows that these "higher" structures, sublimations, intellectual structure and character, have been won over from sexuality (or the component instinct sources of sexuality) by an early and protracted process of denying the latter its unrestricted enjoyment.

Notice that the patient here referred to only ceased his pubertal masturbation when the exigencies of cultural life intervened.

A part of the primitive process of suppression of a force within the psyche consists in a denial of its existence. This is merely the process of preventing its admission to consciousness, since it is along this route (admission to consciousness) that instincts normally obtain their active expression in behaviour.

Normal man, particularly cultured man, has achieved his culture and the ingredients of his intelligence at the expense of these more primitive forces, which tended otherwise to flow into an instinct level of life such as sexuality. As there exists a parallelism between the patient's symptoms and his earlier instinct life or sexuality, so there exists a parallelism between the investigator's sublimations, character or culture, and his own abandoned early instinct pattern. His mind is still automatically guarding the former from any possibility of a relapse to the latter level. The conscious sense of the outrageous is the parallel on the intellectual and conscious plane of this early mechanism of guarding or protecting intellectual sublimation from a relapse into its primitive instinctual or sexual form.

Though we have reached a stage where we need no longer exercise it, this early repressive force continues to stand between us and a recognition of the primitive origins of our higher mental processes.

As we apparently must hide from ourselves the lowly origin of our sublimations, so we must hide from ourselves the sexual origin of psychoneurotic symptoms—with the result that such illnesses continue to mystify even the most intelligent amongst us.

## Conclusion

The material of this paper may start us upon a line of investigation which, if followed to its ultimate conclusions, would suggest the following theories:

(1) That the primitive mind consists largely of an organization of vital forces having a biological purpose, expressed in sexuality.

(2) That these same forces in their more or less organized form can become deflected from sexuality and obtain their expression in:

(a) symptoms, or

(b) sublimations (character, culture, etc.).

(3) That some force within the mind (clinically detected as a resistance to sexuality) that was responsible for this deflection, still has its "sublimated" equivalent in the form of a blindness to psychosexual parallelism, and as a bias against its acceptance.

## THE TRANSFERENCE NEUROSIS

IN the course of the psycho-analytical method of treatment, the patient eventually reaches a stage called the *transference neurosis*.

It is not unusual then for all the ordinary symptoms to disappear, but this stage itself is called a neurosis because another symptom takes their place. This is the symptom of irrational emotional attitudes towards the analyst, as illustrated in the case history below.

Next follows an attempt on the part of the patient to resist against this unsatisfactory emotional state. With this, in so far as he resists the transference, the old symptoms tend to recur in an acute but temporary form.

It is as though a struggle were taking place between the old illness and the new, the old one being his original symptoms—particularly in their earliest or infantile forms—and the new being a childish preoccupation with his feelings towards the analyst.

In some cases the fight is not very frantic, but in most curable forms of psycho-neurosis—especially hysteria—the struggle may become very fast and furious.

Analytically, there is this advantage: the patient has already experienced a period of absence of the ordinary symptoms while he (or she) was engaged in his new emotional preoccupation during the transference neurosis.

After a struggle between the old symptoms and the new, a relatively mature attitude to life is usually adopted.

This is the case of a woman of thirty-five who was so ill when she first came to the clinic that her case was considered hopeless, and treatment was refused. This was done in spite of the diagnosis being that of hysteria, the most favourable type of illness for psychotherapy.

When I questioned the clinic's decision I was told that the hysteria was so severe that her reason seemed to be clouded by it so that she presented more the aspect of acute confusional insanity. The outcome was that I decided to try the effects of treating her myself.

There was some justification for the clinic's point of view, for if there is insufficient ego or reason to fall back upon we are deprived of that very instrument which we require to cure the patient.

Nevertheless, the treatment was attempted and in due course this patient reached a thoroughgoing transference neurosis.

Wherever she went, and even during long intervals between analysis, she could think of little but the analyst. Apart from this, she felt that all her troubles had been solved. Sleeplessness and other symptoms had practically disappeared. There was some phantasy that she would live happily with him ever after.

But hope does not spring eternal in the human breast, and in the session here recorded we are well in the throes of the struggle between the new illness and the old. She is trying to cast off the new illness, and the old symptoms are temporarily returning in a brief, but perhaps heightened, form.

She starts by saying that for the first time since she began treatment she has forgotten to bring her money (this patient has always paid at each session). She goes on to say she has had the most violent attacks of acute abdominal pain. These are so severe, and becoming more frequent, that her doctor has sent her to hospital where she has been X-rayed. They have been suspicious of gallstone or gastric ulcer.

She says: "The most severe attack was only last night. I rolled about in agony for three and a half hours. Finally, I was given some morphia and thereby got a little sleep. It seems there was a terrific shindy going on in my stomach. Nevertheless, I had a dream.

"I dreamt that I went to a public house for a drink. To get to it I had to go down a hill, and up a hill, and then down again, and then up two steps into the little bar. A hefty barman came to serve me, and I asked for a whisky. He went away and took a long time to come back. Finally he put down the 'whisky' and I paid.

"Presently I saw that it was foaming; it was not whisky at all, it was mineral water. I called out to him. He took it away and put another on the counter, and I paid again. Then I found that this was still mineral water.

"I shouted for him and made a fuss, but he didn't come. Throughout he was treating me with contempt. Finally I dashed after him and made a row. At last he said to me: 'We do not sell whisky.' I demanded my money back. He said, 'You can't have it.'

"I shouted for the police; then we both went to fetch the police. It was a long journey, down steps and up hills. Finally I woke up still suffering from feelings of tremendous anger, and as though the fight were going on inside me. It seems I was still demanding my money back."

Two points should be noted at this stage. One is that the patient for the first time forgot to bring her money to the session. The second is that she described her attacks of acute abdominal pain as "a terrific shindy in the stomach."

She continues: "I have been very miserable for some time, feeling my end was near. It is a terrible lonely feeling as if I haven't got anyone in the world. I cannot be bothered to think when I am in these moods. Even you do not come into the picture.

"I believe it all started two weeks ago when I made up my mind that you will never be any use to me. Then I found I could dismiss you. Soon after that the pains started, and since I have been in this pain it seems that you have failed me. Previously, I was feeling that you were something to me, but when I get this depressed feeling you are like the rest of them. I cannot be bothered to think even of you. It was as though there was one thing worth living for —you, and when I lose that idea there seems nothing at all worth living for.

"The doctor thought I was worried about this pain, but I have no worry about that. I wouldn't mind being dead; I would only dread the experience of dying. It seems there is something I have wanted and I have given up the idea that I can get it.

"I feel now that I can never gratify my wishes. Of course, I do not know what these wishes are, but somehow I was hanging on to you. And then, two weeks ago, I came to the conclusion that you had refused me.

"As a child, if I wanted a thing, once I knew what I wanted and then they refused me there would be a terrible shindy. It seems I would rather die than be refused, or I didn't know whether I wanted to live or die. I have never asked you for anything because I dread refusal. If I were refused I think I'd die. So instead I have turned the wishes away; I have turned you out of my mind, and since then I have had this agony."

*Analyst:* "Is it the agony of refusal?"

"Yes."

*Analyst:* "Free association to the burly man in your dream?"

"You."

"Did he refuse you anything?"

"I asked for whisky and he gave me mineral water—a poor substitute. I wanted my money back."

"And you haven't brought your money to-day?"

"I do not know what I need of you. Spirits—something internal, but I get nothing, not even mineral water. There is a heavy pain inside me that I cannot dismiss from my mind; sometimes it is a pain in the groin like a menstrual pain, a dull pain which gets worse and worse, then it goes up to my stomach.

"When it is at its worst there is a feeling as if it will burst. It's as though I am waiting for it to burst. I keep forcing myself to break wind but nothing relieves it. When the doctor pressed it at hospital it felt like a pain lower down in my vagina. Of course, I could not tell the doctor that; he would not understand.

"This something that wants to burst out is like a feeling of anger. At one time I had a terrific angry feeling with you. It was bad temper, as bad as I felt in that dream with the barman. I wanted to row with you, tear you to pieces and that's when I get these hysterical attacks and screaming at night.

"Always in my ordinary life I go *frantic* if I cannot get what I need. I used to do this before I ever saw you; then later it was those hysterical attacks. I kicked up a shindy all round, but then since I got used to coming to see you all those quieted down; for months I did not have any; everyone thought I was cured, but now I have subdued all this, even the anger and bad temper have gone.

"It seems I have cased it up inside me; it is imprisoned internally. Is that the shindy that is in my stomach?"

*Analyst:* "Did you ever get attacks like this as a little girl?"

"That's when I always got them, but then I used to get what I wanted through making these outbursts. If mother ever refused me anything there would be a devil of a shindy. I'd scream and kick until my father came along and then my father would always see that I got what I wanted against my mother's wishes.

"You may think that my father spoilt me Well, of course, he did, but then you see, I don't know what would have happened if I had not got what l wanted because l would go so frantic and scream so much that I think l would have died.

"Mother did not seem to get alarmed, but father did, and that's how l always got my way.

"It never went so far and I was never deprived for so long as I am being deprived now." (If the barman wouldn't give her "whisky" or her money back she'd see that the police—her father—would make him do it.)

Perhaps enough has been said to indicate that what the patient now calls the "shindy in the stomach" may be a converted expression of the shindy that used to be created by the hysterical, spoilt little girl.

The reliving of these hysterical experiences of childhood under analytical conditions will give the adult ego a chance to make a fresh adjustment between emotional demands and inexorable reality. But of course this is providing that there is sufficient ego in the personality to assist in this operation of adjustment.

The reason the clinic refused to treat this patient was because they suspected insufficient ego ability in this case.

The position is far stronger than it was in childhood, for the patient has now had an experience of several months of ordinary good health, that is, while the transference situation was in full swing and before she realized the hopelessness of her phantasies and tried to resist or repress them.

She may now see that it was the frustration of similar wishes in childhood or infancy which made such noisy complaints, and which unfortunately succeeded in procuring her ends.

She will see that she is still behaving as this child behaved, but that whatever requirements she may have in life they will not now be achieved by these methods.

In short, sooner or later, she will learn to make a better adjustment and to abandon her illness.

## WAR IN THE MIND AND IN THE WORLD

IN the case here described we learn again the primary lesson of medical psychology: namely that symptoms have their *source* in the *unconscious* mind. It will further be suggested that this is commonly true of other behaviour besides symptomatic "behaviour." Specifically will it be suggested that it is true of sexual behaviour, of aggressive behaviour, of fighting, and of war.

Under analytical conditions (free association of thought) this patient produces a superabundance of aggressive material; much as the average person produces a superabundance of sexual material.

We may detect in this contrast the opposition of the two most fundamental instincts: Eros and Thanatos. The one produces life (reproduction); the other produces death (destruction).

The average person, in obedience to deep-seated or unconscious compulsion, plays his part in the biological scheme by reproducing his kind, the next generation. But here we see at work forces that produce war—in the mind, in the home, or, if on a national scale, in the world—forces that may well *destroy* the next generation.

We may reflect, also, that little "wars" are going on everywhere, in every household.

Some persons destroy others; some destroy themselves.

In all cases the *source* of the destruction may be as deepseated and unconscious as the source of sexuality in the average person, as unconscious as the source of the symptoms in this patient.

His symptom was *not* acts of violence upon others. On the contrary he repressed all such impulses and phantasies and suffered the violence within his own mind and body. The outward and visible sign of the battle within was epileptic fits.

It is often by the most acute or violent outbursts of illness that we can best understand life and health. In the course of treatment as the emotional origin of the fits came to light, they became hysterical (i.e. conscious) instead of epileptic (unconscious) in character. That is of special scientific interest. Here, however, we will see that "war" in his home during his infancy led to "war" in his mind. Later on, we will discuss the question as to whether war in the world at large has its source similarly in war in the mind.

Analysis reveals behind this patient's superabundance of aggression, experiences of childhood that stimulated, developed and brought to fever pitch his innate aggressive instinct.

Here is a verbatim extract from one of his sessions:

"I was a little boy. We lived in a tenement—two rooms. Night after night, peeping through the crack of the door between the bedroom and the living-room, I saw father struggling with mother; father shrieking and running round the room after my mother. Mother shrieking, too, and running round the room. He would catch her and swing her round by the hair. Something terrible was happening to my mother! . . . Or perhaps it happened to me. . . . I felt it was happening to me. I was in terror."

(For a moment he chokes and cannot speak) ". . . perhaps it was a plant-pot came through the window.

"I have got a job to speak sometimes. I feel the cause of the trouble is not far off. I had a terrible time when I was a kid. Night after night I had to listen to this horrible row, violent quarrelling, shouting, raving, screaming. I looked through the crack—I was terrified.

"Perhaps it was on one of these occasions that something happened, or perhaps it was the life I led day after day, year after year. The continuous terrible strain, the continuous scratchings on the memory of all that sort of thing. It caused a deep wound in the memory.

"I do not understand how any human being could be like it. He'd come home drunk night after night, shouting, raving, quarrelling—quarrelling with a defenceless woman. He would only come home for this and his food and his lusts. He didn't care a damn about his wife and the kids. He had the trump card because he was stronger and because he earned the money. He would use his trump card by shouting that he was going out to drown himself. Then he would disappear and leave us all starving.

"That Christmas! No food in the place, rags and starvation and one orange in each of our stockings. My mother was starving, but somehow she had managed to get three oranges, one for each of our stockings. That she, a good mother, should be treated like this! Should suffer! It's agony! . . . Crucifixion! . . . Like Christ on the Cross! He gave up the ghost. It is like my dream . . . nightmare. I feel curling up like a worm that has been cut in half. It is more than being hurt—it's agony—it's like the fit."

The patient writhes on the settee while he remembers these acute emotions of his childhood. His action is a mild but distinct reproduction of movements that take place in or after his fits. The fists are clenched and he appears to be wrestling with himself with slow, clonic movements of the arms, at the same time emitting guttural sounds.

It will be understood that with a father such as this it is more than likely that the patient inherited certain violent aggressive tendencies. In addition to the hereditary factors these emotions were, no doubt, abnormally stimulated from an early age by such scenes as he has just described. But the point is that he did not give vent to them as did his father. What he did with them will be revealed in the discussion at the end of this chapter.

In the meantime we will pass on to a revelation by the patient of his struggle with his aggressive instincts: "I had been thinking of the office manager. I had been working out a phantasy of revenge on him because he had prevented me from getting promotion. I'd go to the office while he was alone. I'd hit him on the head. I'd take four rusty nails and nail him to the floor—that is, crucify him to the floor. I'd bite off his ears. Then I'd take the office thing for making holes in paper and I'd make holes all over his back so that when he was in hospital he couldn't lie on his back. He doesn't believe in psychology, so I would leave a note with him to tell him while in hospital that here he had a practical demonstration of psychology.

"Then I went on to a phantasy where I'd tear him to pieces. I would cut his arms off. Stab him. Torture him. I thought of taking out his eyes, but I couldn't do that. That was too terrific. If they took out *my* eyes it would be terrific, I couldn't bear that."

He squirms on the settee for a few minutes.

He then continues. "I know it is abnormal. I know it is murdering the father [cf. childhood memories of his father]. But I don't want to *act* a play. I want to *do* it. I don't want to be a Hamlet. I really want to murder him (the office manager). Rip him up. *Murder has got to be done.* If only I could have my revenge, murder him, *then I would get well.*"

It appears that this patient is suffering from a state of most acute mental tension. This condition has come about largely through a lifelong bottling up of violent revenge impulses against his father. His condition is so tense that the lightest stimulation of these impulses by, for instance, a current injustice, is like a spark to a powder magazine. He almost gets a fit on the spot. He nurses the idea that if only he could carry out the aggressive act which has been arrested since his childhood, he would immediately relieve his state of tension, and be cured of his illness and his tendency to get fits. In the face of continued and perpetual frustration he feels there is no other course but to endure internal agonies and to be a victim of fits.

A little reflection will show us that such a state may pre-condition an individual to crimes of violence. Is it not possible that many murderers have a similar psychological basis for their violent anti-social behaviour? It is, perhaps, the urgent need to obtain relief from agonizing internal conditions that practically compels them to seek relief by some such compulsive act.

Reflection which may be of even more widespread social significance, and even more deserving of our interest and study, is that some of the historic aggressors, or would-be conquerors of the world, have been known to have had not only the epileptic character, but in some cases to have even been subject to actual epileptic or hysterical fits. For instance, Cæsar and Napoleon were reputed to be epileptic, and it is whispered that Hitler at one time was the victim of hysterical blindness. Has he ever recovered?

It may well be asked whether the blindness is not still present, though now of a mental nature. Hysterical "conversion" symptoms are known to be a conversion of their mental equivalent into its physical symbolic form. Perhaps it requires a considerable degree of "blindness" to believe we are doing good by substituting destruction for procreation. Perhaps it requires a certain clouding of consciousness to be unaffected by admiring or hostile worlds and to be incapable of self-criticism. The disease is sufficiently satisfying to be infectious.

Medically and psychologically we can see a relationship between the epileptic fit that knocks out the whole of consciousness and a "fit" of blindness (cf. rage) that knocks out a special sense, or a portion of perceptual consciousness.

The eruption of a fit is, however, only the end product of a conflict (internal war) which has become too strong for conscious control.

Accumulated tension within the instinct levels of the mind has not been allowed to discharge itself by the primitive instinct paths, aggressive or sexual.

But what if an aggressive outlet *can* be found? May not the internal fit-producing situation be relieved—at the expense of the external?

Are all these "conquerors" and similar super-aggressive persons unconsciously trying to rid themselves of such intolerable tension as our patient reveals? If we pass on to further extracts from his clinical material we will find that this problem becomes even more interesting.

The circumstance that most easily arouses him to the greatest frenzy is one in which he conceives of the mother, or her symbolical equivalent such as a "pure" woman, being ill-treated or attacked by a father equivalent. All humanity is apparently divided in his mind into two contrasting opposites. There is a very sharp line between them. On one side of the line are innocent or good people, such as the Christ, his mother, himself, his doctor, etc. On the other side of the line, contrasting with the former as black contrasts with white, are the bad people or "devils." They include his father, office managers, all those who are in the slightest degree unjust or powerful, and sometimes merely rich. In fact, there is a tendency for them to include almost all males, as on the white side of the line he tends to include almost all females. His psychology is so built up that he must spend all his life protecting the mother equivalent (with which he identifies himself) on the one side, from the diabolical father equivalent on the other. Towards the former he must be nothing but tenderness, so much so that he suffers from grave inhibition in his sexual life. Towards the latter, and towards them only, he is psychologically free to vent the great mass of hatred and aggression bottled up within him. It is the equivalent of letting loose the frustrated revenge against the bad father who so diabolically ill treated the good mother.

Of special interest in international politics is the psychological reflection that in the unconscious mind one's *mother*land or *the place of one's birth*, is symbolically the equivalent of the good mother. Of course, it makes no difference if it is designated as one's fatherland! It is still a mother equivalent. It will thus be seen that for a person with this type of psychology any injury to his mother country will be resented as the most heinous outrage. Those who perpetrated such an act would be unconsciously identified with the diabolical father and no degree of revenge or punishment would be too severe for them. We may reflect on the apparent psychology of certain figures in the world of European politics and wonder whether we are not being confronted with a similar epileptic type of character. Is there not, perhaps, the same feeling of outrage against the enemies of the mother country—the same feeling that all the bombs procurable are not too many for the enemy? Is there not, in some cases, even the same inhibition of normal tendencies to sexual relief? Are such persons suffering from such an intolerable degree of accumulated mental tension that they are practically driven by it to seek relief in such an enormous, aggressive orgy? If that is so we may understand that, in the meantime, they are working in the only possible way which can give them an anticipated satisfaction.*

The fact that it may be possible to justify (or appear to justify)

* This paper was written early in 1938.

such behaviour on reality grounds is no refutation of its real source
from *unconscious* psychological forces. Every medical psychologist
knows that the intellectual (or reasoning) faculty is often merely
the servant of the deeper (unconscious) levels of the mind and is
rarely at a loss to find "reasons" or rationalizations for carrying
out and justifying the latter's behests. Thus one patient can find
"reasons" for murdering his office manager, and one section of the
community or one nation can find "justifications" for attacking
another. Is the instigator of the attack driven by unconscious mental
forces similar to those revealed in our patient?

The avenger or punisher has in his unconscious those very tendencies the expression of which he is so ready to avenge or punish
—and in a strength proportionate to the strength of his revenge
tendency. Occasionally they reveal themselves. Thus we see him
who is filled with indignation and revenge at the rape of his mother
country himself devoting his life and all his energies to the systematic
rape of his neighbours' mother countries. "Justice," or at least punishment, was always another way of performing the very same crime
that we profess to avenge or destroy.

Now the difference between such persons and our patient is that
he himself has, in a sense, *locked himself up*. He does not commit acts
of violence upon others nor does he make elaborate preparations in
anticipation of committing such acts and thereby obtaining the
desired relief. His "war" goes on under his own skin, or within his
own mind. For the clinical material of the session last quoted continues as follows:

"If only I could have my revenge—murder him. *Then I would
get well*. But what am I to do? I am in a helpless position. I cannot
do anything at all because of my wife and child. I wouldn't mind
paying the penalty myself if only I could relieve myself by doing
this murder. If only the wife and child met with a fatal accident
and were out of the way. But, under the circumstances, I am in a
helpless position, like I was as a boy, watching that swine murdering
my mother. I'm whacked. I've no further card to play. I must be
an enforced pacifist. I must be tortured and say nothing. Because
I was helpless I had to stick my crucifixion.

"But then I went back to my phantasy and thought of him lying
there helpless, with his arms chopped off and in agony. I suddenly
thought, 'Perhaps he is not a *bad man after all*. Perhaps he is a good
man and I have done this to him.' I thought of his eyes coming out
or bursting, and then I flopped out and started having my fit."

Or again from another session: After five minutes' silence he
begins the session with a fit. On recovery he explains it as follows:

"When you said you would give me only half an hour I had to tell you about your b—— Harley Street snobbery. I felt a great feeling of rage against you. I felt b—— you. While I was lying on the settee in silence I murdered you—as I have done the manager, and as I have wanted to murder my father.

"*Then*, I thought of all the hours you have spent with me in order that I shall get better. I thought, 'could ye not watch with me one hour?' You have watched with me, you have been kind to me to make me better. It was an awful smack in the eye for me. I had murdered you because you had got on your hind legs and you were the good one after all. I had murdered the good one, the innocent one (mother). I should have murdered myself. It's one long terror. Then the fit arose at that point. It's like hot meeting cold. It's as though two contrasting things (incompatible) came together. Something very hot meets something very cold, and the fit results. Black meets white. I rush all hot to murder my father. Then I find it is an innocent person (mother) whom I am murdering, and the murder feeling turns inwards. I murder myself. I suffer agonies. I beat myself, clench my hands and fight myself. I twist and wriggle in agony, kick myself, break my arm. It's an agony—that's what the fit is!"

Perhaps enough clinical material has been given to justify us in discussing the possible psychopathology of this condition.  In considering inherited characteristics we must remember that this man's father was in the habit of reducing his emotional tension by the most violent behaviour towards his wife (the patient's mother) and others. Evidently sexual relief was not enough for him. He had periodically, if not nightly, to fight and to raise pandemonium in the house.

May we not assume that this patient has been endowed with the same sort of tensions as his father and with the same tendencies to reducing them—by aggression rather than by sexual relief? In this connection it is worth remembering that this patient's fits actually began after a period of aggressive behaviour towards his wife. For some years he had become increasingly aggressive and objectionable towards his wife. Then he made a successful effort to suppress this tendency. The fits followed almost immediately. We might even suggest a comparison between the violence displayed by his father outwardly and the violence displayed by our patient inwardly in the form of a fit. His father broke everything and everyone in his environment—our patient broke his own arm.

Why did this patient come to differ from his father? I think the answer is perhaps—*through the influence of his mother*. As a child he witnessed his father's behaviour, naturally sided with his mother, and directed all his violence against violence. The thing he wanted to smash up was that violent aggressive thing (namely his father) whom he saw smashing his mother. He felt that the only relief for his state of tension would have been through aggressive action against his father. Unfortunately for his mental health, such an outlet was not possible for him. But that the bottled-up tendency lost none of its strength, even with the passage of years, is evident from the fact that in adolescence he carried out his long-cherished resolve and actually did fight his father. Also, his clinical material has shown him to be strongly possessed of the phantasy that he could only be cured if he actually did murder the manager whom he felt to be oppressing him.

The psychology of the fit is rather complicated, but put as simply as possible it is as follows:

The bottled-up aggression had been at last loosened from its tension in order to destroy the bad father. Suddenly he discovers that it is the mother whom he is so attacking. Immediately the aggressive outlet is stopped. But it has already attained too much headway. It is, as it were, in motion and all he can do with it is to reverse its motion, and, as it were, turn it back upon himself—himself, whom he now recognizes as the bad aggressor. The force of the impulse is sufficient to knock him out, as he says, like a "punch on the jaw," and he falls down in a fit.

If only some of our would-be world aggressors would so treat themselves!

An interesting and relevant reflection is that his father, whose tendencies this patient has presumably inherited, did not behave thus. On the contrary, he did not so inhibit his aggressive impulses and suffer from epileptic fits. He let fly with them against his defenceless wife and family. In that case the "war," as depicted in the opening paragraphs of this article, was outside himself though still confined within the family circle. Does it not appear evident that, up to a point, these two types of warfare, that in the world and that within the mind, are the equivalent of each other?

# WAR NEUROSES

*War is a condition which exists in the minds of all persons. The psychologist who is dealing with mental conflicts cannot disregard the theory that an external or real condition of war is, like patterns of culture, a projection into the outside world of reality of a condition which already exists within the mind of man.*

*In turn, this external condition reacts upon the minds of certain persons and we are here concerned with the effects which it produces. There are cases of severe fright, anxiety states, anxiety hysterias, conversion hysterias, confusional states, stupor and psychoses all indistinguishable from those which we commonly see in peace time, except for the precipitating factor of war conditions.*

## MAN WHO SWAM IN A SEA OF BLOOD

IT is some years now since I was consulted at a clinic by a tall, gaunt man, roughly dressed, and with a muffler around his neck. He looked a tough customer, aggressive, and with a square jaw. His appearance was in contrast to the impression created by the first words he spoke, for he had a marked stammer.

A second glance revealed that he was in an acute anxiety state, for his legs were trembling. He complained somewhat sullenly and aggressively that he could not sleep: "It is years since I have had so much as one hour's sleep."

He complained, also, that he could not cross a road alone for fear something would come up and hit him in the back. He complained of frequent sweatings: "If I do go to sleep—if you can call it sleep —for so much as half an hour, I wake up in a bath of perspiration, wringing wet and cold as though I had just come out of cold water. But more often I cannot get to sleep at all, for just as I am dozing off, I leap up in a panic, choking for my breath. I am sure if I didn't wake up at that moment, I would be a goner.

"When I joined the Navy before the war I was as fit as a man could be, athletic and a good swimmer. I soon became first-class boy, at eighteen, and when the war broke out in 1914 I was a stoker on H.M.S. ——.

"It must be this —— war that has brought me to this condition —fit man that I was. I got wounded in the head. Doctors have told me that it was only a scalp wound and that I ought to be quite well, but all I know is that I am still a helpless wreck—and that was years ago. Sometimes when I get up in the mornings my legs give way under me. I feel dead from the waist downwards.

"And this is a funny thing, doctor. I sometimes dream that I am in the water, and—would you believe it—when I awake in the morning I have a bad cold. It is a real cold which lasts for several days. This happens every few weeks. I never had a cold in my life before the —— war. They have reduced my pension again. All I know is that I was fit before the war and am so helpless now that I often think of finishing it off. Coming to this hospital is my last hope.

"You have listened to what I have to say, but at the pension office they put a bright light into my eyes and take out little hammers and start hammering me all over. I have had enough of that for years and 1 swear this, that if ever those —— plumbers with their —— hammers come tapping around me any more, I will knock their blocks off."

(Apparently the patient had experienced repeated neurological examinations, obviously on the theory that this head injury [scalp wound] may have caused some organic lesion of the central nervous system which was responsible for his numerous symptoms. Though one or two of these symptoms might by themselves suggest an organic causation, to the psychologist the conglomeration of them certainly was diagnostic of functional or psychological causes.)

There is no doubt that the neurological approach had, to say the least of it, entirely failed to get rapport with the patient. It had increased his feelings of hostility towards the world in general and towards doctors in particular. Reductions of disability pension had had the same effect.

Though he dated all his symptoms from the war, this man had not clearly connected them up with his war experiences, and he was not even certain that the war was responsible for them. At first he did not mention any specific war experience, but on the analytic settee, under free association of thought, he presently began to produce several curious dreams.

In one of these he dreamt of a field of red poppies, and, at the same time, he could hear a band playing military music. Associations to this were most dramatic.

He remembered an outstanding date—April 25th, 1915—"The time," he says, "is 4 a.m on Sunday morning. On the battleships the bands are playing military music; the soldiers and sailors are mustering for a great task for which they have been preparing for several weeks. The landing at the Dardanelles was about to take place."

The field of poppies brought to his mind visions of a "sea of blood" in which he says he had swum for hours. They brought also associations with death and graves.

Later he says: "I shall never forget that landing; I can still hear the band playing the lads to their doom. The bands were playing aboard the ships to cheer the lads up before they got into the cutters. We all thought we were going to have a picnic; we were going to have it all our own way and go right to Constantinople. But we had given them two months to prepare for us, and what a welcome we got!

"I shall never forget it. I was only twenty years of age at that time and thought it was great fun. I was one of the oarsmen in one of four cutters towed by a tug. We were sheltered behind a larger ship, the *River Clyde*, which was to run aground on Sedd el Bahr. As the *River Clyde* grounded, the tug pulled us out further along the Bay, turned away, and we continued with our oars. A moment later we were caught by submerged barbed wire, only a few yards from the shore, but in sixteen feet of water.

"It was at that point that hell was let loose on us. All that the Turks had accumulated in the way of machine-guns and small cannon, for two months, seemed to go off suddenly together. It was sheer murder—that is what it was.

"I can still hear the hammering in my head, the banging and pinging—some nights no sleep at all—terrible dreams—fighting for breath—thinking one's going to drown.

"When I picture the war, my whole inside turns, I get frightened (I don't mind saying so). From my feet upwards I get a lot of needles reaching even to the top of my head, to the roots of my hair. Some days I do not know how to walk, and think that everybody is looking at me or that somebody is behind me. It is a rotten feeling. Sometimes, in bed, I hear a sound of somebody shouting, and a pinging, as plainly as if the whole thing were in front of my eyes.

"That boat was a slaughter-house. I was struck on the head with something and there was blood all over me. I jumped out of the boat to save my life, and down I went in the water. I tried to come up again, but a drowning soldier was clinging to my legs. I kicked him off; it was a fight for life. When I came up I sheltered behind the boat.

"Later, with another man, I tried to tow it out of the range of machine-gun fire. He was shot, and I swam for my life to a K lighter. There I can hardly remember what happened. I think I lost my head completely. I was in a terrible panic.

"I saw a man on board whom I took to be a Turk, and I attacked him with a shovel. Then I had to lie down beside his body to avoid the firing. Finally I rolled off this into the water and swam for the *River Clyde*. Here I was hanging on with two soldiers until the darkness overtook me.

"When they pulled me back into the boat, I had been swimming for so many hours that I couldn't stand up. I fell overboard again and though I could not stand, my legs went on moving and I went on swimming. That is how I finally got rescued.

"For weeks afterwards everything seemed like a nightmare; I think I must have been raving mad. I was kept in bed in hospital. I can remember that all my hair fell out and it was a long time before it grew again. I returned to duty some months later, but

I don't think I was ever any good. In the boiler-room, at every moment, I would run out and run up the steps to the hatch. I kept thinking my last moment had come."

Many more details could be given of this remarkable case. Suffice it to say that every one of the symptoms of which he complained at his first and subsequent interviews was correlated to feelings which he had experienced in the course of his tragic sixteen hours of war experience at the Dardanelles.

The numbness which he still occasionally feels from the waist downwards—even all these years afterwards—was connected with an identical feeling which he experienced after hours of swimming in cold water.

The choking which wakes him out of his doze so as to prevent him from getting any sleep was associated with the sensation of drowning. He had found a device to assist him against insomnia. This was to roll the top of the bedclothes into a hard bundle and to tuck it firmly under his left armpit. Then and then only could he secure a little sleep.

Free association under analysis brought to light an experience of acute anxiety when he had been drowning; though a strong swimmer he had been pulled under water by a drowning soldier. Exhausted and nearly drowned, he had finally succeeded in reaching a boat and getting his arm over the gunwale so that it supported him firmly under his left armpit.

In this comparatively safe position he had at last been able to take breath and gain a few moments of rest. This was over twenty years ago; and without knowing the reason, he had, until recently, been adopting this device with the bedclothes to secure his sleep. He gave it up when this associated experience was remembered.

Fear of crossing the road was associated with the experience when he was expecting every moment a bullet from behind.

Most curious of all, the colds from which he frequently suffers have been shown to succeed dreams—remembered or forgotten—when he had been repeating the experience of being chilled to the bone in the water.

When all these details had been brought back to his memory and the full story of his experiences, and particularly of his emotions during that sixteen hours of panic, had been accurately associated with them, he found himself relatively free from most of his symptoms.

It appears that there had been a compulsion within his mind. Whenever he relaxed, or attempted to sleep, he returned to the tragic scenes of his panic to re-experience those crowded hours of agony. Why the mind should behave in such a manner it is difficult to say, unless it be that there is an impulse to go over material which has not been mentally digested, in order to digest it; or to sort it out and reconstruct it in such a manner as to nullify its injurious effects; or we may suppose that these traumatic experiences create by their violent stimulation a sort of wound, rut or channel within the mind—called by some psychiatrists an "engram." Along this channel thereafter the dynamic currents of mental or nervous energy tend to flow whenever the mind is disposed to relax its concentration on current events—or, rather, the energy *constantly* flowing along this channel tends to *become conscious* on relaxation. This deeply pitted portion of the mind seems often to be separated from the rest of the mind and often to lead a more or less independent existence. Particularly is this the case when there is complete amnesia (memory-blank) for the events. As this portion of the mind is by virtue of its separation inaccessible to the main portion of the mind—its current experiences, sense of reality and reason—it remains unaltered by the latter, and nervous energy continues to flow along it *in perpetuam*. That is why the process can still be going on even twenty years after the events.

It is conceivable that this man was everlastingly engaged upon such a task whenever he let his mind out of his conscious control. For many years he had been doing this, perhaps nightly, without successful therapeutic results. On the contrary the compulsive habit seemed to reawaken the injurious results of which he wished to rid himself.

It is only when by the technique of analysis or by some other psychotherapeutic measure the forgotten events and their associated emotions have been recalled to consciousness and fully remembered that the banks of this traumatic channel are as it were flattened out, its content dispersed over the entire mind, and nervous energy is no longer prone to find its isolated way along it. This is apparently the psychology of how cure is brought about.

Our theory gains support from the fact that when he was helped to remember fully every detail of these experiences, it seemed his mind was relatively able to leave the matter alone. Perhaps some degree of mental digestion had at last taken place. The pathological channels in his mind had been flattened out. His sleep improved very considerably; he was no longer awakened from it by terrifying dreams or feelings of choking.

With this improvement came a general improvement in his physical and mental health. It appears that he is now safe from ideas of suicide and from the nightly torments which he had endured for so many years.

# CAMBRAI 1917—LONDON 1938

THIS case concerns a condition which had become increasingly rare since the Great War ended, but which, as this instance shows, can crop up again in the most surprising and unexpected manner, even after all this lapse of time.

The mental mechanism here portrayed is a common one in nervous illness. Severe fright or "mental trauma" experienced at any stage of one's life, especially in infancy, *and subsequently forgotten*, can later cause a nervous breakdown. The sufferer has, of course, no knowledge of how or why the symptoms arise.

A point of special and topical interest in this case is the rôle played by the increasing international tension with its threat of war, culminating in the recent crisis.* This rôle should be distinguished from the *cause* of the neurosis. However important, it is merely a stimulating or precipitating factor, not a cause.

The lesson which this case holds for the psychologist is that he should, as far as possible, have no preconceptions or theories as to the possible cause of a neurosis, but that he should allow the patient's own free associations of thought, under analytical conditions, to lead spontaneously to a revelation of the origins of his condition.

A man of forty-five came to my consulting room because he was suffering from very severe attacks of depression. These periods of depression lasted from a few hours to several days.

He complained also of insomnia and various apparently hysterical outbursts. These hysterical outbursts we found later to be compounded of acute attacks of anxiety together with a display of violence.

You will understand that it is not unusual for fear and fight to be linked together. Occasionally they reach the violence of a fit.

The condition of depression had existed with this patient for a considerable number of years, but to a degree that was almost imperceptible until the six or twelve months immediately previous to when he first came to me.

The theory he advanced was that his current life with its increasing financial worries and its absence of a satisfactory marital state was responsible for this progressively severe condition.

His first and second consultations were occupied with a long

* This paper was first published in February 1939.

recital of all his current emotional difficulties, financial worries, social misfits, etc. He had a feeling that *disaster* was imminent in all his private affairs. A personal crisis, he thought, would soon arrive and be the end of him.

At first he said nothing of international war crisis, but later on it becomes apparent that the world unrest, and particularly the recent crisis, was a very specific stimulus to his anxiety and depression.

Indeed, the subject was so extremely stimulating as to be *intolerable.* In consequence, his mind performed a mental operation with which the psychotherapist is familiar; he *displaced* the anxiety of these matters on to similar feelings about his private affairs, although the latter did not warrant it.

Displacement in this direction is the reverse of that usually encountered. It is more usual to displace or *project* private anxieties on to public or international matters.

At the third session he told me of a dream which was as follows:

*He is in jail and is very distressed. He is begging to be let out—to be given his liberty. Finally, they do let him out, but only to rearrest him and to flog him. He can feel the pain of the flogging.*

He awoke terribly distressed. This heralded several days of deep depression.

At first he had no idea of the meaning of the dream. He had never been in jail nor had he ever been flogged. He laughed at the idea. But lying on the analytical settee, his associations of thought to the *feeling* of this "being in jail" were quite surprising. They brought to his mind a terrible experience:

He is completely paralysed, unable to move a muscle to help himself. He is lying in a narrow recess in a dug-out, terrified that he will be forgotten and left as in a living tomb.

This is in 1917. The horror of his position is that, though fully conscious he cannot move—for the shell splinter that has wounded him has also given him spinal concussion, resulting in a total paralysis of every locomotor muscle.

He lies in this crypt in great terror and utter helplessness, shrieking to be taken out (begging to be let out of jail). But nobody pays any attention. Eventually he is taken out (the release from prison), only to be admitted to an operating theatre in a field hospital (rearrest) where they operate upon the wound in his back. On account of his weakness the operation is performed under a local anæsthetic.

As the effects of the anæsthetic wear off, he feels the agony of the operation (he feels the pain of the flogging in his dream) and is still helplessly paralysed in bed (still in jail). It is twelve months before he leaves hospital.

These associations to his dream heralded several sessions with me in which he produced the most astonishing memories of war experiences. This man claimed that, unlike most of his fellow soldiers, he had experienced no fear or anxiety during his abundant battle experiences.

Nevertheless, after a few sessions in which his mind had relived some of these experiences, I observed him surreptitiously glancing at the clock during his session.

On being asked "Why do you look at the clock?" he admitted, "I was relieved to see only ten minutes left of the session," but he did not know why he was in such a hurry to get away.

The next day he took the coach as usual from a country town to London, but his state of anxiety was such that he could not approach my consulting room. He got out of his coach and got straight into another one back to his home.

It was with difficulty that he was persuaded to come again. At his next attendance he admitted that since he had taken to remembering his war experiences in my consulting room, he suffered acute anxiety and discomfort at the very thought of entering my room. He was in a state of fear, counting every moment when he would be able to escape.

A further agony in his mind was the thought that if he missed the coach he would have to wait in a fever of anxiety for half an hour before he could get out of the neighbourhood.

This was nearly a year before the present war and air-raids.

Association revealed that my consulting room, where his war memories had returned to him, was emotionally equivalent to the front line where these terrifying experiences took place. The bus stop was still not out of the danger zone. It appeared that if he missed the coach and had to wait there for half an hour, at any moment the shell that wounded him might come over and the whole dreadful experience be repeated!

In other words, it seemed that this man, who had no recollection of fear during battle, must have experienced the most tremendous fear, however successfully he may have repressed it from consciousness or, alternatively, have forgotten the memory of his terror.

But the most traumatic or injurious experience of all was apparently that of being totally paralysed and helpless as a result of the spinal concussion accompanying his wound, of lying so helpless in the field under fire, of being confined in the tomb-like dug-out while in this helpless state, of the operation and his subsequent experiences.

Gradually, every one of his neurotic symptoms, including his insomnia, came to be related to repressed memories of acute emotional experiences during the war.

This was a case of war neurosis, commonly known as "shell-shock," in which the patient had been tolerably well for all the years after his release from hospital in 1919.

The added current stresses of the last year or so had stimulated the buried anxieties in his mind; and the rumours of imminent war and war crises had apparently proved to be the last straw. They had put this little extra strain upon his nervous stability and had stimulated the hitherto more or less successfully buried or repressed emotional experiences of the Great War.

The censorship between conscious and unconscious mind had in consequence been relatively weakened and the old feelings or emotions had broken through.

The main forces responsible for his illness were therefore the bottled-up emotions of his repressed and forgotten war memories. He and his friends had no idea that his present breakdown had any connection whatsoever with the events of so long ago.

Only by pursuing the technique of free association of thought and association to current dream material were all these memories and their emotional accompaniments brought to light. His bouts of depression were the consequence of his *reliving*, during his sleep or in his unconscious, the experiences of those helpless wounded days.

His anxiety symptoms were similarly the re-expression of the repressed and forgotten anxieties generated during the same period. Only when he had gone through all these again and brought them fully back to memory, was his mind able to distinguish that these things took place over twenty years ago and were no longer a part of his current life.

At his last session he said that he had no thoughts of the war in his mind, no worries, no unpleasant dreams. He said he felt perfectly comfortable and happy and the only thing he could think of was that he wanted to spend the evening at a cinema where he antici-pated thoroughly enjoying himself.

This programme he carried out with much relish, though he had not hitherto been able to enjoy himself in such a dark and confined place.

## PSYCHOPATHOLOGY

The psychopathology of such a neurosis as this may be explained very simply by the aid of a few diagrams.

Let us draw a line and regard the space above it as representing the conscious mind (see Fig. 1).

The conscious mind contains all that we are conscious of or can ordinarily become conscious of by such processes as voluntarily recalling something to memory. We commonly identify ourselves with this portion of our mind.

Below the line we represent the unconscious mind. The unconscious is ordinarily inaccessible to consciousness. We only know of

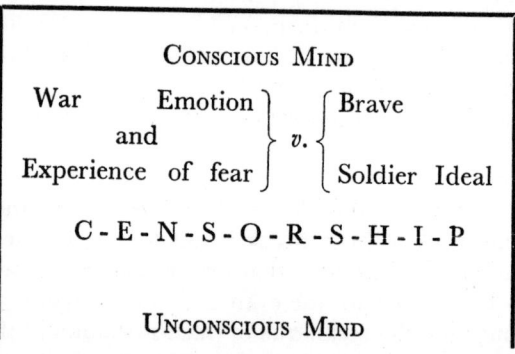

FIG. 1.—*During the War years (1915–17) his experiences aroused emotions of acute fear. It was intolerable to remain conscious of this distressing feeling, both on account of the discomfort and also because it came into* Conflict *with his ideal of himself as a brave soldier. Therefore he tried not to think about it, and he succeeded in repressing it from memory, and submerging it into the unconscious. See Figure 2.*

its existence by certain inexplicable feelings, ideas, or impulses which periodically break through the line or barrier and appear in consciousness.

Now if we broaden this line and call it "censorship" we can envisage it as a custodian of consciousness, keeping or endeavouring to keep unwelcome thoughts and feelings from breaking through and disturbing our conscious mind and our idea of ourselves.

Every thought or experience arouses in us certain accompanying feelings or emotions.

For instance, our patient comes under fire and this experience arouses in him the emotion of fear (Fig. 1). But to be conscious of fear or to remain conscious of having experienced fear is incompatible with the "brave-soldier-ideal" of himself which he also carries in consciousness.

For this reason and because the fear emotion is intolerably uncomfortable, he censors or turns out of his consciousness these unwelcome memories of the fear-provoking experiences. He *represses* them into the unconscious and they no longer exist in consciousness, so that he can now maintain his "brave-soldier-ideal" with ease.

Moreover, his conscious mind is free from the acute discomfort of the feelings of anxiety and no longer afflicted with disturbing memories (Fig. 2).

This happens in 1917, and apparently all is well. But later on— sometimes a year or so later, but in this case as much as twenty-one years later—the additional stress of current events may turn the

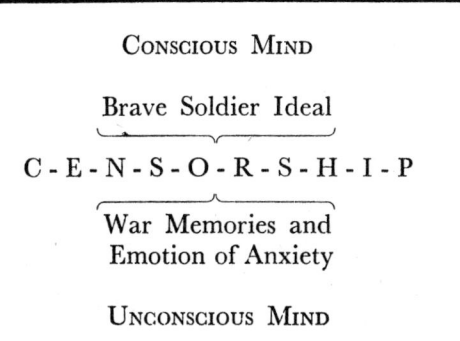

CONSCIOUS MIND

Brave Soldier Ideal

C - E - N - S - O - R - S - H - I - P

War Memories and
Emotion of Anxiety

UNCONSCIOUS MIND

FIG. 2.—*The period of 1917-18 and after. He has succeeded in repressing the unwelcome memories of the War together with the intolerable emotions they aroused. This is the period of apparent health. It is maintained for over twenty years—but at the price of the continued expenditure of mental energy from the censorship continually pressing down the dynamic energy of the repressed emotions of anxiety, which fain would rise.*

balance either by weakening the repressing (censoring) forces or by stimulating the repressed emotions.

Thus, these repressed emotions break through the barrier and *something* appears in consciousness. At first this something that appears in consciousness is a disturbing emotion such as depression or anxiety—divorced from any memory of past events (see Fig. 3).

It gives the impression of floating freely about the conscious mind ready to attach itself to relevant or apparently irrelevant ideas or current events. This is how phobias are commonly formed.          ·

Thus it comes about that this patient consults me on account of bouts of inexplicable depression and attacks of inexplicable anxiety. He has at first no memory of terrifying experiences during the war, or if he has memories they are entirely free from terrifying accompaniments.

If originally both memories *and* their emotional accompaniments had been repressed, it is as though the repressed *emotions* were more dynamic than the *memory of events* which caused them.

It is as though the emotions were for ever pressing upwards trying to break through the barrier of the censorship. It requires ever-lasting energy on the part of the repressing forces to keep them under (see Fig. 2).

When, even years later, these repressing forces weaken their constant vigilance or if the repressed emotions receive some extra contribution from current events, up burst the old, out-of-date

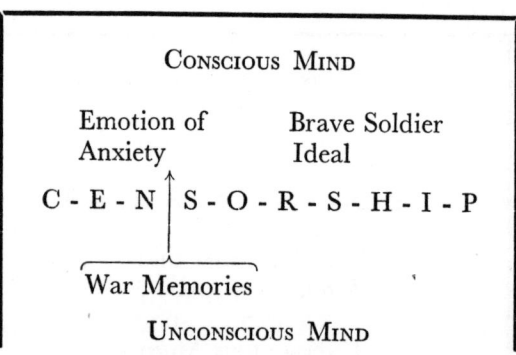

FIG. 3.—*Period of illness, 1937–8. At last the dynamic emotions of anxiety and depression break through the censorship and appear in consciousness. This is the period of illness. The patient complains of inexplicable depression and anxiety—inexplicable because the experiences that caused them are absent. This state of affairs has come about either through a weakening of the energy of the censorship or through recent stimulation of the hitherto unconscious emotions, or through both. Recent "War-scares" put the spark to the magazine and exploded the state of apparent health represented in Figure 2.*

emotions, having apparently lost nothing of their virility in twenty-one years; the man becomes *conscious* of depression and anxiety (see Fig. 3).

It appears that the mere *memories* of events *divested of their emotions* are neither here nor there. They matter nothing and can easily remain repressed from consciousness or forgotten.

The tragedy of the situation is that without recalling these memories and without attaching the distressing emotions to these memories, the conscious mind is unable to appreciate that the occasions for them, the occasions for depression or anxiety, are no longer current, no longer belong to the present day. And so our patient is in a fever of anxiety to get out of my consulting room and the district around—just as though it were Cambrai in 1917 and not London in 1938! (see Fig. 3).

When, under analytical conditions, anxiety is sufficiently allayed for him to relax the repressing forces of censorship, the memories of the occasions when he originally experienced this anxiety also come up to consciousness (see Fig. 4).

As he remembers that this anxiety is none other than the identical emotion he felt during those experiences, he at last realizes that it belongs to 1917 and accepts the terrible memories in preference to living the terrible emotions in his present-day life.

Similarly, the depression that accompanied the period of his

CONSCIOUS MIND

War Memories              Brave Soldier
with Emotion              Ideal Modified

C - E - N - S - O - R - S - H - I - P

UNCONSCIOUS MIND

FIG. 4.—*Restoration of health in* 1938. *The missing or dissociated memories have at last become linked up with the emotions which properly belonged to them. He has adjusted his conscious mind and his idea of himself as a brave soldier to accept all these facts and feelings. Therefore there is no further need to maintain the repressing energy of the censorship. This is the final stage of health and ability to live in the present day. The censoring forces are relieved of their constant vigilance and expenditure of repressing energy, and the mind is relieved of strain.*

wound and long months of paralysis becomes a memory instead of a living actuality.

*At last he is living in* 1938, *instead of living emotionally in the horrible years of war and helplessness.*

EPILOGUE

In spite of the truth and satisfactoriness of the above explanation, in practice it is frequently revealed to the psychotherapist that the war experiences which seemed to be the cause of the patient's condition are nothing more or less than the stimulating or precipitating cause. One man can have such experiences and suffer no consequent neurosis, whereas another will merely hear of war and become invalided. There is thus something already inside the psyche of the person who breaks down which predisposes him to break down under these particular conditions. This "something" should be regarded as the real cause, though admittedly he may never have become *manifestly* ill had it not been for war rumours or war shocks.    If a deeper analysis is required, as often becomes necessary, whether we wish it or not, it is always revealed that these deeper, predisposing or real causes of the "war" neurosis are the familiar repressed conflicts of *infantile* amnesia rather than those of war amnesia. These are the conflicts which form the pattern of the individual's character and which are responsible for the emotional nature which predisposes him to feel and act in a particular way towards current events. It is on account of this that he may be unable to tolerate, for instance, large doses of love, hate, and violence, such as he is likely to encounter under war conditions. This, and the undercurrent of unconscious homosexuality stimulated by war (and perhaps responsible for it) are dealt with in greater detail in a long clinical case-sheet by the present author, entitled "The Analysis of a War Neurosis" (Case XXIII in this book).

## BOMBS AND SHELTERS

WHEN air raids and bombs are the main mental preoccupation of a large proportion of Londoners, the difference in the nervous reaction of various persons to this new condition of life must be of paramount psychological interest.

Some of us may be amazed at the apparent indifference of some persons living perhaps in the centre of the most bombed areas. We may admire it, but at the same time we should not be too condemnatory of the highly sensitive, excitable, or overstrung persons whom we constantly meet.

It is essentially with the psychology of these latter that I propose to deal.

Some people with highly strung nerves, who are even in ordinary times in a state of tension, cannot bear the suspense when air raiders are about, guns are fired, and occasional bombs may fall.

It seems almost that something in them may be unconsciously wanting the explosion, and cannot bear to wait for it.

The problem of fear and bravery is a very big subject, and we cannot hope to deal exhaustively with it in one short article. We hear so many persons who have not thought at all deeply on the subject, and who have acquired their "knowledge" from the most superficial sources, speaking dogmatically on these subjects, with, I am sure, a quite unjustifiable degree of conviction. All I propose to do in this article is to give some of the verbatim remarks of an ordinary cultured and sensitive individual under the conditions of free association of thought.

The patient is by no means a nervous invalid. Curious as it may seem, he is a competent member of H.M. fighting forces and one who volunteered for service long before conscription. No doubt some of his reactions are common to a great many of us. He says:

"My anxiety state continues. It started a week ago, corresponding to the mass air raids on London. Yet I am convinced that it is not due to the air raids. It goes on all day.

"My forty-eight hours leave began yesterday. I went to see my young lady, and spent the night sitting in an Anderson shelter with her and her mother and the two women from next door. It was a noisy night. Sitting in an Anderson shelter waiting for the bomb to drop is the worst. Four women and myself. I was in a state of anxiety all the time, and, of course, dared not confess it.

"I scratched my finger in getting into that Anderson shelter. The next night I went back to the camp where there are 500 soldiers, and there we took no shelter and I was less anxious about the raid—but I did become anxious about my finger, and feared that I might get lock-jaw from the scratch.

"Sitting in an Anderson shelter waiting for the bomb to come, that is the worst. I have a phantasy that a great bomb will come down through the opening of the shelter, and then come *up* and get me. Somehow I feel the sensation in my body. It seems to me that I would not mind being bumped off, but I cannot bear waiting for it."

He is asked to give free association to this feeling. He starts laughing, and says:

"I see, it is not dread, but impatience. Impatience feels very like anxiety. *When it is not too great* this anxiety is accompanied by a definite sexual itch. I feel desperate. I feel I could commit rape. I would be too impatient for any preliminaries. You see, it seems that something terrific is going to happen. Then I feel that I could turn the tables on it, and do it myself.

"You see, there is so much tension that something terrific has *got* to be done. If I sit in an Anderson shelter I feel that it is going to be done *to* me, whereas, if I could fight it would be much better. Then I would be doing it to somebody.

"Punching somebody on the nose or raping would be turning the tables on sitting down and waiting for a bomb. There seems to be some high explosive energy in me behind all this, and if I cannot use it myself then I get this terrible anxiety that it is going to come along in the shape of a bomb and blow me up.

"All my feelings tell me is that it might go off. It must go off. And if I am tied down and cannot do anything then it is going to blow me up instead of my blowing somebody else up with it. I'd be a damn sight happier in a Spitfire than in an Anderson shelter.

"Even the Anderson shelter would not be so bad if only the blessed bomb would come soon and blow me up. The thing that is intolerable is the suspense. It must be that there is something in me that wants the explosion, that must have the relief at once, but cannot bear the agony of waiting for it.

"When I first came here for treatment I was in a suicidal state. And this is the point of interest: I thought of committing suicide by a *violent* method. I got over all that, but now that these air raids have been intensified, I feel that there is, after all, some promise of this violence which some instinct in me must be wanting. I cannot bear the agony of waiting for it."

At another session he says: "I have a feeling that there is a special bomb marked for me and it *must* get me. Yet on the other hand I wish I could get blown up and put an end to all this anxiety. A feeling that I am going to break down and burst into tears about it—a feeling that I can't go on much longer . . . yet when I come to think of it I have had a feeling just the same as this for years and years, long before it became materialized in the form of these air raids and my reaction to them.

"There seems to be nothing in life for me but anxiety. No doubt these raids have made this psychological state of mine much more real, and, as it were, justifiable and believable—going to bed to the sound of anti-aircraft fire and bombs and feeling very sorry for myself. The anxiety seems to be coupled with the air raid.

"As the siren time approaches I get a state of suspended anxiety. I am all ready for something to happen. Then at last the sirens go, and I jump and my foot trembles. Everybody around me is joking. I try to joke and hide the anxiety.

"Then in half an hour I feel very tired. Then I think, 'Let me be blown up and end it!' I feel something terrible is going to happen to me. I am going to be destroyed. I have to go to bed like that. If there is a noise I feel something is going to come through the ceiling, so I lie on my side so that it will have to smash through my hip first.

"At last I think, 'Let it come! Let's have a great smashing roar and end it all!' "

*Analyst:* "Free association of thought to this feeling."

*Patient:* "A desire for sexual relief. I think of the first orgasm I had, and the almost unbearable tension that preceded it. That terrific climax has never happened since, and now it seems I am waiting for it, and expecting it, and the air raids excite me to a pitch of unendurable tension as if something terrific like that is going to happen again.

"That seems to be the only comparison to that first experience. It frightened me then and it frightens me now. But I must have, through fright, repressed all that, and now I feel I am going to be blown up by it. I am in front of that bomb instead of behind it. It's wind-up I've got.

"I can't say I feel sexual when I am like that: I feel it in my belly. I wish to hell it would go off.

"And now I will have to drag through another week before I see you again. Here I can let fly with my own feelings, but back in camp I can't. I am in a subordinate position, being treated as any illiterate corporal wishes, and no power to hit back—being bombed and no power of hitting back.

"I am impatient. I can't stand the waiting for it. Give me something that will get rid of this anxiety. I can't go on like this week after week. Give me a tablet that will cure me to-day."

## Psychopathology

Several interesting psychological speculations may be based on even the trifling clinical material on this and the previous pages.

First we may observe that the patient is ordinarily in a state of nervous tension. This, he says, has always been his natural condition. Nervous tension means an uncomfortably highly-charged condition which is instinctively striving towards discharge, and relief of the state of discomfort.

Such a relief is normally attained when any instinct which has reached a high pitch of desire is gratified. Satisfaction or calm and comfort is the natural result.

The problem as to why this man is highly strung, why some instinct within him is constantly at a high pitch without attaining relief, must be referred to his deeper psychological make-up.

No doubt we would find conflict which prevents an ordinary heterosexual adjustment. Perhaps deep down in his unconscious mind we would find that he has never successfully dealt with his relationship with the father-figure.

As a result he cannot happily conjugate psychosexually with the female (the mother-successor) but is instead left with his undischarged tensions, and pre-occupied with his relationship to the male (the analyst, the father-successor). He is vainly hoping for some relief of his tension, some solution of his conflict in this unsolved and unsatisfactory relationship.

This is his condition before the war and the air raids came along —I almost said "before the war and the air raids came to his assistance."

With this "help" from reality his deep-seated anxieties can easily be rationalized and dramatized.

Here too the Anderson shelter comes into the picture as an excellent symbolic representation of that feminine interior (mother's) which he was always afraid to enter (even in phantasy), and inside which little Œdipus always knew disaster would befall him.

And that particular Anderson shelter *with four women*! Of course, he felt most uncomfortable. Of course, he felt that the bomb (specially marked for him) would come in there after him—would come through the opening and then *up* to get him. He says: "Somehow I feel the sensation in my body."

This is indeed unconscious homosexual conflict seizing upon the reality basis of bombs in order to rationalize and dramatize itself.

If it won't hurry up and bomb him and get it over (relieve the tension) then he himself will be forced to do something to give himself relief. At one time he thought of suicide. Now he says, "I'd be happier in a Spitfire than in an Anderson shelter." And perhaps so would all males worthy of the name.

It is when the positive drives to relieve instinct-tension have been unduly checked in early life by fear of the father-image that we get this state of suspended animation or of tension passively and fearfully awaiting its discharge by the active intervention of a more powerful image—for instance, a bomb.

Perhaps this in the male is the unconscious homosexual component. And perhaps this homosexuality is brought about through fear (arising in infancy) of normal heterosexual development with a failure adequately to discharge psychosexual tension and a consequent accumulation of such tensions in the form of highly-strung nerves.

In this connection we should remember that fear is also the common cause of attack. More than one psychoanalyst has held that the phenomenon of war is fundamentally due to the repression of sexuality.

The stages through which the repressed libido (sexual instinct) would pass before its emergence in the form of war include first: repression of heterosexuality, then with accumulation of undischarged tension a state of fearful expectancy—expecting the tension to be discharged by another (e.g. by a bomb) and finally the inability to endure the suspense, being oneself forced to attack and get the thing over.

Certain changes in the intrapsychic disposal of libido occur coincidentally with the above stages. First, it regresses from what is called a genital disposition to an anal, bodily or bowel disposition. Bombs are expected to get at one, or even to come up at one. Subsequently it (libido) may re-emerge in the form of aggression, which, like the latter, is a more primitive mode of expression than is sexuality. We may relieve tension and compensate for anxiety by dropping bombs ourselves or by shooting from our Spitfires.

Poor humanity, so much in the toils of its unconscious conflicts that it must disseminate and suffer their agonies, even to the extent of jeopardizing its very existence!

War in the mind, like all unconscious material, tends to dramatization. In all human behaviour, whether individual or collective, we see as in a mirror the unconscious mind of man. At the present time what we see is war. War in the mind becomes war in the world.

# CLINICAL NOTES ON A COMPLETE ANALYSIS

Most of the cases hitherto recorded have been confined to a description of preliminary or very early sessions. But in all cases in which *a complete cure is attempted* analysis is carried to a very much deeper level, so that the whole aspect of the treatment and the type of material produced at the sessions undergoes a very dramatic change.

A stage in the treatment is reached which is called the stage of the transference: or even, by some analysts, the stage of *the transference neurosis*.

This is a stage at which all or most of the patient's symptoms of which he originally complained have now disappeared, and in their place he is concerned only with emotional feelings towards the treatment and towards the analyst himself. Unlike earlier sessions, emotions colour the entire picture most vividly, and, in the most successful cases, often most violently.

Transference may be defined as the transferring on to the analyst of the patient's emotional patterns of infancy, which were at that time concerned with his parents. The patient is, of course, unaware that he is doing this, or he only gradually becomes aware of it. To him the analyst really merits the invective or the esteem and love, or curiously enough both together, which he levels at him.

In psychoanalytical treatment proper, the analyst is in no hurry to get rid of this situation, nor has he tried to avoid its development.

On the contrary, psychoanalysis, as distinct from other forms of psychotherapy, has been defined as *the strategic development of transference and of transference analysis*.

The former process, the development of transference, is achieved by the fundamental rule of free association of thought, and at the same time by excluding all other relationships with the patient. The second process, the analysis of transference, is achieved by interpretation after transference has been established.

The essential characteristic of psychoanalysis is that everything else is subordinated to these ends; that is to say, interpretations are not made just for the sake of interpretation, but only with an eye to the strategy above defined.

The danger is that in the process of transference development negative transference, or hate feelings, may accumulate undetected. If these undetected and unexpressed negative feelings should exceed in quantity the accompanying positive transference, the patient is liable to express his negative feelings, not by coming to the session and speaking them, but simply by staying away. If the unanalysed negative transference be excessive, he may never reappear.

In the light of these remarks it will be appreciated that the expression by the patient of his negative feelings *within* the analysis is the most important essential in ensuring the continuation of his attendance and the success of his treatment.

So much for the importance of negative transference and the danger of the failure to express it within the sessions.

The question arises as to whether there can be any more difficult task in analysis than getting the patient to attend in spite of hate feelings and getting him to give analytical expression to these feelings. What else may there be that may escape both his attention and ours? What else may he resist and refuse to express to his analyst?

The answer is: Love.

A man is not readily going to admit even to himself that he loves another man and passionately desires that man to love or to make love to him. If he succeed in maintaining his repression of these tendencies, if they escape his notice and that of the analyst, analysis will cease as surely as it will cease if he refuse to attend and express his hate tendencies.

The following case-sheet article illustrates in a most dramatic fashion the difficulties caused by the transference on to the analyst of the patient's infantile loves and hates. It shows us that the interpretation of these affects is essential to the uncovering, not of the war neurosis, but of the far more important original emotional situations of earliest infancy which formed the pattern of his mind and laid the foundation to his emotional character and were the essential causes of his breakdown.

## THE ANALYSIS OF A WAR NEUROSIS

WAR Neurosis, as an investigation of this case shows us, is not a specific entity, but merely the precipitation of a latent state of psychoneurosis or psychosis in an individual already potentially ill, and only resisting breakdown in the absence of exceptional stress. This being so, we may presuppose a ratio between the degree of tension already existing and the severity of the trauma required to precipitate the illness.

The special nature of the condition to which the specific designation "War Neurosis" is applied consists diagnostically in the precipitating factor of war, and therapeutically in the fact that in the forefront of the analytical material are partially or wholly repressed traumatic war experiences or war phantasies which must fully emerge into consciousness before the deeper psychological conflicts, the real and predisposing causes of the condition, can be approached.

In this paper Section I is concerned with the early part of the treatment, when the analytical sessions are almost exclusively filled with this material and an overcoming of the resistances to its emergence. Subsequently the deeper and more essential causes of the abnormal condition and its specific susceptibility to stimulation by war trauma demand analysis before the patient can be sufficiently restored to health to enable him to resume military duties.

His emotional fixation to infancy, with its primitive love and hate conflicts, his unconscious homosexuality, and the sources of his psychosexual impotence, are matters which demand analytical attention immediately the traumatic war experiences have been released from repression. The situation which arises suggests that the analysis of war neurosis should not be undertaken unless one is prepared and competent to complete the therapy and to unearth the neuclus of the underlying psychosis or psychoneurosis.

### I. THE WAR NEUROSIS

A man in the early forties, an officer in the Regular Army Reserve of Officers, is sent to me by a doctor in whom he has confided that he cannot face the prospect of overseas service. Since being called to the colours, and, more specifically, since hearing that there was a possibility of his being placed in command of his regiment and being sent overseas with it, he has had a succession of minor illnesses, has been continuously on the sick list, and the question has arisen as to whether he should have a Medical Board. In fact, the wheels had been set in motion, and shortly after I saw him he was invalided out of the Service.*

At the first interview he says it is most strange that he should have misgivings at the prospect of active service, particularly as in the last war he had earned a reputation for daring.

He has no family history or past history of nervous illness and hotly denies the suggestion that he felt fear in the course of his former war experience, but admits that his *present* condition might be described as acute "wind-up."

"As soon as I thought of going overseas to fight I was laid up with a cold. Since then I have been in hospital with what I thought was a succession of influenzal attacks. Now it seems that I am terribly afraid of something—goodness knows what. If I had to give orders to men in action I feel that there would be a quaver in my voice, and that would give me away."

"When did you speak in a quavering voice and reveal fear?"

"Never, to my knowledge. I would hardly have been given the V.C. for a show-down like that. What I am afraid of is that I shall do so *next* time."

In view of this preliminary statement, the dramatic story that emerges will seem particularly astonishing.

Like all analytical case material, this is an account of a struggle against resistances. The early sessions are naturally filled with rationalizations covering his emotional state. He considers that he has grown older and slower in his thought and action, and therefore is neither physically nor mentally fit to lead men in the field.

Other rationalizations include such statements as the following:

---

* Attention has been drawn to the large number of resignations on health grounds in the Regular Army Reserve of Officers. For instance, in an issue of the *London Gazette* taken at random, the only announcement made under this heading is that no less than eleven reserve officers have resigned on grounds of ill health. In the same issue, in the two hundred and fifty announcements concerning the regular army, there is none of resignation on account of ill health.

The question arises as to why there should be such a relatively large proportion of invalidism in the R.A.R.O. as compared with the regular army. One reflects that the R.A.R.O. consists largely of men who have seen service in the last war who preferred civil life to soldiering, and who were automatically recalled on the outbreak of the present hostilities.

Has this ill health anything to do with their experiences of 22-27 years ago? In other words, is it due to latent and undetected war neurosis? Investigation of the above case is very suggestive.

"You see, I don't know in which direction my duty lies—duty to my ideals, or duty to my uniform. Perhaps that is all my present trouble is—doubt. It is a conflict between my ideals. How can I fight when my heart isn't in it?"

These remarks may be compared to those of conscientious objection. Perhaps we shall see in the investigation of this case that the apparently sound arguments of the conscientious objector may have their real source in unconscious conflict.

Within a week or two the patient becomes less cautious. His ego-resistances begin to weaken, and sessions assume a more emotional quality.

He says: "I cannot bear the thought of breaking down in front of the men." (Then, more emotionally) "I do wish I could be a brave soldier, but I just can't—I can't—I can't do it!"

Here he bursts into a flood of hysterical weeping, then shouts: "I am not going to go mad again! I refuse! Nobody is going to make me do it!"

After more weeping, he says calmly: "I would not mind being killed or shot. It's madness I will not bear."

"When were you mad?"

"I may be mad now. Or perhaps the war is mad. I have never been mad before. These feelings I've got have nothing to do with my experiences in the last war."

As he continued his daily attendance it became increasingly apparent that he was making no reference to his actual experience in the last war. In particular he made no reference to how he gained his decoration. When, after his above remark, he was asked what these experiences were, he insisted that there was nothing worth relating in his past war experiences: "I had no very strong emotions —a bit of excitement I expect, which would be only natural. But nothing out of the way."

He prefers to come in mufti. He says: "I loathe decorations, and I would far rather throw them away, and for that matter, throw away the whole uniform . . . the army and the war."

Finally, I have to ask him point blank how he obtained his V.C. Otherwise it appeared we might have continued for several more weeks without any reference to the last war. He said: "I got it for being in charge of a blockhouse in Serbia in 1915. I had fourteen men with me when we were attacked. We killed seventy and captured a hundred. But it was all over very quickly."

"Give me details."

"There were no details."

He nearly forgot his next appointment, and was fifteen minutes late for it. He confessed his reluctance to come: "My enthusiasm for soldiering certainly left me after the blockhouse experience, and my enthusiasm for coming here to see you has also gone since you brought the matter up. This morning I thought to myself, 'Good Lord! The doctor has got me cornered on the blockhouse, I feel l don't want to remember it. I can't face it.' "

After a brief silence, he shouts: "This damned war. It has got me trapped in the army. I will get ill. Cornered! Trapped! That's what I am. Trapped!" And he suddenly bursts into a paroxysm of tears. In the middle of this he lets out a howl loud enough to disturb the house.

Presently he dries his tears and declares that he feels better. He then asks if he may sit up and smoke. I tell him he may if he really cannot bear being trapped in my consulting room any longer, but that it would be better to bear it, and tell me his associations to this feeling of being trapped. Presently he says: "I was trapped in that damned blockhouse. I was the first to see them coming. I was looking out at dawn, and I saw the figures moving out of a wood and deploying across the countryside in the snow. I remember how I caught my breath and held it, and the chill that came over me . . . *like this damned 'flu*. My first impulse was to call the sergeant but I stopped myself, because I had to *make sure I could speak without a quaver in my voice* before I called him. And, my God! we had a busy time after that! That's all I can remember about it."

Later he says: "There was an awful moment when our machine gun and both Lewis guns were all jammed at the same time. If they had made one of their rushes at that moment we *would* have been done. Anyhow, we got them working again in time."

Suddenly he bursts into tears and howls again, without being able to offer any explanation of why he did so: "What was I doing looking out at dawn? How was it that I was the first person to see them? There were two men on watch. I was too anxious to sleep. And then the terrible feeling, 'Here it is at last!' I remember now that I knew we had to prevent them from assembling their machine guns. That was a frantic struggle. It was touch and go.

"Then it seemed that hundreds of them got into a hollow and I phoned the artillery. The artillery officer said it was too near us for shelling. It must have been pretty close because we got our trench mortar working on it. They told me afterwards that I was swearing like a thousand troopers on the telephone, and that seems to me very odd, for I never swear in the ordinary way. Perhaps I was more excited than I remember. But there was the devil of a din practically all the time. It must be all that shooting that has put me off shooting, for now, when the sergeant at the range asks me to have a go with the Bren gun, I always refuse. I don't want to fire anything. That reminds me that at the blockhouse I did have a go at them myself with the Lewis gun. It was easy to see where the bullets went in the snow and therefore easy to find one's target. They were lying there in lines only two hundred yards away.

"It must have lasted longer than I thought, because it certainly started at dawn, that would be about 5.30, and it was 9.30 that they surrendered. They came out of the hollow with their hands up. I can remember one of my soldiers shooting a wounded man, and I laughed."

"Why did you laugh?"

"I haven't any idea. Perhaps I was crazy."

To show that even these dramatic recollections do not do justice to the emotional intensity of his experience, I will give a few extracts from subsequent sessions. It appears that his initial anxiety has not been adequately remembered or described. He says:

"I am not a coward. To be a non-belligerent under fire would not be an impossible situation."

"What would be an impossible situation?"

"Fighting—the blockhouse—fear."

He starts weeping and howling. "If I try to force thoughts my mind just clamps down on me. I feel trapped." (Silence.)

"Can we finish now?"

"Are you feeling uncomfortable here?"

"I feel I want to run away. I wanted to run away and couldn't. There was nowhere to run."

"Is this the place you want to run away from?"

The patient yells at me: "*No! This isn't the place. How dare you suggest that to me!*"

He breaks into hysterical weeping and howling. Later he said: "Your suggestion made the walls of this room go red and for a moment I felt I was going into a trance.* I felt I was going mad. I felt angry with you. I had to yell—like I yelled in the blockhouse."

In the light of the intense emotion displayed at this and subsequent sessions we can at last appreciate why the beginning of treatment was occupied exclusively with calm unemotional rationalizations. We can understand also why there was little or no reference

---

* No attempt is made here to explain the phenomenon of "seeing red." It is clearly related to extreme emotional tension—sudden in onset and as yet undischarged. It might be suggested that "seeing red" may have a physiological basis in sudden congestion of the retina or/and other parts of the optical apparatus, preparatory to the relief of tension by weeping—as in this patient's case.

to past war experiences. The patient was naturally reluctant to allow himself to be overwhelmed by these repressed emotions.

He starts the next session with a flood of tears. "I've such a lot to tell you. It's not going to be easy. It starts off with dawn at the blockhouse. I was outside alone in the snow, before dawn; it was scarcely light. I saw what looked like a few figures—silhouettes in the distance. I wasn't sure that they were men. Gradually I looked round. In every direction wherever I looked there were men. Men everywhere—hundreds of them."

"*I wanted to run!*" he screams at the top of his voice, and bursts into a flood of hysterical tears. "They wouldn't let me run. Never again. I'll never do it again. No power on earth will ever make me do it again, I tell you.

"After that I wanted no more heroics. I'd been in search of them, but that pricked the bubble. I refuse to admit that I was frightened. Anyhow, I did not show fright. I had to do something with my pent-up emotions. I couldn't run so I turned it all over to the killing side. I tried to deflect the disappointment in myself on to the killing. The killing was really due to my being so frightened. I was mad to kill and kill; that's why I seized the Lewis gun myself. That's why I phoned the artillery to shell the hollow. I wanted to see arms and legs blown up. I wasn't sure our trench mortar was killing enough. That's why I yelled at them to shoot anyone who tried to run away. That's why I laughed when the wounded prisoner was shot. I was a mad killer.

"No one is going to make me mad again. I refuse. I'll get ill, I'll die. But that! Never again!"

Some of the automatic habits of his calmer moments are of interest, and confirm that he is still unconsciously reliving his blockhouse experience. Possibly he has been doing so for the past twenty years. For instance, whilst talking quietly he was balancing a penknife on his fingers and slowly moving it downwards. When I called his attention to it, he admitted that he was sighting with one eye shut down the corner of my room. He explained, "The danger was that if they got too close we couldn't fire through the slits at a sufficiently acute *downward* angle to get them."

Like the story of his soldiers shooting the wounded prisoner, this memory was accompanied by insufficient resistance and insufficient affect to be convincing as the important repressed material responsible for his unconscious pantomime. Both these stories were shown later to be "screen memories." In the mental economy they had the advantage of releasing some of the affect belonging to an incident which he had found truly intolerable, and by this release assisted

N

him in keeping the really painful matter from memory. It emerged at a subsequent session. After a long silence he says:

"The other day in imagination I was again bringing my hand down to shoot. There's only one thing you shoot from coming down—and that's a revolver. Then I thought, 'It would be strange if you'd deliberately shot a man.' Then my mind said to me, 'You shot a wounded man.' And I said, 'No, you can't have done that.'

"As I tried to think about it my mind would work only very slowly, and that reminded me of my slowness of thought and action which I have told you would prevent me from being any good in this war. Eventually it came back, and I thought to myself how nice it had been of my mind to refuse to work fast, and so save me from a terrible shock. Now I'll tell you the episode.

"When the fighting was over and we went out to look at the dead and the wounded . . .(here the patient starts whimpering and crying) . . . there was a man with the back of his head blown off, yet alive and conscious. The sergeant told me I ought to finish him off. I just made myself do it. I had to come down with the revolver because he was on the ground. I'd like to have comforted him, but I deliberately shot him. Blew his brains out. I wish I'd said 'No.' Was it murder? I know it wasn't . . . and yet . . . and yet. . . ." (He weeps.)

Later he remembers that when he came home he used to sleep soundly for fourteen hours out of every twenty-four. This continued for months. His relations joked about it and called it "sleepy sickness."

"But there was something odd about my health for much longer than this. I can remember now that for some years I did not want to do any work at all. I felt I should be pensioned or given an income and just allowed to do nothing. I expect I was trying to recover from something—goodness knows what. I was restless and depressed. Many people are restless and depressed after a war. It is quite usual and recognized."

The patient was evidently in àn unrecognized "anxiety state," followed by exhaustion, for a considerable period after the war. This diagnosis is confirmed by his further remark, "I was impotent for some years after the war, and then I lost all sexual desire for several years."

I asked if he could remember any dreams he had had at this period. At the next session he says: "I can remember now that I had a continuous waking nightmare during that time, and for years afterwards. I dared not pass a policeman. I've looked round in the

street to see if the police were watching me. I'll tell you. . . ."
(Here he starts gasping for breath.)

"Yes, I looked round to see if they'd spotted me as the man they
wanted. Wanted for murder . . . murder . . . murder," he shrieks
at the top of his voice. Then there was a burst of crying and howling.
"You see, I was out to kill in the blockhouse—to kill all 1 could.
1 went mad with a lust to kill. I wanted to see them all smashed to
smithereens. I was terrified lest one should escape and get me afterwards. And I shot a wounded man. Then for years I feared not
only police but gangs of loafers. I thought they were Germans
spying on me to get me. I lived in fear. I feared everybody and
everything. Nobody knew. Years of it." (Tears.) "Only now am I
recovering. I'd forgotten it all before I came to you."

Presently he asks: "Can one's fate be told by the look on one's
face?"

"Why?"

He bursts into a paroxysm of weeping. "Because for years I used
to go about thinking that my face showed that my fate was to be
hanged—hanged for murder. I even had thoughts of committing a
murder in order to get the whole ghastly business over. Let's leave
this subject." (He dries his tears.) "I'm beginning to feel that happiness is just round the corner."

Enough material has been given to show that we are on the track
of the traumatic factors in his present invalidism, and to justify us
in drawing some hypotheses about war neuroses in general.

It appears that in so far as repression of traumatic war experiences is effective it is inevitably accompanied by repression of other
psychic elements, including sexuality and aggression. In all cases
there is no doubt that the conflict between repressed and repressing
forces absorbs a variable amount of potential psychic energy. The
"war weariness" referred to may be a symptom of this absorption.

In so far as repression is unsuccessful, the affects stimulated by
war experiences break through and occasion a crop of anxiety
symptoms.

There is always some evidence both of repression and of its failure.
Thus, in this case, the patient suffered from an inhibition of energy
(inertia, slowness), psychosexual impotence, and what might here
be called the symptom of pacificism.

His anxiety symptoms, reprecipitated by the mere anticipation
of war, were evidence that this had stimulated the repressed material
sufficiently to occasion a partial failure of the repression, with the
result that the repressed emotions broke through while their related

memories remained repressed, until the resistances to them had weakened as recorded in this section.

## II. THE ILLNESS TRACED BACK TO ITS EARLY FOUNDATIONS

The importance of repressed material (and the strength of its affects) may be gauged by the degree of resistance opposed to its emergence, and by the severity of the disturbances caused by the accompanying conflict.

Measured by this standard, it would appear that the war memories which this patient has so reluctantly produced, however dramatic, are merely the prelude to an even more disturbing drama, a drama which causes such an upheaval in its uncovering that it temporarily overwhelms his ego and incurs a risk of analytical catastrophe.

It is clearly a mistake to assume, as some do, that war experiences, the experiences of adult life, however unsuspected and dramatic in their emergence, could themselves be the essential causes of a psychoneurosis or psychosis. It is safer to regard them as only precipitating factors, perhaps as a special variety of "screen memory," though carrying sufficient affect to be themselves resisted and even subjected to some degree of amnesia.

As this obstacle to further memory work emerged and was removed, even more highly charged material, conflicts that had their origin in the early development of the psyche, became progressively uncovered, and the emotional intensity of these nuclear Œdipus conflicts shows them to be the true causes of his abnormal disturbances. In fact, they reproduce identical disturbances for our immediate observation in the course of their emergence during analysis.

This heralds the transference situation and betrays the resistances to it. Thus the nuclear causes of the illness become accessible only after it is possible to analyse the transference and its resistances. This possibility was very nearly precluded by the suddenness of the emotional eruption which temporarily overwhelmed the patient's ego and caused him to suspend treatment.

We can describe only the comparatively calm approaches to these events, for analysis was suddenly swept aside by the violence of the emotional outburst. The psychopathology of this was only revealed after the resumption of treatment.

It proved impossible _before_ these happenings to discover the Œdipus material responsible for them. All that appeared to be taking place was that, his war experiences having been fairly exhaustively worked through, he was beginning to get associations that led him back to memories of his early life. These eventually proved to be the unsuspected reservoir of the disrupting conflicts.

He arrives at his session full of excitement, due to an association he has formed.

"I have discovered the origin of the howl. I was thinking about the blockhouse, when suddenly it came to me and clicked very strongly in my mind. I am sure it is the incident we are in search of, although I do not remember the details.

"It was a good beating I got from my mother with the cane. I remember that my howling could be heard the best part of a mile away. I would say that it was the most powerful howl that had ever been heard for many a generation. I was only about five or six at the time. I had stayed out enjoying myself when I should have come home to be put to bed. I can remember some of my feelings now. I resented what was demanded of me. I did not see why I should be beaten. Finally I submitted.

"I feel sure that this has a bearing upon subsequent events. For instance, the blockhouse. Even then it made me feel: 'I am aching to take this out of somebody.' "

(It seemed subsequently that perhaps during earlier canings he developed the belief that he had killed his mother.)

"I have had beatings at school, but they were nothing to this. Perhaps I howled so hard that mother, too, lost her head, and tried to murder me with the cane. Anyhow, the next morning the cane was ceremoniously burnt in my presence. I feel now that that howl could have been heard all over the world. I can still hear it in the blockhouse. I feel that I have never ceased howling and sobbing since then. It is all linked up with my mother, and love, and hate, and killing and being killed. I wonder if, when I shot the wounded soldier, I was really killing mother, and that if all those years when I expected to be hanged, I really felt that I was going to be hanged for having vented my murderous hate on mother."

(It appears subsequently that in this act he was performing the two essential acts of the Œdipus situation: destroying his father and ejaculating into his mother.)

"I know that this beating is the right incident behind the yells and sobs, just as I know that the blockhouse is the right incident behind my nervous breakdown after the last war. So, you see, there was a blockhouse before the blockhouse.

"If only my childhood had been happy, with everybody being kind to everybody else!" (Here he starts whimpering and crying.)

He says: "You will never get me there" (to the blockhouse). "I could not do it. At the thought of overseas service I feel myself go quite immobile—still, and howling like I was at that beating. I cannot fight any more: I am tired out. It is just possible that I said these very words in the mess after the blockhouse experience. It is possible I said it with similar emotions. It seems nearer now. It seems I had been expecting to be told off about it, but instead I got sympathy, and then I broke down and sobbed and howled.

"I think of that habit you called my attention to—the habit of stroking my chin to see if it is shaved. I have thought, similarly I have a habit of putting my hand to my sex organ, and that is, definitely, to see if it is still there.

"I think that at the age of five I set out trying to be a man, but mother took it out of me. She wanted a daughter.

"When I saw the Medical Registrar at the hospital, I started off by trying to be the male. I felt he was a father-figure. I kept it up as though I also were a man. He was brusque and I was aggressive.

"Then I could not keep up the fighting any longer. I broke down. I felt I was cutting myself up to be tortured. It seems I felt like a female. It was then that his whole manner altered. He took me by the arm, and seemed to like me. I broke down and sobbed, and we have been pals ever since then.* I probably was pretending to be a man years before I was." (He breaks down and cries.)

At another session he says: "As a little boy, do you know what I was frightened of ? Of my father coming back. And do you know what the blockhouse was? I will tell you. It was the country cottage we lived in after my father had left us. He had to be kept out. You see, if he got in he stole mother. If he got in he stole my happiness." (Hysterical crying.) "The blockhouse was a perfect reproduction of childhood. It is just like that country cottage. As a child I felt I had no one to turn to. This may have been after I had the beating from mother."

From another session: "The howling and crying must have happened in the blockhouse. I cannot have scrapped like that without howling and crying. I have got to be absolutely tired out after it, because I have put too much into it. Tired out . . . that is, collapse. That is when I weep. I feel sure I broke down in the company mess, and had to be put to bed. Otherwise the Colonel would not have said that I was not to volunteer again. And yet something in me had gone raving mad. It is a conflict between fear and fight. You turn fear into fighting. If you let them loose it is possible that something in you gets a most acute enjoyment, but you are terrified of being in the same position again, because the release has been so

* These events have reference to the Medical Board which invalided him from the army.

mad that you are afraid that you will never get out of that state. It is something that you must not do again. And 'it seems that I insured against doing it again by nervous breakdown—by impotence." (By castration.) "The experience may have been even more acute than I have yet remembered."

Presently he starts sobbing and crying. On inquiry he says: "I was thinking of that occasion when I was beaten by my mother with a cane. The thought is that she should never have done it. The result was that mother burnt her cane, and I became impotent. Ever since then my impulses and instincts have had to be locked up to maintain a world of peace with mother."

A curious feature about this case is that, in spite of nearly three months' analysis, and a very full emergence of the disturbing war memories, he had mentioned nothing about his current sexual life.

At last be brings me a dream which gradually opens up the subject of sexuality. This in turn heralds the development of transference and transference resistance, and the emotions of love and hate (the nucleus of his illness), which had once previously overwhelmed his ego, and which now threatened to disrupt the analysis itself.

The unsatisfactoriness of his adult rôle of husband reveals itself, followed by the revelation of the all-important conflict between his libidinal tendency to submit himself to the good father-image, and his intense fear and hatred of the bad father-image.

"I dreamed I was shown into a very unsatisfactory billet. You opened an oak door, with a round top like a vault door. Behind this was another door like a grille. We got into a little whitewashed prison compartment with a tiny barred window. There was not enough room to lie down. In the side wall there was a passage-way through a cubby hole. There were steps up and down. It had a concave floor. That was my billet. Of course, it was an impossible situation. You could not lie down. You were shown in and there imprisoned. The upshot was, I was wondering whether to try and stick it or whether to run away. It is like the blockhouse all over again. The modern equivalent is being in the army. If I stay in that little space I shall go screaming mad, like I was in the blockhouse."

Although he produced no sexual associations to this dream at the time, he arrives for the next session full of associations to his bridal night and the defloration. He continues: "The position now is that my wife is not easily satisfied, and therefore I hold off from orgasm as long as I can. I feel it has all got something to do with these doors and steps in the dream. I am satisfied some time before her. I try to go on after orgasm if she is not satisfied. It goes against

my grain: but there is anxiety to please her. I practised this method
of satisfying my wife the morning before I had that dream. It
certainly does not leave me with a feeling of satisfaction. I cannot
explain my feelings very well, but they are the same feelings that
I had in that horrid dream of the billet. A sort of despond and
oppression."

At the next session he talks of teeth extractions and goes on to
say: "I started losing my hair twelve months after I got back from
Serbia. Also it is only since Serbia that I have taken to catching
influenza every year. It was six or seven months after the blockhouse
that I got my 'sleepy sickness,' when they could not arouse me for
breakfast. Then I lost my hair and got thinner and thinner. Eighteen
months after that I was looking round for the police, and thinking
I was going to be hanged. That lasted for over a year. The impotence went on for much longer."

It would appear that the conflicts precipitated by the blockhouse
were at first too active to be dealt with in any other way than by
protracted periods of stupor or clouding of the ego. Subsequently
they were dealt with by physical conversion—the loss of hair and
flesh. Still later they had undergone repression sufficient to cause
only a mild degree of paranoia. Their most persistent functional
disturbance was psychosexual impotence, a degree of which still
persists, as revealed in the depression that accompanied the billet
dream.

"That horrid dream of the billet has reminded me that I am a
bit wrong on the sexual side, not getting the satisfaction I ought
to from it."

He goes on to say: "I had a dream this morning. I dreamed
there was a big dam and I was putting in the final block of concrete
to hold back the flood."

Evidently there is no satisfactory "flood" of emotion in his relationship with his wife. Then what is this "flood" which he is so strenuously engaged in holding back?

In spite of the apparent calmness of recent analytical material,
or perhaps because of it, when the analyst hears such a dream
fragment as this he should be warned. Some catastrophic tidal
wave is about to overwhelm the situation.

In spite of attempted transference interpretations the patient
holds on to his block of concrete. At the next session he says: "I
feel the analysis is finished." It certainly made no progress on that
occasion. Evidently the prospect is considerably worse than that
which confronted him when he was forced into a revival of the war
memories. On that occasion he said: "These feelings have nothing

to do with my experiences in the last war." But he did not threaten flight from analysis. On this occasion he says: "I feel the analysis is finished." But the next day he betrays himself by weeping: "It's going to be a bad time letting the waters of that dam out."

The attempts to let them out were not very successful. The material he produced, although subjected to transference interpretations, was well entrenched and defended behind concepts of his wife, his former mistress, and his mother. He says:

"It is the sex side that has gone wrong. I've noticed that a lot lately. I had a terrible time last night: part of me wanted to make love to my wife, and part of me didn't. Somewhere I was feeling cross with her. Hate seemed to spring up and get in the way. Then I thought of my mother. What a pity I can't be myself and do murder—like I did in Serbia. Then I thought of being hanged. Then I thought of obeying mother, and being good—and—impotent; absorbing mother's mood instead of being myself—but there's a tinge of sadness... depression." (He is weeping.) "I have got bottled-up sadness. It is going to be a bad time letting the waters of that dam out. Then I could be myself—blast mother!—kill and be potent . . . go mad! No, I mustn't do that. I think of my former mistress. She has intruded herself into my sex life, though I haven't seen her for ten years. That will break the crust of my marriage if I go back to her. I was potent with her. But it was her mood, not mine, that I absorbed. She was a stronger character than my wife. . . ." (Strong enough to make him *feel* potent!)

The interpretation of this material is that he is tempted to abandon his ego-supported though libidinally feeble rôle of husband to his wife, and to adopt the inverted Œdipus rôle towards his analyst, whom he disguises in the concepts of the strong mother and mistress. At the same time he is holding back (behind the concrete of the dam) his hatred for the analyst and his love of the analyst. The hatred is due to the fact that the analyst appears to split the transference to his wife. This transference, however strong, has a weak sexual urge, but that urge, now dominated by the transference to the analyst (the father—strong enough to make him feel potent), strengthens his desire to be a little boy, and weakens his rôle as a husband.

In spite of these attempted interpretations, his resistance was maintained throughout the session. It was during the interval between this and the next session that the flood waters burst through repression and swept his ego aside.

The dramatic psychological experiences with which he was overwhelmed for two weeks are told when he revisits me. On this occasion he refused to lie on the settee, but stood before my chair, towering over me with blazing eyes. The dam has burst. The transference hate which he refused to admit at his last session is now all too evident. He says:

"I have been very ill since I last saw you. That day I left you I went home and told my wife that I loved her so much it hurt." (Attempt to conserve transference unsplit.) "The next morning I hated her, and I had a high temperature." (Orgasm of hate.) "I also hated my mother and I hated you. I had a high temperature and then three nights of insomnia. A doctor was called in and I was given tablets to put me to sleep. While I was going to sleep I was being caned by my mother, and I was catching my breath and screaming, 'Don't do it, Mummy!' I woke up thinking 'Don't blame me, mother, if I cannot go on with this marriage. I did it largely to please you.'

"I have had two or three dreams:

"First I was back in Serbia. Three of us were skating along, and one of us says, 'Paul, Paul, I have lost my eyesight. I have gone blind.'" (His Damascus! He now surrenders to the Father.)

"In the second dream I am pouring out tea. The teapot lid slid, but seemed to catch by a little thread at the end." (Penis nearly falls off.) He goes straight on to his free associations as follows:

"Ski-ing along took me to Serbia. I did a damn silly interpretation of my own. I connected eyesight with syphilis. I thought: 'I was impotent after the last war. I am impotent now. I lost my hair just after that war, and so i thought: I have got syphilis.' I had to send for the doctor last week to get him to confirm that I had not got syphilis. It was agony waiting for his verdict.

"Then I had a curious memory. I remembered that I had not previously remembered the chief part of that billet dream. I remembered what the steps were for. *If I had climbed through the cubby hole, I should have become a cockerel. I would have flapped my wings and crowed, and it would have been a nice billet.*" (Potency.) "Instead of doing this, I just stood looking round bewildered. Is it possible I am not letting myself love my wife fully? Is it to do with something I am repressing? Yes, I know I ran away" (from analysis) "and I got a temperature. The main reason of my running away is the fear that it" (analysis) "will upset my married life. The whole point is this: Can you give me a guarantee that, if I go on with analysis, I shall be able to go on with my married life and make my wife happy?

"Waiting for that doctor to confirm if I had syphilis or not was just about as bad as waiting for the guns to restart in the block-house. And that cockerel flapping his wings! I might have got like

THE ANALYSIS OF A WAR NEUROSIS

that if this war had not come along. The trouble is that I cannot jerk the semen out. It just dribbles.

"I cannot make up my mind whether to go on with analysis or not. I am afraid if I do I might leave my wife and go back to Lucy (his former mistress)—and I'd rather remain unhappy myself. I am going away to think it out and make up my mind. In the meantime I have closed my house in London, and I have gone away to live at X."

*Analyst:* "How far is that from London?"

*Patient:* "Two hours' journey."

*Analyst:* "Is that to keep you far from Lucy or far from me?"

*Patient:* "Well, my health is not very good, and I think the air will be better for me."

*Analyst:* "You mean the amount of air between you and me. So it seems you are still busy running away from yourself."

From an early age this patient has been extraordinarily frightened of his libidinal and aggressive urges. As a boy the mists along the country road assumed the form of spectres from which he fled in terror.

In order to preserve his sexually weak transference to his wife he is now engaged in an ego-supported effort to hold up the flood waters of his natural libido and aggression. As the dam bursts, his ego, still clinging to that block of concrete, is temporarily swept aside with it.

Thus, while he goes to doctors to confirm that he is not castrated (syphilis) or blind (cf. Œdipus castration), he avoids the doctor who can see that the bogies from which he is fleeing are merely the deepest emotional experiences of his infancy. One of the earliest of these, remembered with such dramatic effect, relates to a time when he was feeling bold enough to ignore his mother's command, and to stay out beyond the permitted time, perhaps to mount those steps, flap his wings and crow. This exhibition of potency was immediately followed by the most devastating experience of symbolical castration. Thus the phantasy that libido and self assertion must be repressed, or projected and fled from on pain of castration, is again confirmed.

The Œdipus nucleus of his condition is the one from which he is at present engaged in fleeing. He has not yet given us an opportunity to analyse it fully. But I fancy that he already almost does so himself. *The analyst is no doubt the latest father-figure, whom he is avoiding lest he should otherwise yield to the libidinal pull of a homosexual transference which is stronger than that to his wife.* He brings as his excuse or reason for not continuing the analysis the fear that if he does so he will not be able to go on with his married life. Thus he must remove the father by putting himself out of the reach of the analyst.     .

He is acting out the resistance to his unconscious phantasy in extra-analytical life, feeling that he will thereby be fighting disaster, and unable to see, in spite of interpretations, that this is the very way to court it.

In this irrational behaviour, and in the outcrop of symptoms, including temperature (cf. his former influenzal attacks), paranoid state, hypochrondria, insomnia and impotence, we see the recurrence of an illness similar to that from which he originally suffered during the years of undetected war neurosis.

It was not the emergence of the content of his war amnesiae which reproduced this condition. It was a revival of the unresolved conflicts of the Œdipus situation. Thus we may conclude that it is the nuclear conflicts rather than the war experiences which are the real and predisposing causes of his abnormal condition, and we can hope for true and permanent amelioration only by the resolution of these conflicts.

### III. Transference resistance

He resumed his analysis after a further two weeks' absence. Apparently his efforts again to repress the forces that were welling up in him had not proved satisfactory. Finally, he had gone from one friend to another, demanding advice as to whether he should resume or not. A struggle was going on between a deep-seated compulsion to resume, and a fear of what would happen if his repressed tendencies broke through.

It appeared later that this four weeks of resistance, accompanied by acute emotional disturbances, was nothing more or less than a simple resistance to transference. He said the fear of resuming was the fear that analysis would cause him to leave his wife in favour of his former mistress, but he was unaware that this "former mistress" was none other than the father-image (in the shape of the analyst), the libidinal attraction of which he had unsuccessfully endeavoured to repress throughout his life.

In the end he found that his nature could no longer be denied, and he presented himself for treatment. He had been told by letter that if he felt hostility towards the treatment or towards the analyst, he should come and aim at expressing everything he thought and felt.

Again he arrived in a fighting mood, and it was evident that he had regressed to the impotent rage of childhood.

He says: "Blast you! You have messed up my married life now! I have had insomnia ever since I saw you."

"You mean, ever since you refused to see me."

He throws himself on the settee and moans: "I got no sleep last night in spite of sleeping-draughts."

Suddenly he shouts: "It is all your d——d fault."

Then at the top of his voice: "Why couldn't you —— well leave me alone when we had finished with the war business? Now all this hatred has come up."*

Here he starts howling and yelling: "How I hate you! If you knew what I'd like to call you!"

He clenches his fists and beats the air. Presently I say to him: "You had better say it. What would you like to call me?"

He stammers and stutters, spitting with rage. Then he ejaculates: "Bastard!"

His next remark may seem surprising: perhaps his hate for me has faded with my passive reception of it. He says:

"If I had let *myself* alone I'd have hated my mother. That is what my nature would have done after the caning . . . only I would not let it. I was frightened to hate her. I was frightened some weeks ago to come here, and tell you how I hated you. Now I have given vent to this hate to you. I can remember what a struggle I had not to hate my mother.

"Some nights ago, going to sleep, I kept crying: 'Don't do it, mummy! Don't do it, mummy!' When I was put to sleep with those pills the other night, I was gritting my teeth and bearing it." (He starts crying.) "Just gritting my teeth and bearing it."

*Analyst:* "What were you bearing?"

*Patient:* "I was bearing being hit with that cane, and I was crying, 'Don't do it, mummy!' I did not know why I should have been caned. Then all this hatred surged up in me. I could have murdered her, but I was terrified—terrified of my own hate. If I had let myself alone, if I had let myself go, it would have been murder. You bastard! I would have liked to have killed you. Only once before did I let myself go. That was in the blockhouse. Then I killed. I see now what I should have done. I should have killed my mother as a little boy."

* It will be appreciated that there is no question of the analyst having deliberately drawn into consciousness ideas or affects to which the patient's mind was unduly resistant. In the course of the loosening of resistance to traumatic war memories, resistance in general is inevitably loosened, and no limit can be placed on what will eventually emerge. Hence in analysing a war neurosis, however simple, there is no safeguard against the possibility of patient and analyst being committed to a deeper analysis.

*Analyst:* "And then?"

*Patient:* "*Then I'd have flapped my wings and crowed.* There'd have been none of this damned impotence about me, nor would I have been afraid of the war. V.C.s would have been nothing to me. I'd be a real soldier, a real fighter, to-day."

He puts his hands to his head. "No! No! I can't! I can't! I get frightened. Coming here is an emotional treatment. I wanted a sedative. I didn't want this. I can't sleep. The top of my head burns. Things keep bubbling up from inside somewhere. I don't think they are ever going to bubble right through, because I feel they are more than I can stand. I am frightened . . . frightened. That's what's the matter." (Silence.)

Suddenly he flings the ash-tray across the room with such force that it shatters against the wall. Then comes screaming, weeping, and a flood of abusive language.

*Analyst:* "What is the violent act you wish to do?"

*Patient:* "Killing her. Giving mother a good hiding."

*Analyst:* "Are you killing me as a successor to your mother?"

*Patient:* "My wife and you are both in the same boat. To-day I could have smashed your faces in. It was the same hatred that came out in the blockhouse—then I killed. If you had both been on the other side of the front line to-day you would have both been shot, and I would have risked my life to shoot you. Love, hate, and fear—somehow I think of that caning. I imagine I was sullen for years after it. I used to be an affectionate little boy. I think that caning killed it. When I felt this hate and the impulse to murder my mother I got frightened. Instead of doing it and flapping my wings, I collapsed and howled. It was too much for me.

"My poor head! Oh, doctor, do you really think you can help me? I am putting tremendous faith in you, although I feel unwell. I am in a terrible mess. Can you ever get me out of it? Here I am clinging to you, like I clung to my mother after that caning—clung to her and sobbed. I wanted to kill her, like I wanted to kill you, and here I am, just the same, clinging to you instead. Will it ever come right?

"Do I cling because I am afraid of hating?

"I have been going through my whole life afraid of hate coming up . . . terrified of it . . . crying and clinging instead. That is why I haven't dared to let myself go. I haven't had the guts to obey my instincts freely. That is why I have been impotent or half impotent with my wife. That is why in that dream of the prison-like billet I did not go through the cubby hole and crow. I am holding something back. I am holding everything back. In consequence the billet dream was dull and miserable, like my life under the surface. I dare not live. It was only when I felt cornered in the blockhouse that I turned it all over to the killing, and the hate came out, as it is coming out here in these sessions. But no sooner do I do it, no sooner do I kill mother, than I get frightened, and collapse and cling to her—or cling to you. That is what I am doing with my wife lately. Before, I had never been absolutely natural with her. I have been trying to *make* myself love her instead of letting myself love her."

*Analyst:* "Or is it that you have been holding back the hate?"

*Patient:* "Yes, yes, certainly! That is better, that's it. I have held back everything with her, including sexual potency. In holding back the hate I have been holding back the erection too. I remember now, when I started being ill and had insomnia there was an urge to hate going on inside me. I was saying: 'I hate her! I hate her! I hate her!' It was shouting inwardly, and I was trying to keep it down."

*Analyst:* "Who comes into your mind in association with this feeling?"

*Patient:* "My mother! It was when I was being caned. . . . It won't hurt me if I have a little cry now." (He weeps.)

Presently the session is over. He gets off the settee, drying his eyes, and moves towards the door with funny little steps, his legs wide apart, and his toes turned out, as if he were still a tearful little boy of five.

At the door he says to me: "Can't we have some other sort of treatment—Adlerian treatment, or hypnotism, or suggestion, or something? Is it necessary to bring up all this disturbing stuff? I can't stand being upset like this. I want a sedative. If something must come out, can't we limit it!"

The reply I gave him was this: "If your bowels are full, so that you dare not move freely, and cannot be natural, is it better to evacuate a measured quantity, making sure that you can control and stop the rest, or is it better to let nature take its course, and turn the whole lot out?"

The patient wishes to deal with his hate and hate transference by repression—or, as he has dramatically revealed, by flight. Hate without conflict causes eagerness to destroy. That is its most natural tension-reducing outlet.

The difference between this and negative transference is that the latter, however negative, is still transference, and includes positive elements as well as negative. In destroying the object of it (e.g.

by absenting himself) the patient is destroying the loved object also.

It is this *conflict* which may be the cause of breakdown after such war experiences as this.

It is one thing to destroy a hated enemy and quite another thing to destroy a loved one. Intense hatred or fear may of itself cause the hated or feared object to fit into the early infantile emotional pattern, and thereby attract the positive transference also so that it becomes the loved parent. In infancy he dealt with this situation by repressing the hatred, and bolstering up by ego-emphasis the love. In his war experience he was forced to deal with a situation unconsciously identified with the infantile situation, by expressing the hatred and ensuring that no portion of the loved parent escaped destruction. The sequel to destroying the loved object is to be oneself destroyed. The super-ego will not permit such an act with impunity. Thus he believes that his fate is to be hanged for murder, and he declares that never again will he allow himself to be in a position to give vent to hatred. He says regarding his refusal to fight: "It is not that I was afraid of injury, or death. I would not mind doing non-combatant work under fire. The point is that I will not fight again. I will never again shoot a man. I refuse. It is not death I fear. It is madness."

His original unstable solution was a repression of hate and an attempt on the part of the ego to reinforce the love. His block-house experience undid all that and landed him in the throes of the unsolved Œdipus struggle between love and hate.

The new transference situation is a dramatization of this identical struggle. Essentially it is an id conflict between love and hate. But here it appears to be the love which is more strongly resisted while the hate obtains some degree of expression.

Is this a resistance of the adult ego to love the father-image *in the shape of the analyst,* or is it that the unconscious infantile ego feels that it is more dangerous to yield to the libidinous tendency to love the father-image than to attack and destroy him? He says later: "You see, I don't know whether you are a friend or foe— whether you will pick me up and carry me until I am strong enough to stand on my own feet, or whether, by possessing mother and attacking you, I have forfeited my right to your protection, and you will in consequence exterminate me."

That this conflict was the essence of his transference resistance, and of his neurosis, is made clear by the material he produces at his subsequent sessions.

## IV. Positive transference

Hate was so difficult to express within the sessions that for some time the patient adopted the more natural course of staying away. In this section we shall see that beneath the emotional upheaval is love; and that the patient's resistance to this, or to its recognition and expression, still tends to be shown by a hope that he can escape, that the treatment will end immediately.

In the meantime, owing to this resistance, the analysis slowed down considerably. The patient was giving little material for interpretation. He is trying to convince himself and me that there is no more material. He wants to get away without recognition of his positive transference and of his homosexuality.

He starts his session by saying: "We are finished: there is nothing more to analyse. Treatment is at an end. Why don't you let me go now? I do not require to come here any more. What I want to do now is to settle down happily with my wife. It's her I want. Not you. Shall we say that to-morrow will be the last session?"

The untrustworthiness of the ego in its function of denying libido immediately became evident. It will be noticed that there is no mention of a wife-figure in the dream of that very night. The transference situation is complete.

"To-morrow" he began the "last session" by saying: "I had a dream last night. I dreamed I went on a visit to Serbia. While there I was suddenly seized by the scruff of the neck and the seat of the trousers and lifted right into the air. When I came down there was a gang of three brigands, comprising a leader and two nondescripts. The leader said to me: 'You have been in Serbia before, and have killed my friends.' I denied it. He said: 'If we can prove it was you, you are for the high jump: so stick around.' I thought I had better get away. I tried to get on a tram, but it started and left me. I waited for another. Again I was suddenly lifted up by the neck and the seat, and they said to me: 'We are not going to let you out of our sight.' I offered my parole (never meaning to keep it) but they refused, saying that I had to stay with them. I resigned myself, and we began to have a good time. We all got quite merry, and laughed and joked together, but of course, all the time I was with them I knew that if they could catch me out they would kill me. Still, the leader and I became great pals, but while I was being hilarious, and even perhaps a bit bumptious, it was all rather a strain, because I was feeling that I was playing on the edge of a volcano. One slip—and it would have been the high jump for me. Still, it was not all bad. I managed to have a cheerful time with them."

He professes to have no idea of what the dream means, except for the fact that his war neurosis, precipitated by the machine-gunning of enemy Germans (of whom some got away), seemed to have developed into the fear that they were after him, and meant to get him. With this he loses interest in the meaning of the dream, and goes on to talk about his feelings regarding the analysis. It will be seen that, nevertheless, he is unconsciously giving us a very full interpretation of the meaning of the dream. He says:

"When I am away from you there is a feeling of depression, but when I have to see you there is a feeling of anxiety. This anxiety takes precedence over all other emotions. I cannot relax here. I think relaxing seems a bit too dangerous."

*Analyst:* "Am I a danger to you?"

*Patient:* "Yes. The possibility is that I shall let out what I am wanting to keep in. Then I'd be for the high jump."

*Analyst:* "That is your dream. What is it that it is so necessary to conceal?"

*Patient:* "I am concealing something the whole time. I have got to lead a very careful life so that the secret is not given away. I am pretending the whole time. I am pretending to be top dog when I am really wanting someone to lean on."

*Analyst:* "Is that how you were with the brigands in your dream? You were bumptious in order to cover up fear."

*Patient:* "If I revealed weakness or anxiety I would give away something which I am trying deliberately to conceal."

*Analyst:* "What does this bravado mean? One can see through it that you are really in a state of anxiety. What are you pretending all the time?"

*Patient:* "I am pretending to be a man . . . a strong man with nothing to fear."

*Analyst:* "What would happen if you ceased to exercise this strain, and just relaxed?"

*Patient:* "It was a strain all the time keeping up a pretence of merriment with the brigands, and it is a strain here also keeping up this pretence with you—pretending to be a man when I don't feel like one."

*Analyst:* "If you gave up the pretence what would you reveal?"

*Patient:* "I would reveal that I was only a little child."

*Analyst:* "Well, wouldn't that be a relief?"

*Patient:* "Yes, it would, but I seem much too frightened."

*Analyst:* "Why frightened?"

*Patient:* "Well, it would be all right if I knew positively that you were going to pick me up and carry me. I liked being picked up, like by the brigands. It was quite a thrill. But I can't say I felt secure, or relaxed, nor do I feel relaxed here." (Silence.)

"You see, it might have been all right. Perhaps, daddy would have picked me up, and carried me *provided I had never tried to be anything else except a little boy.* The trouble is that I had been pretending to be a man. I had usurped father's position. I felt that I had taken possession of mother. God knows!—perhaps I felt I was her husband. At any rate, it seems that I had been up to something that made my position with daddy very problematical. I didn't know what to do. If I confess that I am a little boy, heaven knows what will happen to me. They said, 'You have been in Serbia before and have killed our friends.' Such a confession from me would mean that I was for the high jump. So I am concealing something all the time."

*Analyst:* "Well, what is the situation with *me?* You come here blustering and bumptious, and yet anybody can see that there is anxiety beneath it. Why must you pretend to me?"

*Patient:* "If I relaxed, which would be such a relief, and you saw that I am not a man at all, but only a child, I should have no defence against you. I have been keeping you at bay by pretending that I am as strong as you, as well armed. If I show you that I have no arms, that I cannot protect myself, what will you do to me? That seems to be the dilemma that I am in. That is why I can't relax here, and am in a state of anxiety all the time. You see, I don't know whether you are friend or enemy; when you see I am a little child . . . whether you will pick me up and carry me, which is what I want, or whether you will just pick me up and throw me out of the window. It seems that I must have done something that has forfeited my right to be protected or treated kindly by you. But, whatever I do or don't do, I can't get away from it. I suffer a terrible state of anxiety whenever I am coming to see you.

"You have created a conflict in me, a conflict between staying with my wife and going back to Lucy (his former mistress). My anxiety in coming to you is that you will separate me from my rôle of protecting my wife, by showing me that I am not man enough, and then I will go back to Lucy, because I felt she played the rôle of protecting me."

*Analyst:* "Remember that when you were so frightened that you broke off treatment you declared that you would only resume provided I promised you it would not cause you to leave your wife and go back to Lucy."

*Patient:* "Yes, I remember that, but I thought that anxiety had gone."

*Analyst:* "That anxiety was never there. What you were afraid of was that you would leave your wife and come to *me*."

*Patient:* "Yes, that is the situation which we were fencing with all the time."

*Analyst:* "What were you afraid might draw you away from your wife?"

*Patient:* "Love of Lucy."

*Analyst:* "But it was not Lucy whom you insisted should make that promise to you."

*Patient:* "No, but it was Lucy I wanted to go to. It was not *you*."

*Analyst:* "Wasn't it? Yet you hadn't seen Lucy for ten years, and it was only while you were seeing me that you got this anxiety."

*Patient* "Yes."

*Analyst:* "In other words, you called me Lucy?"

*Patient:* "Yes, you are quite right."

*Analyst:* "You have told me that you come to me with anxiety, and that you go to your wife with anxiety."

*Patient:* "Yes. And the conflict is *what*?"

*Analyst:* "*Which of these shall I choose?*"

*Patient:* "Yes."

This patient's strongest resistance is against recognition and admission of the transference, therefore it has often to be forcefully and repeatedly interpreted. Even after he has seen and accepted such interpretations he constantly goes back on them.

All this is in keeping with the truth that transference phenomena are the essence of the analytical situation. It is transference which he is constantly dreading (while refusing to admit its interpretation) —for instance, when he breaks off treatment and runs around amongst his friends threatening to attack his analyst, and when returning to analysis he succumbs to phantasies of being lifted up and carried about by this same father-image. In short, it is the father-image towards whom he has the strong ambivalence which he enacted in the blockhouse, and in the subsequent breakdown. Failure to interpret transference, failure to interpret it repeatedly, with confidence, vigour and insistence would assuredly lead to analytical failure in this case.

The analyst has to continue his insistence upon the transference interpretation.

*Analyst:* "What you are afraid of is the strong pull of your instincts towards choosing me."

*Patient:* "Yes. You are big. This is where I can be myself without having to pretend."

*Analyst:* "And what is 'yourself'?"

*Patient:* "A little boy without any protection."

*Analyst:* "And so your anxiety is that while you are going through life pretending to be a man, pretending to your wife, and to everybody else that it is her and her alone whom you desire, your feelings are that you are acting a part, and that it is all a terrible strain. Actually, the real relief would be to give up pretence, to admit that you can get relief only in being a little boy and having a daddy to love you. In fact, your fear is that your instincts will win and that you will come to me instead of to your wife. The position is simply that that is what you want so much, and that is why you are afraid of it. Of course, your delusion is that if you succumb to these instincts of yours you will never be a man again."

*Patient:* "You know, some time ago I expected fireworks if we went on with this analysis, but this that we have been interpreting just now isn't fireworks; but I am sure that it is absolutely the goods.

"I can see what this Serbian dream means. I really needed a father very badly, but when he went away and left my mother and me, though I was only four years old, I thought it was my duty to take his place. It was my duty to take all risks for the protection of my mother. The fear arose that father might come back and take her from me. Father would do dreadful things to her, and she would die. I am sure I did sense some special relationship between father and mother. Previously I had felt that father was a protection for us both. But when he went this is what happened. I had to be a man, and therefore I had got to pretend to be big enough. If the pretence is successful the home is protected, but if a real man comes along, if I come to see you—and this is why I feel anxiety on my way to every session—you will challenge my manhood, you will say, 'Oh, no, you are only a little boy, you can't bluff me like that. Because you have been taking my place,' you will say, 'I will oust you.' That is when you pick me up and throw me out of the window. That is when you seize mother and run off with her. Her end is to submit to you. Because she is certainly not strong enough to resist. If I give up all my defences and relax here, that means I submit to you. And for all I know you will not protect me like father did originally. But you will seize me like you seize her. Perhaps something in me wants even this to happen. But I am afraid, because I do not know what happens to little boys if a man gets hold of them like this.

"That reminds me. I had another dream since I last saw you. I know it was important, but I have forgotten it. All I can remember was that there was a long red strip of carpet running out of a church at a wedding, and I slid down it. I know I had my legs on each side of it.

"If I could snap out of this anxiety I think I could be a big cockerel, but that is a station I can never hold. I start with it, but that anxiety arises, and anxiety and virility are not good companions. I suppose it is a fear that I may be castrated. You see, when I am the cock I am too cocky, and somebody downs me and I go all over on the other tack. Perhaps I feel like a little boy. There is no fight left in me then. At Sandhurst I was such a martinet that the others got together and downed me."

*Analyst:* "What are you here?"

*Patient:* "Here you can see what I am. Not relaxed—afraid to relax—in a state of anxiety. And yet putting on a lot of free and easy bravado. My position is that unless I am the cockerel I am finished. I am dead. I am the hen.

"Have I got the wrong psychology to be a soldier, or even a husband? Is it that I just want to be a little boy, and I am afraid to be that and to relax here, because if I give up my defences I do not know what is going to happen? I don't know what you are going to do to me."

*Analyst:* "What you do not know is what you are going to want me to do to you. You are putting me in the rôle of this father phantasy, and there are apparently two father-images, one the father who will pick you up and carry you until you are strong enough to stand on your own feet, and the other the father who will never forgive you for usurping his place, for having been in Serbia (i.e. in mother), for having killed his friends (i.e. castrated him), and who will in consequence lift you up not only by the scruff of your neck, but also by the seat of your trousers. You are afraid that you will be for the high jump, that you will suffer orgasm, which will be death.

"This was the little drama which you were enacting in that blockhouse. There you had made real the phantasy of the second father-image—the father whom you must fight and kill in order to survive yourself. Afterwards came the phantasy or belief that *he* must win, that he would seize you and destroy you for your attempted destruction of him.

"You have yet to learn that none of these things will really happen, except as an expression of your thoughts and feelings within the analysis. You will learn that your phantasies can be indulged in and even enjoyed without danger. What is the phantasy you are enacting here?"

*Patient:* "I suppose I am playing some sort of game with you." (Here he puts his legs over the side of the settee preparatory to leaving.)

*Analyst:* "We have a few minutes left—why are you in such a hurry? Perhaps your dream tells us what this game is. What does it suggest to you?"

*Patient:* "The red carpet was the red cockerel."

*Analyst:* "And you are sliding down it with your legs on each side of it?"

*Patient:* "That sounds like buggery."

## V. Psychopathology

The psychopathology of this case, which at first promised to be a simple war neurosis, takes us to very deep levels of the mind. It appears to take us even to that point where sexuality diverges into its two main branches—masculinity and femininity. The intimate emotional mingling of one person with another, which began (apart from intra-uterine sustenance) with the sucking of the infant at his mother's nipple, and the consequent gaining by the more feeble of strength on a physical plane from the stronger, gives rise to an equivalent psychological pattern.

The child is drawing, as it were, strength from its supporting parents. Their strength is for its good. (But, of course, the same strength may in infancy be used against it for its destruction. Infantile cannibalistic phantasies may have the advantage of mastering the bad and ingesting the good in the one act.)

Feminine sexuality appears to be a transition from this stage. The female feels a need to receive psychosexually from a stronger or more forceful power, while in her turn she gives of her strength to a weaker and dependent creature, her child.

On the other hand, male sexuality includes primarily the giving or forcing of his strength into the weaker female. At the same time the male has not lost, he can never outlive, his original psychological pattern of requiring in turn to be fed as it were from a force still more powerful than himself. Thus, even the most virile willingly gives allegiance to some more powerful body, be it state, church, God, or king. This latter trait in his character may be even stronger than his masculine sexual tendency towards the female.

Considered biologically it would seem that mere special separation of the "branches" from the "stem" does not entail psychological independence. It seems the offspring still needs to draw from the strength of the main stem or roots. This dependence upon the source from which he grew, which is so marked in mankind, may show its equivalent in the animals in the form of the so-called herd instinct.

The case with which we have been dealing throws some light on the psychology of unconscious homosexuality, and its sublimated equivalents.

There is evidence of positive feelings towards his father whose psychological support he had lacked from the age of three years. For instance, he was found on more than one occasion at the local railway station awaiting his father's return from the office. Very soon after this his father abandoned the family, leaving a troubled and almost destitute mother to bring up the two boys. From that time the infant seems to have felt a premature responsibility coupled with a precocious possessiveness of his mother. He assumed maturity before he was ready for it. He repressed his deepening need for a father to lean upon, to relieve him of the anxiety of pretending to be a "man," whereas being only a child his feelings were really more those of passive femininity towards his mother's domination or masculinity. In so far as he pretended to a male rôle the father was represented as an enemy to his security, and unconsciously as a rival to his possession of his mother. In other words his infantile tendencies of father dependence were never lived through; they were repressed, and he was in consequence constantly looking for a father-image to fulfil the desired rôle, namely, that of a good object to satisfy his feminine need. At the same time this father-image was apt to assume the rôle of a dangerous enemy.

The following material is evidence that the positive feelings towards the mother (female) are not sufficient to relieve anxiety and to establish a protection against the possibility of a hostile father—and evidently of a hostile world. He dreams as follows: "I booked a room at a hotel and put my things in it. Then I left my room. When I wanted to find it again I couldn't. I was going up and down every corridor looking for it. Then I was running hither and thither looking for it. I had to get to it in time, because there was a dangerous man about, and the room that I had booked was Sanctuary. Then some hotel attendant wanted to know what I was doing rushing about up and down the corridors. He said: 'All right! I'll find it for you.' And he found it for me."

Immediately after telling the dream he complains he had sexual intercourse with his wife and got no satisfaction from it.

"It started calmly, and then it became hectic—like the rushing about the corridors in the dream. There was no ejaculation. Also, I am not sleeping well these nights."

*Analyst:* "What would the Sanctuary be?"

*Patient:* "It would be relief—orgasm—sleep."

*Analyst:* "What prevented you?"

*Patient:* "I didn't know my way to the room, and there was somebody after me."

His interpretation of the room that is Sanctuary is: The woman—wife—mother—the womb. The corridors are the passage that leads there. The things he had left there are: "Bag and baggage," to which he says "penis and testicles." The man who was after him was father or the analyst as the bad father-image, and the attendant who shows him the way is the analyst as the good father-image.

But the point I wish to make here is that it is not a completely satisfactory solution merely to find the "Sanctuary" (protection of the woman) if there is a hostile man still about in the passages. This is because the man is stronger than the woman. Friendship with him is essential for complete protection and permanent relief of anxiety. Nevertheless it should be remembered that the mother's domination or masculinity can play a similar man-like rôle.

The patient's feeling is that real security and freedom from anxiety can only be achieved by dealing with the man. This can be done in one of two ways, either by fighting and killing him—hence the patient's truculent manner at analysis and in his blockhouse fight—or by making friends with him, being forgiven and carried about by him until "one is strong enough to stand on one's own feet"—that is to say, by discovering the good father.

*In short, a satisfactory father relationship is essential for the disappearance of anxiety.* The patient says: "To fight father is to be killed, but with a good father behind one, one has real security, so that one can sally out and make raids, one can kill with safety, because, if ever danger should arise, one has only to run back to father, and he is adequate protection against everything. If you are on father's side you are quite safe to fight all battles." We may reflect here upon the heroics of religious—and state—fanaticism.

That this condition is productive of heroism is clearly due to the belief that being on God's side (or on the right side), defeat is impossible.

> My strength is as the strength of ten
> Because my heart is pure.
> Sir Galahad in Tennyson's *Idylls*.

Djengis Khan, founder of the first Mogul empire, in spite of the loss of his real father at a similarly early age as the patient, had evidently built up psychologically a more than adequate substitute to uphold him and underlie his valour. *This patient's breakdown after the blockhouse battle was due to the absence of such a psychological background.*

Another patient, also a soldier, reveals in the analysis of his unconscious homosexuality that strength is acquired frcm the father, which cannot be gained in any other way. This patient is more candid than the one with whom we are dealing in this case history. He is less on the defensive, because the affective material is less anxiety-ridden. It is on this account that he can reveal it more freely.

He says: "While I was at the door waiting to come in here I had a helpless feeling, as though I were unarmed before an aggressor. Then when I walked in front of you into this room I thought of what one of the men in my section said to me, 'Don't you wobble your bottom when you walk!' I am sure I was wobbling my bottom when I walked in here, and try as I might, I could not stop it from wobbling. I thought to myself, 'I'm doing this—for the attention of Dr. Berg.'"

*Analyst:* "And then—if we continue the phantasy?"

*Patient:* "The obvious thought is buggery. That is why I had that helpless feeling before coming in here. I must have felt that all my defences would give way before your sexual aggression. At the same time there was a feeling of impending doom. Nevertheless, I walked in front of you wobbling my bottom . . . apparently inviting buggery."

*Analyst:* "What is buggery?"

*Patient:* "Satisfaction. Orgasm. A relief of tension; relief of anxiety. Peace and calm."

*Analyst:* "And after this has happened—what then?"

*Patient:* "Then I would have some hold on you—some hold upon your affection. You see, the relationship of physician and patient is inadequate. If you had buggered me, it would be incongruous for you to say at the end of the hour, 'Shall we say, four o'clock on Monday? Good afternoon.' We should have advanced beyond that point. I'd have got you. I'd have a right to your affection. Our relationship would be more satisfactory to me."

*Analyst:* "What is the position that is so satisfactory—a right to my affection?"

*Patient:* "As you were speaking I thought of my father. In my later childhood I missed his friendship. And that is largely responsible for my present difficulties. Most people have a feeling of their family as a background. They feel they belong somewhere and that gives them strength and ability to fight life's battles without fear. Otherwise one might break down if one were hard-pressed through feeling one had no support. The anxiety would be too great to bear. This is the explanation of why I have the phantasy of an intimate relationship with you. That is, if you buggered me I should belong to you, in the sense of the saying 'he possessed her.' You would represent the strong background of which I feel the need.

"One's military superiors ought, I suppose, to supply that need, and to give me that confidence. But all the time I descover signs of inefficiency—futile orders. The result of my lack of faith in them is that I have a sense of the futility of life, at the same time I seem to have no energy or initiative of my own."

In free association of thought to this feeling of futility he says: "It occurs to me that I have had no sexual intercourse for a very long time. Also I have not been to see you for two weeks. I suppose I have been thinking of you as the efficient father physician.

"It may be that if my superiors were really efficient, I might feel some enthusiasm in their service. I would not have this feeling of futility. It would seem almost that I were acquiring efficiency myself. *At present, I suppose, I feel that I have not been accumulating potency from a potent father, and therefore I don't feel potent myself.* If life isn't going to be futile or wishy-washy it must contain some efficiency, strength or potency. Either you must be ruled or you must do the ruling. Potency must be present. You must be either the object of it or the subject. It is no good being impotent yourself and the love object of an impotent father. Nothing happens. It is all futile. That is why I come to you and wobble my bottom."

Thus it appears that in order to be strong, to feel confidence in battling with one's fellow-men, it is necessary to feel that one is a part of the omnipotent male, the almighty father. Otherwise anxiety is liable to become excessive, breakdown is liable to supervene.

If this is true in peace time, when the battles are merely economic and social competition, it is even more important in time of war, when the primitive phantasies may be only too adequately supported by the reality of physical danger.

The essential infantile or Œdipus factor in the case of war neurosis here described was that the patient had prematurely attempted, forced as it were by the artificial pressure of circumstances, to take on, at least in phantasy, the masculine rôle before he was mature enough to fill it without strain. Hence there was an ever-present harking back within his mind to that easeful or restful position of dependence upon a stronger figure, which he had missed, and of which circumstances had robbed him.

In the course of his analysis he re-lives that omitted part of his psychological development. When he had successfully gone through it, with all its concurrent deep phantasies of a psychosexual nature, he found himself more comfortable at man's estate.

Nevertheless, it is all rather a strain. He feels that he is playing on the edge of a volcano. One slip, if he relaxes for only a moment, anything may happen. The best he can do is to keep up this pretence.

His second dream, given towards the end of the session, shows that deep down he is still seeking a solution by union with the father-image, again represented by the analyst. He had his legs at either side of the red strip of carpet. Interestingly enough it was running out of a church. Bearing in mind that a church is almost a classical womb symbol, a possible interpretation of this dream, coming as it did in the terminal stages of analysis, is that this patient was experiencing an analytical re-birth with the analyst in the rôle of mother at the mother-with-phallus stage of phantasy.

One of his earlier attempts at a resolution of his anxiety was that if he could not be the man, marry the mother, and get away with it, he might at least surrender to father and perhaps attain security and strength by marrying him. His conflict at an earlier stage of his analysis when he felt the treatment might take him from his wife (to the analyst) was a resistance to this attempted solution.

It would seem that many alternative attempts have been made to resolve anxiety. We might tabulate them briefly in this order:

(1) Whether to fight father, destroy him, usurp his place, be a man and possess the woman (mother wife).

Or (2) Whether to give up the strain of this unequal struggle, surrender to the more powerful father and seek security (relief from anxiety) in his love.

In short, these two represent the classical conflict between the Œdipus and the inverted Œdipus situation. When he first came to analysis he was psychologically playing the female rôle to the mother-image to his mistress and to his analyst, in spite of the fact that he was acting out a relatively weak masculine rôle to the femininity of his wife. The point is that these masculine images were feared as a bad object and he was consequently resisting with much anxiety his feminine rôle towards them.

With the progress of analysis the analyst became the friendly receptive father and in consequence the patient was able to feel growing masculinity unaccompanied by his former castration anxiety. The little boy was growing to manhood. The war neurosis, the anxiety neurosis, the homosexual conflict, the paranoid tendencies and his psychosexual impotence were progressively disappearing.

Throughout treatment there had been evidence of a strong pull towards inversion, of his resistance to it and of his anxiety in connection with it. This raises the question as to how large a proportion of cases of war neuroses have similarly strong unconscious homosexual tendencies. It may also raise the wider question as to whether the phenomenon of war is fundamentally a dramatization of such unconscious phantasies—a homosexual substitution. It is certainly an emotionally all-powerful (an orgastic) dealing with *men* rather than with women.

If the objection is made that destructive violence and the fear of it is pre-pubertal and at a level with animals' food-finding efforts, I would add that feeding and self-preservation in general is not dissociated from the necessary sense of security dependent upon being loved by the more powerful adult. In all animals as well as humans this love has a basis in the gratification of the stronger by the weaker. The weaker monkeys, male and female, present sexually to the more powerful male whenever they seize any food within his reach.

Re-living his unconscious phantasies within his analytical sessions, and obtaining insight into them, released this patient from their domination and enabled him to give up pretence and strain in favour of natural development and masculinity.

That these results were more than theoretical is borne out by his re-joining His Majesty's fighting forces, from which, prior to treatment, he had been invalided.

## YOU AND YOUR HAIR

WHILE it is generally recognized that psychotic or "mad" behaviour has relatively little reality causation, typically "normal" behaviour is readily assumed, even by some psychologists, to be amply conditioned by environmental reality. It is, however, sometimes instructive to attempt to define the rôles played by the pleasure principle and the reality principle respectively in some well-established form of "normal" behaviour.

The attempt to explain such "normal" behaviour as our daily habits of dress and toilet in the terms of logical response to reality demands can be shown to be a process having the defensive advantage of enabling the instinctive basis to be ignored.

For instance, from the most primitive times, man has given much time to various forms of interference with his hair. Let us turn to some clinical material to see if we can throw any light on the source of these daily activities.

A patient dreams as follows:

"You" (the doctor) "were rubbing some stuff into my hair—like a white lather of soap. My mother was there and was very anxious to help."

Some associations of his to this dream are:

"The first thought that came to me was that you may have been cutting my hair, but it was not you, it was my father that wanted my hair cut shorter. I used to hate it. You were doing the reverse—making it grow.

"Now, I have my hair cut as I want it—not too short. I thought my father noticed this the other day when I visited him, and I thought to myself: 'He can go to hell!'

"I have thought that you were restoring my hair in the dream. Treating it in some way . . . and now I remember that my hair was short—shorter than I ever have it nowadays. I have a feeling that it had something to do with castration. Short hair is in the nature of a castration. It is part of discipline. In prisons the hair is cut short, and monks used to shave the head completely.

"In my dream the anxiety was my mother's, but it actually indicates *my* real emotions and anxiety. I keep thinking: 'How can I get some progress? How can I get better?' That, of course, is what you are doing in the dream. Rubbing my hair to make it grow."

Another patient dreams as follows:

"I had my hair cut, and somebody (a lady, I think) remarked that it was very nice. Then I went out and had it done again. The barber cut off the same amount again. As a result it was very short, I put plenty of grease on it and plastered it down. People thought it looked absurd and laughed at it."

His associations to this very striking dream are so voluminous that I shall have to select and condense, although the result will not do it justice.

Briefly, the woman is his mother; the haircut pleased her, so he went still further and had still more cut.

He says:

"I have brushed down what was left for the same reason. . . . To please the woman. I think I must have some sort of ideal woman in my mind." (The ideal woman is the mother to achieve whose love he must discard sexuality.)

With regard to the haircut in general, he says:

"Haircut is conforming to an ideal that civilization has built up. Haircut, like other civilized acts, is the desire to conceal the nakedness of emotions and desires in order to please somebody."

Other remarks of his are as follows:

"I don't like to see hair standing up on end." (He then remembers a man whom he knows, whose hair stands on end. He dislikes him for this reason. He says:) "He is a gay dog, especially with the opposite sex. I was just the reverse of this type.

"In the dream, after the second haircut I became an object of ridicule, *and that is what I am at the present stage of my life when I cannot enter into the fun of things, and cannot find a word to say if there is a girl about.* I am in a ridiculous position.

"It is rather a low-down business to have erect hair. Not the sort of hair that stamps a member of the upper classes. Makes me think of the 'Bill Sikes' type of individual—anti-social.

"*I suppose the association to hair is really pubic hair—and thence sexuality.* I might not please a woman if I were overtly sexual. I would hide the fact and control the desire. I would plaster it down like I did the erect hair.

"I now see more or less what the dream is about. I don't like my hair for the same reason that I didn't like overt sexuality. It was *rude,* so I had it cut and my mother was pleased. I wanted to please her so much that I went too far, and ended up in this ridiculous state of almost complete baldness."

It is unnecessary to call attention to the relationship between this patient's associations to his dream, and the usual social behaviour towards hair. We are all familiar with the objection to erect hair.

We are all familiar with the tendency to plaster down the hair to prevent it from being unruly or untidy. We know the father who cannot bear to see his sons allowing their hair to grow too long.

The double haircut in the dream, representing extreme politeness (or castration) reminds us of the social convention of being completely bald about the face and chin—of shaving.

Are we, in shaving, doing the same thing as this patient did in the dream—to please the parents (i.e. to renounce the Œdipus desire for the mother)? I have much clinical material to support this idea.

Our clinical material need not be limited to dreams. One gets actual symptoms, or even whole cases, which throw light on the subject under discussion.

I am reminded of a female patient, at the menopause, who came for treatment on account of a habit of rubbing her hair in one place. This habit was so persistent that she rubbed a hole in every cap she wore (she was a housekeeper). The history was significant:

The habit began at fifteen years of age. She had been masturbating. (She had been rubbing her genitals—she has been rubbing her *hair* ever since.) She struggled against the impulse to masturbate, and suppressed it. It was then that she went into an orchard and stole apples. While doing so she fancied that an earwig had crept into her ear. In consequence she felt an irritation and rubbed her head above the ear. This rubbing had persisted ever since—a period of thirty years.

We can only think of one source from which such an absorbing and persistent energy could be derived.

The unconscious mechanisms at work are sufficiently clear. The unconscious incestuous phantasy accompanying the masturbation was repressed on account of strong Œdipus guilt. It escaped from repression in the form of apple stealing. The incestuous wish with its impregnation corollary expressed itself in the delusion of the earwig having penetrated her ear (vagina). Erotic (masturbation) impulses were expressed (and partly gratified) in the hair rubbing. The guilt attaching to the whole Œdipus phantasy is easily detected in the patient's state of mind and in the punishment which the neurotic habit inflicts upon her ego.

The symptom is (as are all symptoms) a compromise formation or a condensation of (genital) libido and its repression. Its relevance for our purpose is that again it is to the hair that the genital conflict has been displaced.

Dr. Eder describes how a woman suffering from a pronounced castration fear (anxiety hysteria) kept putting off her shingling appointment. When at last she kept it, she was taken ill with the first cut. He refers to similar experiences in normal people and quotes a hairdresser as saying he is accustomed to his clients failing to keep their appointments. A normal woman, on the night prior to her appointment for shingling, dreamed that her son was drowned in the swimming bath, and awoke with the anxiety of a nightmare.

We see in all these cases the conflict between the sexual impulses and the repressing forces. The field of battle is displaced to the hair of the head. Can we not see the same conflict being worked out, without ever reaching a solution, in our normal daily hair activities? They bear the characteristic of every hysterical symptom, namely that, in some displaced or converted disguise, the original sexual conflict at the genital level is fruitlessly seeking solution.

Perhaps it should be a matter for commendation of the ego that such primitive and powerful instinct drives have been so skilfully deflected into such a harmless field of conflict, as shown in the ritual of cutting the hair—as one of my patients expressed it "to please the woman."

It is as if the little Œdipus conceived the hair (phallus) as a menace to his mother, which would meet with her disapproval or with a withdrawal of her love. Therefore he cuts it off to please her. Similarly, the reaction formations are expressed in endeavours to keep the hair tidy, flat, etc., and perhaps most conspicuously in the ritual of shaving. We thereby become at peace with our various social parent-substitutes.

I have had dream evidence to show that the custom of covering the hair with a hat is an expression of each side of the conflict. In so far as the hair is hidden, it shows a fear of its exhibition. In so far as the headdress is itself exhibitionistic we have the positive impulses gratified by means of this displacement.

A patient dreamt that he was a soldier in uniform walking through the woodlands with his helmet missing and his hair blowing about in the breeze. He knew in consequence that his uniform was not in order. Eventually, as he had feared, he was arrested by the sergeant.

His associations to this dream destroyed any doubt there might have been as regards the phallic significance of his untidy hair-behaviour, and also of the castration significance of his arrest.

But this is not the whole story. Certain factors remind us that the aggressive impulse is here also. Aggression, or sadism, appears clearly in my clinical material. May it not also be detected beneath the prevalent cutting, singeing, and especially the shaving of the hair?

Is it not against our aggression, rather than against an otherwise harmless phallus, that we are directing insistently the sharp blade of the razor? Do we not intuitively detect something of this objectionable quality in our fellow man who has neglected to shave?

In shaving and haircutting we discharge our aggression by directing it against our aggressive hair.

If it is granted that hair is conspicuously a genital symbol, and that our mental attitude towards hair and our activities with it are a displaced expression of our sexual conflict (at the genital level), the problem then arises as to why it is *hair* we have picked upon for the symbolic expression of this conflict.

A host of other objects can be, and are, freely chosen for its expression and relief, but perhaps the true explanation of why hair should be singled out as a phallic substitute *par excellence* may be in its *physical* relationship to sexual maturity.

Havelock Ellis points out that hairiness is commonly recognized as indicating sexual virility. In confirmation of this we have an example of the opposite in a patient who lost his hair (alopecia) when he was unconsciously convinced of castration. This is a common phenomenon of which many clinical psychologists have had experience. A large number of shell-shock cases (i.e. persons whose state of fear represented unconscious phantasy of castration or loss of life) suffered from alopecia, sometimes amounting to complete baldness during the weeks of mental illness following their traumatic experience.

It appears that conventional hair-behaviour, the periodic hair cuttings, the daily hair brushings and *particularly the daily shave*, are a present-day ritual-*symptom* exactly analogous to many savage and ancient customs.

All this may teach us nothing more than we have already suspected, namely that our hair activities are but another substitutive expression of our sexual conflict. We have merely drawn attention to another habitual method of expression of well-known unconscious material.

This study will have served its purpose if it makes us realize once again the truth that our behaviour, whether "normal" or "mad," is essentially an expression of the various opposed tensions of our unconscious conflict.

In this paper we see this conflict displaced upwards to the socially visible hair of the head and face; and so our preoccupation with the unsolved primitive past has found its way into our modern civilized life, in a form which by virtue of its symbolism ensures it against any likelihood of solution. Is this normality: to go on repeating our old struggles with obsessional persistence until death overtakes us and ends the matter with a final castration?

*N.B.*—A paper dealing with this subject more comprehensively and from a more technical viewpoint was published by the present author in the *International Journal of Psychoanalysis*, Vol. XVII, Part I, 1936.

# CHAPTER THE FIRST AND THE LAST

TWO thousand years ago a Roman general wrote to Cæsar from Spain: "This is a people very prone to civil war."

The practice of medical psychology similarly convinces us of the extraordinary conservatism of the human mind.

If we begin our psychotherapeutic endeavours filled with optimistic ideas of effecting facile changes in the minds of our patients, if we feel that we have only to encourage them to give up the folly of their ways, or even if, not going so far as this, we assume that we have merely to get them to obtain insight into the irrational mechanisms at work in order to effect a cure, we are going to be bitterly disappointed.

In so far as, by advice, encouragement and persuasion, we use only the instruments of reason, our endeavours are directed to modifications of the reason or ego of the patients, and the changes, if any, that we may achieve are going to be at the best merely superficial and of short duration.

In the end we shall discover that instruments other than those of reason are required, that our technique must of necessity be based upon an understanding of the deeper mechanisms hidden within the unconscious structure of the mind, mechanisms which influence or coerce reason itself.

We shall discover that the mind is fundamentally instinct driven and that reason is a relatively weak instrument of cure, that on the contrary it is designed specifically for achieving the gratification of the instincts rather than for the purpose of altering their nature or modifying their dynamic energy. In fact, it may be the attempt to use reason too much in this very unnatural way—against the instincts—that was the very thing responsible for the patient's nervous breakdown. In trying to be too reasonable he unduly ignored the demands of his primitive, unreasoning nature, and this nature reasserted itself in spite of him and against him. The symptoms of which he complains are the consequences of this conflict.

If this is the cause of his illness by what means then can we hope to achieve a modification or cure of the illness?

If the process is to be at all scientific, that is to say, if the therapist is to understand and control the measures he uses, it is essential that he himself has thorough insight into the hidden mechanisms that are responsible for the patient's illness. But this is not enough; he must understand also how to bring about changes in those mechanisms or in the results thereof.

*Technique*

In the early days of psychoanalysis the technique consisted principally of active interpretation by the analyst of the patient's unconscious material whenever the latter betrayed what he was *not* saying, and perhaps not even consciously thinking or daring to think. This method was abandoned by psychoanalysts thirty to forty years ago. It did not lead to the desired therapeutic results.

However clear the pathology of the case may be, it is not psychoanalysis to offer psychopathological explanations to the patient during the early interviews. It merely tends to rob the patient of necessary modes of relief (under which term we may include symptoms), while offering him nothing in place of them.

This is the sort of thing which was done in the case I have recorded under the title of "Self-cure by Asthma." The patient was "robbed" of her asthma, and given nothing she could put in place of it.

One should admit, however, that a more common mistake may well be to refrain from giving interpretations at a time when the need for them is ripe or over-ripe. In other words, the experienced analyst is more likely to err on the side of restraint than on that of premature interpretation.

The next important step in the development of the technique of psychoanalysis was to allow, or to encourage, the patient to make his own interpretations as the time became ripe. This was better, and had a less shocking effect upon the patient, but it did ot lead to a complete analysis, nor usually to a complete cure.

These two procedures are still placed in the foreground by some hools of psychotherapy, for, however desirable, it may not always be possible to insist on a full psychoanalytical technique. If treatment is to be undertaken, it may be necessary to decide at an early interview which particular method of treatment is best suited to the psychological nature of the case and to the material situation of the patient.

As space will not permit even an outline description of every method, I shall here limit myself to a description of the psychoanalytical method, as initiated and developed by Freud and his school. This is undoubtedly the most advanced, the most far-reaching, and the most ambitious method. Those who employ it insist that the patient should attend daily for at least five days a week.

The psychoanalytical method is based on the theory, itself the fruit of much experience, that the root of every neurosis lies in the Œdipus complex, deep down in those unconscious emotional patterns which were formed and fixed by repression during the early years of the patient's infancy, when his mind first began to develop emotional attitudes (love and hate) towards persons in his immediate environment, such as parents or parent surrogates. These patterns and their earliest modifications, like all repressed material that is highly charged with emotion, repeat themselves in all subsequent situations throughout the patient's life, however inappropriate these situations may be, and without the patient having insight into the process. It is as though he were under a compulsion from an unseen force over which he has no control to behave in a certain emotional manner. This behaviour will include not only his symptomatic behaviour, but also his love and sex life, and even his way of thinking and acting in every particular.

Whether or not a practitioner uses the psychoanalytical method, it is as well that he should have a thorough training in it. Unfortunately this is the exception rather than the rule. It is as well that a surgeon should be able to perform major operations, even if he is usually engaged in minor surgery.

Psychoanalysis aims at bringing out the Œdipus complex, and with it all the forgotten period of infantile emotional development, so that the ego will be able to direct it, instead of being directed by it.

Psychoanalysis holds that all methods of treatment which do not go so deeply as to expose the Œdipus complex leave the root of the patient's behaviour untouched, and are therefore at best not permanent cures. The sort of factors with which these other methods deal are at most merely adjunctive or precipitating factors in the causation of the illness. Improvement resulting from these other methods is always incomplete, and often only temporary.

The aim of the psychoanalytical method is to achieve permanent eradication of the very root of the illness, and at the same time to put its psychic energies at the disposal of the ego or reason.

The modern step in the evolution of psychoanalytical technique is the one which I shall presently describe. It may be called the *strategic technique of Transference development and Transference analysis.*

It has been said that psychotherapy is transference. I should like to go a step farther than this, and say that the *analysis* of transference and of transference resistance is psychoanalysis.

It is to illustrate this essential process in the psychoanalytical method of treatment that I have included a few instances of the advanced transference stage of treatment in the Case Book material, particularly in Cases XVIII, and XXIII.

There is not space to describe adequately even the general principles of technique in the preliminary stages of treatment as I wish to give a fuller explanation of what is fundamental and essential to the final success of this technique.

Therefore I must content myself by saying briefly that these general principles include extreme passivity on the part of the analyst and the fundamental rule of free association of thought on the part of the patient.

The degree of the analyst's *passivity* and its absolute necessity will rarely be sufficiently appreciated by anyone who has not himself been analysed. It is safe to say that every non-analyst will treat a patient wrongly. He will not discount his own tendencies to emotional reaction even to the mildest thoughts or ideas.

It goes without saying that there must never be any emotional display on the part of the analyst, but more than this is required of him. No opinion must be ventilated, no theories must be propounded —least of all those of psychoanalysis. There must never be the slightest hint of self-assertiveness or dogmatism on his part. He has one function and (throughout the first stage, at least) one function only to perform, and that is to keep the patient doing and expressing free association of thought.

To achieve this it is essential that the analyst shall understand all the infinite varieties of what may be called defence resistance. *Defence Resistance* may be defined as anything which interferes with the patient's expression of his free association of thought and with the progress of the analysis.

*Free association of thought* is the only positive rule for the patient. It may be necessary to explain this at the outset, but the longer I can defer explaining this rule the better pleased I am. A patient often freely associates with less anxiety if he does not know he is freely associating. Of course, if he should ask for instruction, and if he is not content with such a reply as: "Just keep on talking," I go a step farther and suggest that he should tell me whatever comes into his mind. Eventually, however, it will be necessary to tell him the rule. It is: to speak whatever comes into his mind, irrespective of emotional or other inhibitions.

In some cases it may be necessary to enter into further explanations. For example, that in ordinary conversation we direct our thoughts to a definite goal, and censor irrelevant material, whereas in free association this is what we are asked not to do. We should say *anything* that comes, even if it seems irrelevant or absurd.

It is safe to say that once this *fundamental* rule has been propounded and explained to the patient, the analyst's work will consist in trying to prevent its infringement or evasion.

Negative rules for the patient include that he should not indulge

in any physical action or strain. This usually means that he adopts
a recumbent position. That he should not stare or look at the
analyst during the sessions. If this were allowed the sessions would
be spent, consciously or unconsciously, in attempts on the part
of the patient to analyse the analyst.

The idea is to limit the patient's activity to that of a verbal
expression of all his thoughts and feelings, and at the same time to
encourage him to freedom in this respect, and in this respect only.

It is essential that the patient consciously accept these principles,
but this conscious acceptance on his part will not overcome the
defence arising almost from the start. There are few defences inherent in a patient, other than in psychotic (insane) patients, which
will prevent a successful analysis, but the defences inherent in the
analyst may prove to be the greater difficulty. These cannot be
dealt with in this paper, but I may mention here that the analyst
must have a *Psychological Sense*. He must recognize behind every
single expression or activity of his patient and in every abnormal
or normal interest inside and outside analysis, the operation of
unconscious motives, that is, the presence of motives of which the
actor is unaware. He must learn to read, understand and speak
the language of the patient's symptoms, and not to be misled by
the language of the patient's conscious mind. If the blind lead the
blind, both shall fall into the pit.

*For instance*, if the patient should ask, "Is the door shut properly?"
it is not for the analyst to answer, "Yes, I am sure it is shut." He
must be concerned with the patient's phantasy and not with reality.
He should think: "The patient feels that somebody might be listening and overhearing what he is saying, or what he is about to say,
or perhaps what he is at this very moment *concealing*." Therefore
the analyst may answer: "What will be overheard?" or, it may
be, "Who is listening?" or, "What will the consequence be?"
Whether he voices these questions or not will depend entirely upon
the transference situation, for *everything the analyst says must be subordinated to the main strategy of Transference development and Transference
analysis.*

But, in so far as the transference situation has arrived, in so far
as the patient is unconsciously enacting the emotional patterns of
his early life here and now upon the analytical settee, it will be
necessary, in order to maintain progress, to interpret all his drama-
tizations as opportunity offers. For instance (as recorded in Case VII),
it appeared that a patient who had been caned by his father as a
boy was far from relaxed. On enquiry it transpired that he was
lying on my settee with his buttock muscles as tense as he could

make them. He admitted that he was feeling "*as if he were expecting the cane at that very moment.*" He was re-living the old scene, but with me in the rôle of his father. Until this situation had been revealed he would have gone on unconsciously enacting it, his muscles would have remained tense *and so would his mind,* and the result would have been we should have made little or no progress in the analysis. This interpretation is an essential part of transference analysis.

In the earlier stages of treatment the patient will ask questions, but the analyst's concern is not necessarily to answer these, but rather to allay the anxiety which lies behind them, though it must be borne in mind that any untrue statement to the patient would be fatal to successful treatment. There is one question he is sure to ask: "How long will analysis last?" There is only one answer: "We do not know." The relief of the mind, like digestion, is a natural process, and its speed cannot be coerced by the will of man.

Psychoanalysis is not the purposeless interpretation of a patient's unconscious material, merely to show him that we can get at something that is in his unconscious, or to reveal our cleverness. Taking rabbits out of a hat may be an amusing pastime, but it is not psychoanalysis.

As time goes on the analyst will have analysed many dreams and accumulated much material which he will need for future reference, and for use during the next stage, that of the Transference Neurosis. For in that stage he will require all his resources. The success of the analysis depends upon his handling of the transference. In any case, it is probably only transference which ever achieves any therapeutic results.

To deal with the transference it is essential that the analyst should have a very real and personal understanding of it. *From the point of view of technique* it is the most important function of the unconscious mind.

### Transference Analysis

I shall now attempt to give some explanation of the theory of the transference. This may be simplified by the drawing of an analogy with the mental mechanism of a simple war neurosis, such as I described in Case XXI.

We may assume that a soldier has an experience in consciousness: an experience of a violent emotional nature—for instance of a terrifying nature. It may be that these emotions are very unwelcome to this man's consciousness, and to his ideal of himself as (say) a brave soldier. His personality, or that part of it which includes this ideal *cannot tolerate* the memory of these emotions.

The whole thing is forgotten. This forgetting is evidently an active process, it is as though some force, which we may call the brave soldier ideal, has pushed the memory of the experience, plus its accompanying emotions, right out of consciousness—the man is suffering from a period of amnesia, or memory blank.

That may have happened in 1917. How do we know that these unwelcome memories have not been thrust *out* of the mind altogether? Because in 1938 the man suffers from various fears or a state of general fear, which appears superficially to be quite causeless. The theory of what has happened is that the experience, with its affects or emotions, was thrust, not out of the mind altogether, but out of consciousness into the unconscious. There it remained inaccessible to the patient's powers of conscious recall.

Now, we know that ideas and memories are in themselves of little dynamic force—it is the *emotions* that are the dynamic or forceful factors in the mind. The powers of repression, whilst sufficient to keep the memory of the *experience* out of consciousness, were not sufficient to repress the affects or emotions belonging to that experience. These affects or emotions have re-emerged into consciousness after many years in the form of morbid anxiety, while the actual experience and its related memories remain buried.

Now on this simple analogy I shall endeavour to explain the transference:

We all suffer from a period of amnesia, or memory blank. This memory blank relates to the period of life when there was relatively little sense of reality, and life consisted almost entirely of feelings and emotions. I speak of the earliest years of life—the period of infantile amnesia.

The amnesia means that our experiences and emotions of that period were pushed into the unconscious in a similar fashion to that of the war neurosis I have described. As in this case, so with all of us, the affects refuse to remain attached to the repressed experiences which originally caused them.

The soldier's fear in 1938 might be related, not to bursting shells, but to the noise of traffic, or even to such apparently innocent things as open spaces. It is as though the dynamic qualities of affect insisted upon breaking loose from the ideas and situations to which they causally belonged, and insisted upon finding new and often irrelevant situations to which to attach themselves.

Now this is a tendency with all highly charged affects, even in adult life. *How much more must we expect to find it to be so with the most original of all affects (the first experienced in life), and the primary causal situations which gave rise to them at the dawn of life!* It is as though affect or emotion demanded to live and attach itself in the present reality, and refused the memory work which would reveal it to be a product of past and forgotten experiences—and not a justifiable product of the present reality situation.

The experiences of infancy, at the hands of the parents, are thus forgotten, that is, relegated to the unconscious—the emotions that accompanied these experiences re-emerge into consciousness throughout life, and seek various suitable or unsuitable objects to which to attach themselves. The emotional life of the analysand (patient) in relation to his parents, or parent surrogates, begins to be re-lived in the analytical situation and in relation to the analyst. All the loves he felt, and all the hates he felt, re-emerge with the analyst as object. (*Vide* Cases XVIII and XXIII.)

This is the transference situation.

And it is the task of analysis, through these affects or emotions, to enable the patient to recall his infantile memories and experiences. The whole difficulty of analysis lies here. The strength of the analyst's position lies in the fact that he has throughout been passive, he has neither provoked nor deserved any of the feelings, positive or negative, love or hate, which the patient hurls at him.

He must never react emotionally to any situation either directly or *indirectly*, however dramatic and real it may be to the patient.

His task is to get the patient to remember when this emotion was previously experienced, and thus gradually to uncover the amnesia of infancy, *in which the roots of the individual's mental illness, as well as the roots of his whole personality, will be found.*

From a therapeutic point of view it may be said that it is usual for all ordinary symptoms to disappear with the full development of the transference situation. But this situation must then itself be regarded as a symptom: hence it is called the *Transference Neurosis*.

The transference then, from a point of view of analytical progress, may be looked at in two lights—one as a defence, that is to say, *instead* of remembering the patient feels and relates his feeling to the analyst and to the present, and, secondly, it may be regarded as a necessary stage in the progress of the analysis.

For it is only through the unmasking of this dramatization that it is possible for the forgotten period of the patient's infancy to be remembered.

Thus, and only thus, will he be in a position to abandon his infantile compulsions, and able to start, as it were, a new life under the jurisdiction of his adult ego or reason, whose function is essentially to make appropriate adjustments between the necessary demands of his instincts and the necessities of such aspects of his environment that he is unable to alter according to his needs.

With these remarks I must conclude my inadequate attempt to explain in a few words this very complex and difficult subject. The most experienced analyst is always still a student, for ever being made aware of his ignorance, but nevertheless at every turn making inroads upon it.

### Theory

It is now time to ask what *understanding of the mind* has been gained by the employment of this new instrument which Freud originally put into our hands. Common sen e, though said by cynics to be the least common of the senses, can give us merely the most superficial understanding of persons and of things. It will never teach us their inner hidden nature. For instance, it will never teach us that the solid table we sit at consists of revolving protons and electrons. In the light of common sense, that table's behaviour at a temperature of 4,000 degrees Centigrade must remain a mystery or a miracle.

Physicists have their special instruments of observation which teach them more than common sense could ever teach them about the hidden nature of the material world. They have invented such theories as the atomic and electron theory simply because these theories help to clarify their data of observation. The psychological theories I would now describe have an equal justification. They are theories based upon clinical evidence of the analysis of patients and they will help us to understand the hidden mechanisms of the deeper unconscious levels of the human mind in which the otherwise incomprehensible symptoms and behaviour of man have their source or origin. We will see that this is a region where the laws of logic or reason do not exist, but where dynamic impulses, instincts and feelings in conflict with one another produce the manifold phenomena which emerge on the surface in the form of symptoms and behaviour.

### Topography of the Mind

Purely for descriptive purposes we shall begin with a concept of the simplest possible mind which we may represent diagrammatically by a circle. In Freudian terminology this is called the "Id" (or the "It"). Of course, such a mind does not really exist, for even the most primitive animal has some proportion of Ego. We might perhaps conceive of such a mind as existing in an embryo. You see, we are taking a developmental point of view. The Id or primitive mind is conceived of as being a world to itself. It has no organs of perception and no contact with environment or the world outside itself. It is merely a reservoir of innate or inherited urges, instincts, desires and wishes. You can, if you like, call it just body without brain or mind. The word "Id" itself justifies this, it is the Latin for "it."

Curiously enough modern clinical psychology is forced to regard this Id and its functions as more important for its purposes than those functions which we popularly regard as mental. A good analogy would be perhaps to regard it as a sort of spinal cord which was rather more than a mere reflex apparatus in that it embodied those phylogenetically elaborated "reflexes" called instincts.

The Id receives stimulation from all somatic sources and accumulates energy or tension, which, like the spinal cord, it would automatically discharge along inherited paths.

Now, last of all (especially after birth) it is receiving stimuli from the external world of reality. Such stimuli, firstly received from the sense perception organs which are in contact with reality, produce some, shall we say, localized modification of a portion of the Id.

Lamarckian and Spencerian evolution would say that it is by dint of these stimuli that the sense organs are evolved, and thus better convey the stimuli from the external world to this undifferentiated mind.

The new structure thus created by these stimuli is called the *primitive* Ego. In our diagram we may regard it as a sort of bubble, created by these stimuli on the surface of the circle. It is that part of the mind which has cognizance of environment or reality.

Early in individual life a highly organized group of stimuli begin to take effect upon the primitive mind of the baby. I refer to the effect of people, particularly of parents, their ideas and ideals. The specific effect of this new human environment is largely in the form of a prohibition or obstruction to the formerly free expression of instinct urges. The newly developing Ego of the infant, in attempting to adjust itself to the demands of this specific environment, finds itself occupied chiefly in opposing Id wishes, or at least in grossly modifying them. It thus comes about that the function of the primitive Ego is, like the function of the parents, largely one of frustrating or countermanding the impulses of the Id. Thus we come to the important psychological concept of *Conflict*, though this is only one form of conflict. (Conflict can also be between one instinct and another.)

There is evidence in psycho-analysis of an Ego attribute that is less rational in its development than that here described. It appears that an introjection (or incorporation) of a phantasied ogre-like parent-figure takes place and assumes in the mind a tyrannical position towards Id forces. This parent-image is originally a pro-

## TOPOGRAPHY OF THE MIND
### ENVIRONMENT

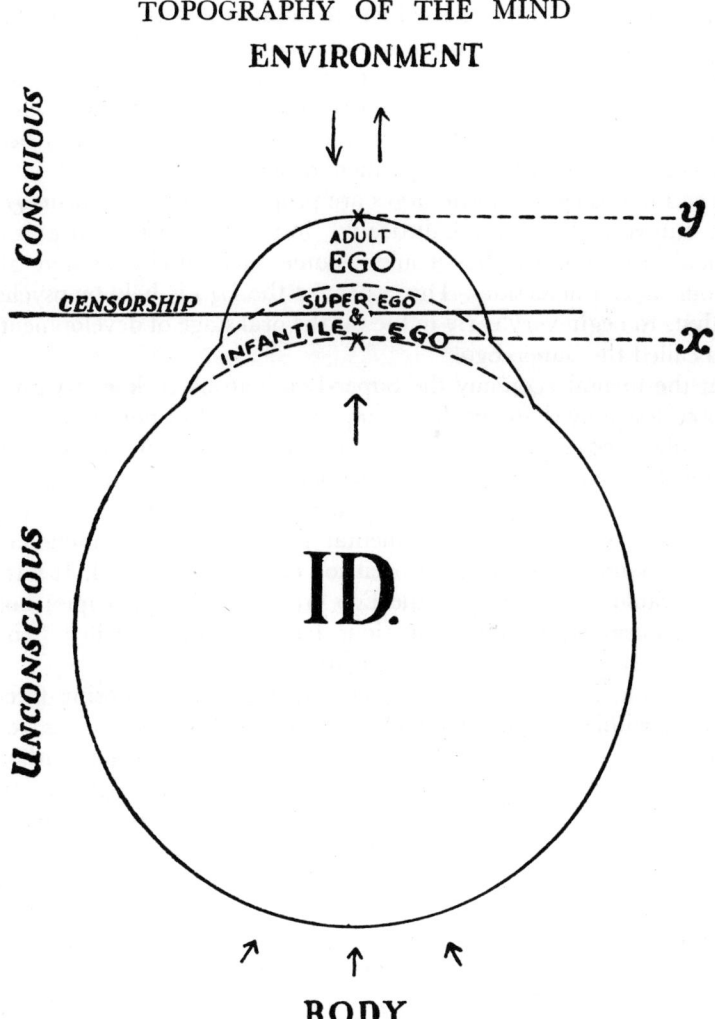

jection of the infant mind's own primitive aggression and sadism, for no real parent could possibly be so awe inspiring. The phenomenon may belong to the cannibalistic level of mental development.

A word about this: psycho-analysts, particularly child analysts, have discovered at a very primitive level of the mind a phantasy corresponding to a stage of development rather suggestive of that of the mind of the animal in the forest. It seems likely that the chief concern of such an animal is to find food to eat, and at the same time to avoid being itself eaten. A child analyst has said that there is a corresponding stage in the infant's development when its world (i.e. its mental world) consists mainly of "breasts" and "bellies." That is to say, things for it to devour and "bellies" which will devour it at the slightest provocation. This is what has been called the cannibalistic level of mental development.

The infant's cannibalistic urges are projected on to parent-images and subsequently (cannibalistically) introjected. Otherwise it is difficult to see how they could assume such terrifying and all-devouring characteristics. This aspect of the Ego is held by psycho-analysts to begin very early in life (at the oral stage of development). It is called the Super-Ego.

In the mental economy the Super-Ego is to be reckoned with as a force less only than the Id in importance. It has power not only to inhibit and repress Id forces, but even to punish the Ego for having listened to them. Its punishments can be of any degree of severity not excluding "capital punishment" (death)—notably in depressive states and in the mental illness called Melancholia—if its demands seem to have been too drastically ignored. It has a considerable influence upon the Ego proper (reality principle) both unconsciously and in its conscious form popularly called "conscience." It is thus the main instigator of conflict.

The mind is now not so simple. There are two opposing forces at work within it. The point of view, or function, of each is very different. The Id merely wishes to relieve itself of tension without any consideration of reality or person, whereas the Ego has the function of adjusting the Id impulses to reality, which means in practice that very often the energy of the Ego is constantly occupied in directly opposing or repressing the insistent demands of instincts emanating from the Id.

Here we have the important psychological concept of Repression. I would like you to conceive of this as a dynamic process constantly at work. The Ego has constantly throughout life to expend energy to maintain repression, because the instincts it opposes are incessant in their demands so long as life lasts. Of course, they may occasionally break through Ego repression, and the task of repression may then be renewed in increased vigour by the Ego, perhaps caught temporarily unaware. This process is in a sense, the essence of the outbreak of symptoms, or of other instinct-driven conduct whether repudiated by the Ego or not.

The repressive action of the Ego is perceptible as one variety of resistance in analytical treatment.

We may pause for a moment to consider where the Ego gets its everlasting energy from. The answer is interesting. The Ego is a modified portion of the Id, and it gets its energy actually from the Id sources which it is occupied in opposing. This process is called Anti-Cathexis. Cathexis is a discharge of Id tension or instinct tension along its original instinct paths. Anti-Cathexis occurs when this energy is utilized by the Ego to oppose the instinct discharge. In consequence we can get an equally powerful and insistent impulse in the *opposite* direction to the original instinct. The process may become conspicuous in such an illness as obsessional neurosis, where the excessive reinforcement of the opposition—opposition to what the instinct wishes to do—is characteristic of the disease. For instance, an obsessional patient with strong destructive and dirtying instincts may be constantly preoccupied with precautions against destruction and with obsessional cleansing, e.g. hand-washing ritual.

A less striking manifestation of the same mechanism is apparent to the psychologist in the violent repudiation of violence, for instance, the conduct of the crowds who lynch (i.e. murder) a murderer.

A similar mental mechanism lies behind all our emotional attitudes towards crime and the criminal, though our practice may be more or less slightly modified by rationalization.

It is noteworthy that, when considering even the foundations of mental structure, we find that our investigations cannot be confined to neurotic symptoms, but that we have chosen the whole of human behaviour as our laboratory. The theories were actually formed from clinical material provided by patients under analysis. The fact that they are subsequently found to cover such a wide field, perhaps a limitless field, only supports their greater credibility.

To return to our concept of Conflict between Id and Ego, and the process of Repression whereby the Ego endeavours more or less to keep the Id in order:

The task of the Ego is a difficult one. It constantly fears being overwhelmed by the more powerful Id. To maintain even a measure of control the new and feeble Ego finds it necessary to adopt very stern, ruthless, and dictatorial methods. It does so in so far as it is opposed to the Id demands. On the other hand, this very early Ego has, perhaps fortunately, so slight an appreciation of reality as we know it that it is constantly being carried along by the Id, without recognizing that opposition is called for by reality. So that the early Ego, in spite of its ruthlessness in places, may still be as mad as the Id in other respects.

This brings me to another concept which is of special interest. It is this. Neurosis or Psychoneurosis (nervous illness) is regarded as being the result of a conflict between the Id and the Ego, in which the Ego maintains its contact with reality relatively unimpaired. Psychosis (mental illness, insanity) on the other hand, is regarded as a state in which the demands of the Id have unduly influenced the Ego—the Ego has, as it were, turned too sympathetic or complaisant an ear to the Id, with the result that the Ego's relationship to reality has been impaired, so that now conflict would lie between the Ego and its environment.

Thus in the diagram the conflict in nervous disturbances would lie at X between the Id and the Ego; whereas in psychosis (insanity) the Ego has already been overwhelmed by Id forces and the conflict would lie at Y, between the Ego and environmental reality.

The primitive mind is relieved to some extent of conflict at the first level, but obviously has a considerable amount of this conflict at the second level. We all recognize that a child's relationship to reality is imperfect and that he may not be unduly conscientious about it. Reality as he sees it is very different from reality as an adult sees it, and this is perhaps fortunate for him, otherwise the burden of conflict between the Ego and the Id would most certainly lead to a neurosis. Briefly one may say that it is psychotic rather than neurotic. *I am rather tempted to extend this generalization to us all, however adult we may be.* Wars in the outer world may save us from intrapsychic wars. Human insanity may be collective, dramatized and manifest. Civilization with all its evidences of neurosis is certainly not free from psychosis also.

To get back to our topographical and functional description of the mind:

As life goes on and as new experiences accumulate, the very early Ego has, as it were, successive layers of further modifications superimposed upon it. The later or *Adult Ego* is developing. There is clinical evidence that a portion of the early Ego remains unaffected by these successive experiences, and retains its primitive form. This early Ego is in closer contact with the primitive unconscious Id. The primitive Ego, particularly the Super-Ego, is now itself largely unconscious, but it still shows evidence that it is very much alive in exercising its early function of opposition, even blind, unreasoning opposition, to Id 'demands. Clinically this would be represented by such a function as conscience, particularly unconscious conscience, which is not in line with the person's reason. He might say to us, "I know that my reason tells me that there is no harm in doing so and so, but I know also that if I did it, I should be very worried, and perhaps lie awake at night." He is telling us something from which we all suffer. Neurosis it is, for it is not in line with our reason; on the other hand, a lot of us have our reason or adult Ego modified by such a primitive conscience or bias so that we rationalize or make excuses for doing that which it dictates, in the same way that we make excuses for doing what our instincts dictate.

We now visualize the adult Ego as mediator between many opposites. Chief of these are:

(1) The Id: instinct tensions and urges within the Id are constantly making demands upon the Ego for their release and gratification.

(2) The Super-Ego is usually making contrary demands upon the Ego and threatening like the imagined parents to punish it if it lends an ear to Id wishes.

These are all intrapsychic tensions and conflicts. There are other intrapsychic conflicts, such as the opposition of one instinct to another within the Id. But we shall not go into this.

(3) There is a third force which the Ego in its permissions and refusals must take into account. This third force is external reality.

It is perhaps small wonder that the Ego occasionally fails utterly in its task of serving these three rival masters. When this occurs we call it nervous or mental breakdown, neurosis or psychosis. That the Ego never fully succeeds is a matter that we are apt to forget. In other words none of us are perfect in our mental functioning. Analysis of the most so-called "normal" person very speedily reveals this to him. Ego-impairment is not likely to trouble him so much as it may trouble others. What will trouble him more will be the conflict and repression within himself. The opposing forces in such conflicts, whether they impair the Ego or not, if they carry the Ego with them break out in the form of some Ego accepted behaviour. If they do not gain Ego acceptance, they are nevertheless constantly breaking out in some form of symptomatic behaviour. We will find in every symptom, as in every form of human behaviour, a contribution from each one of the various topographical regions into which we have here divided the mind.

There will be first of all, as the source of the symptom, the dynamic force of some primitive instinct, or a component part of such an instinct. There will be some element from the opposing Super-Ego. There will be some element, such, for instance, as epinosic secondary gain into which the Ego will enter. And, of course, reality will contribute some little part.

To summarize or recapitulate this very condensed mental topography:

First of all, we have dynamic energy accumulated by afferent impulses from somatic sources. This energy would naturally be discharged along instinct paths—without any consideration for reality.

Next we have the development of the Ego with its reality principle, and with its opposition to this blind discharge of instinct tension. The Ego, then, primitive and adult, opposes the natural primitive process of relief. The Ego takes some of the available Id energy for the purposes of its work. It is always to some degree or in some particulars beaten in its task. It can never succeed in maintaining a perfect reality principle. It has to allow a certain degree of instinct relief, even to the detriment of its reality relationship. Sometimes it aims at a perfection beyond its power, and then the dynamic energy of the instincts may assert itself in spite of the Ego and produce a neurotic symptom—perhaps after a struggle— and with manifestations of anxiety.

Nevertheless, even after the symptom is produced, the Ego, still attempting to make the best of a bad job, may accept this symptom, and, as it were, try to make capital out of it. Here we get the epinosic gain to which I referred in the case of my so-called asthma patient. The phenomenon is of importance only in so far as it makes cure more difficult.

The dynamic forces contending with one another within the mind reveal themselves not only in symptomatic behaviour, but rather in every variety of human behaviour. It is merely that they attract our attention more easily when they show themselves in a form to which we have not grown accustomed. Such forms are, besides symptoms, delinquencies and oddities of every variety.

The description here given is far from complete, and in the space at our disposal we can do little more than mention some of the remaining theoretical concepts.

Topographical concepts include besides the Id, Super-Ego, and Ego already mentioned, the equally important concepts of Conscious (including perceptual conscious and pre-conscious) and Unconscious. These are conceived as cutting across the other topographical divisions of the mind in such a way that while the Id and the greater portion of the Super-Ego are wholly unconscious, most of the Ego, but not the whole of it, is conscious.

*Theoretical Concepts*

In contrast to the simplicity of this mental topography, the theory of psycho-dynamics and mental functioning makes use of a complex number of theoretical concepts. Thus: the instinct forces of the Id have been divided into Eros and Thanatos, or the life and death instincts, which manifest themselves respectively in the sexual instinct on the one hand and the aggressive (or destructive or repetitive) instinct on the other. In this contrast we detect the important concept of *Conflict* at its lowest and most fundamental level, but it should be added that these opposites can in some degree unite with each other—even to the extent of producing the phenomenon of sadism.

Again, there can be a functional conflict between the Pleasure principle (which, generally speaking, means the discharge of energy or tension along the path of least resistance) and the so-called Reality principle. The former is the special province of the Id, and the latter of the Ego.

It has been said that the Id is the reservoir of mental energy. This can be conceived of as the steam pressure within a boiler— the pressure that, passing through various mechanisms, sets the wheels in motion. Now this energy is clinically manifested in two forms corresponding to the two fundamental instincts. The form which manifests itself as repetition seems to be outside the pleasure principle and the reality principle, and is still relatively obscure, but the form which is principally responsible for making the wheels go round, the form which corresponds to the steam pressure in our engine analogy, that puts the whole mechanism into life and activity, is of the utmost importance for an understanding of mental dynamics. For conceptual purposes this energy has been, as it were, extracted from its instinct source, and given a name of its own: *Libido*. It can be conceived of not only as the energy or dynamic force of the sexual instinct, but also as capable of as many transformations, changes of direction and vicissitudes, as the steam pressure within the various tubes of the steam engine. There is a vital quality about it which justifies this special conceptual abstraction. Though it includes the term erotic, it is wider than this, for it is regarded as lying also behind any emotional attachment not only to all persons, but also to concrete objects and abstract ideas.

There is a libidinal feeling-tone in every portion of the living body, and it is conceivable that every living cell and organ contributes to it, even though there is no localization to the source of these contributions. Localization does, however, occur most markedly at specific places or regions, which have in consequence been called

*

by psychoanalysts the erotogenic zones. They include particularly certain regions where the sensitive lining of the interior of the body (the mucous membrane) emerges upon the surface, or forms contact with the sensitive covering of the exterior of the body (the skin); for instance, the orifices of the body where external things can be taken in to affect the vital interior and vice versa. It is probably on this physical basis that the psychological phenomena of *introjection* and *projection* are founded. They reflect the tendency of the primitive mind to regard pleasure-giving objects as a part of itself and pain as due to an external agency.

The most important of these erotogenic zones are the lips and mouth (oral), the anal canal and anus, the urethra, the clitoris, the phallus and vagina. Their erotogenicity may extend for a considerable distance around these, and indeed to some extent it includes the entire surface of the body, and even its musculature and its interior.

From this we can better understand the Freudian conception of *infantile sexuality*, and the concept of the *component instincts*. The idea is that adult genital sexuality does not suddenly spring into being miraculously from nowhere, but that it is, as it were, a final stage of libidinal organization, having roots and origins in the erotogenicity of all living tissues, and passing through many intermediate localizations, such as the erotogenic zones enumerated, before it is finally canalized in its fully adult form. In fact, there is psychoanalytical evidence that it goes through a similar organization in a less sharply marked fashion, even in infancy, much as the adult teeth are previously represented by the milk teeth whose place they take. Indeed, the infant's life is even more proportionately sensuous or sensual than that of the adult.

Whereas in the earliest months of life this sensuality employs the mouth as its chief erotogenic organ, and the nipple or finger as its pleasure-giving part-object, there is analytical evidence that within the first few years of life a certain degree of psychosexual organization takes place, the genital organ becoming at least potentially capable of erotogenicity. In so far as this is the case, the pleasure-giving object, at least in unconscious phantasy, tends to become the parent-image of the opposite sex. Put crudely, it may be said that little boys marry their mothers and little girls marry their fathers. This situation leads to extraordinary, though hidden, psychological difficulties, as it entails conflict between emotions of love, hate and fear. That old classical play by Sophocles, *Œdipus Rex*, itself a product of the unconscious, dramatizes the tragedy that ensues. Suffice it to say that little Œdipus, like his classical counterpart, extinguishes his sensuality and goes out into the wilderness away from the desired object of it. In short, it is said to be a breaking up of the psychological Œdipus situation which initiates the latency (school) period of libidinal sublimation and cultural achievement. The Œdipus struggle becomes repressed and forgotten. But in adult life the emotional tendencies, and even the character, fall largely into these early emotional patterns.

Before infantile libidinal organization developed, before the Œdipus Complex arose, *Fixations* of libido to some of the early erotogenic regions may have become established. These are responsible for the sexual perversions. *Regression* to these fixation points occurs if normal development is frustrated, inhibited or otherwise repressed or discouraged. It is transformations of the *Component Instincts* rather than of genital sexuality that are responsible for neurotic (particularly hysterical) symptoms. Conversion hysteria (*vide* Case XVI) can be regarded as the erotization by regression of that part of the body where the symptom occurs. The hysterical patient whose stomach is so sensitive or ticklish is more or less anæsthetic and frigid in the genital region.

Conflict which we have already mentioned as existing between one instinct and another has a more classical instance in the conflict between instinct and Super-Ego forces, or between these and the Ego (or reason). In the last case the conflict may be conscious or partly conscious. Analysis is chiefly concerned with completely unconscious conflicts.

The Super-Ego or Ego may *resist* libidinal impulses and ideas emanating from the Id. It may impose a *censorship* upon them and cause their *repression* into the unconscious.

If these forces are too strong for it and the Ego is not confident of its ability to keep these unwelcome "enemies" repressed, it reacts with *Anxiety* at the threat of their emergence. This is what commonly happens in cases where the sexual instinct is being unduly stimulated without achieving relief of its consequent tension—for instance, in engaged couples who go in for much courtship and no sexual intercourse (*vide* Case IV).

In any case, it is usual for the dynamic energy of these impulses and ideas to find a way of evading the censorship, as the Id is for ever trying to relieve its tension. They emerge by assuming all sorts of disguises and subterfuges to evade the censorship. The dynamic energy, affect or emotion of these Id tendencies is commonly *displaced* on to ideas or conduct less heavily censored by the Super-Ego or Ego. *Sublimation* is said to occur when these newly energized ideas or conduct are, far from being censored, really in keeping with Super-Ego and Ego ideals, or when they are regarded as serving the reality advantages of the individual and of society. When, however, the repressed forces escape, *in spite of Ego-resistance* they may exhibit some manifestation which is contrary to the Ego's wishes and injurious to its sense of security and well-being. There is then a state of Conflict, and the escaped energy manifests itself in the form of symptoms, and the individual is suffering from a *psychoneurosis.*

Sublimation, substitution and symptom formation and all human behaviour other than instinct-behaviour are thus the result of the mechanism of *Displacement of Affect.* This mechanism, one of the many in the unconscious mind, is most important for our understanding not only of the mode of production of psychoneurotic symptoms, such as phobias, but also of all our sublimations and of the substitution of cultural values for the primitive instinctual and erotogenic valuations. Abundant illustrations of it have been given in the text of the cases described, for instance, in Case VI (Knife Phobia), and its mode of operation has been explained in the psychopathology of a war neurosis under Case XXI.

Suffice it to say that, on account of the resistance or opposition to certain ideas (particularly primitive sexual ideas) unwelcome to consciousness these ideas become repressed into the unconscious, as a result of conflict, while the affect or emotion originally attached to them, being more dynamic, because dissociated and *displaced* on to other ideas which can be tolerated (or even welcomed) in consciousness. Thus the dynamic affect reaches consciousness after all, and gains relief and expression by means of this displacement.

Thus in conclusion we may review the dynamics and mechanisms of the mind as follows:

*Tension arises from somatic sources and accumulates in a sort of instinct reservoir called the Id. Thence it would tend to discharge itself along the established instinct paths and emerge in the form of instinctive behaviour.*

*In the course of development the smooth and ready working of this process is held in check first by external agents such as parents and reality, and secondly by the infantile Ego or Super-Ego developed in accordance with the influence of these external agents.*

*But growing tension is intolerable and the dynamic energy or affect of these instincts is for ever striving for relief of tension. This is achieved largely through the mechanism of displacement of affect whereby it attaches itself to ideas or forms of behaviour which are permitted by the censorship of Super-Ego and Ego (sublimation).*

*If it fails to obtain relief in this way, a state of Conflict will arise. This may resolve itself in one of several ways. Either the impulses and affects will be repressed, in which case there is a constant expenditure of energy on the part of the repressing forces often resulting in mental ineptitude and exhaustion; or, in so far as the accumulation of tension becomes intolerable it may regress and reactivate component instincts: or, with or without these intermediate processes, it will undergo some degree of displacement of affect, and break out in spite of the Ego, displaying itself together with some portion of the opposition in the form of a symptom: or, last of all, it will cause modifications of the Ego itself, disturbing the latter's appreciation of reality to a greater or lesser extent and thereby giving rise to a psychosis.*

It only remains to be added that each and all of these processes are continuously taking place in every mental apparatus, the only difference between one mind and another being the relative energy of the forces at work, and the relative degree to which the various mechanisms are employed.

In other words, all persons display instinct behaviour, cultural or sublimated behaviour, symptomatic behaviour, and psychotic behaviour. There is no Ego whose relationship to reality is not to some extent vitiated by the claims which undischarged instinct tension makes upon it. (*Vide* Case XXIV—You and Your Hair.)

To those without adequate clinical experience much of this theoretical structure will seem unnecessarily confusing, if not altogether unsatisfactory, or positively repellent. Its justification is that it is based entirely upon clinical evidence, and not simply for the purpose of satisfying an intellectual need. If we prefer something simpler, clearer, more logical, and more easily credible, we have merely to ignore all clinical evidence and invent a phantasy satisfactory to our particular biases and wishful thinking. This, I am afraid, is the usual method we adopt when we theorize about things which are not easily seen or which we can avoid looking at. The mind is thus obeying the pleasure principle rather than the reality principle, although its pleasure may be of the intellectual or Ego variety.

Until the time of Vesalius and Harvey, before the human body had been dissected, the intellectuals of that age invented the most fantastic and gratifying theories of its structure and function. Attempts to make real investigations and to correlate their findings, particularly in the case of comparative anatomy as made by Charles Darwin, were strenuously resisted, as they did not enhance mankind's desired self-esteem.

Unfortunately for our medical students, dissection of the body reveals innumerable rudimentary, unnecessary and "illogical" parts. These would be useless for an idealistic theoretical construction, particularly as they can be understood only in the light of evolution from a more primitive form. It is exactly the same when we undertake the more difficult task of dissecting the mind. Its deeper levels are full of the most primitive obsolescent structures, and its mechanisms have nothing of logic or reason or of those principles with which we are consciously familiar, and with which we would like to endow them.

But here we have a particularly difficult task for the forces we meet are just those which in their primitive form are prone to threaten the new territory we have won by means of sublimation and cultural substitution. (*Vide* Case XVII, Part II.) It was on account of their incompatibility with this cultural world that we repressed them into the unconscious.

Nevertheless, if we are to be successful in manipulating these forces and mechanisms, we must investigate, understand and accept them as they are—just as in order to be successful surgeons we must accept the fact that the abdomen is full of bowels—whether we like it or not. In the long run, we may find that it is more comfortable and healthy this way than to deny the truth and perhaps to deny instinct its necessary and permissible modes of relief.

It is only after such reality recognitions that we can adjust our environment to our nature, without unduly torturing our nature to fit an idealistic, fantastic or unreal environment. Health will then take the place of disease—and perhaps a healthy civilization takes the place of a diseased one. Indeed, each event will be seen to be necessarily contingent upon the other.

This brings me to the subject of *prevention and cure*:

Psychological investigation brings the surprising revelation that what we are trying to cure or prevent is often not illness but *health*.

Immediately we were born we set about trying to cure our ills, or to bully others into curing them (which was the only practical technique possible for us in those days) by crying or screaming. If we felt cold or uncomfortable, we cried or screamed until we were made comfortable. If we felt any tensions or discomforts, we immediately "*cured*" the "*ill*" by discharging the tension or gratifying the impulse.

The constantly recurring hunger pains we cured by repeated doses of the appropriate medicine—mother's milk. Or, perhaps, this illness never became very acute; it was prevented by feeding at regular short intervals.

Prevention and cure in these earliest days were a simple process of instinct gratification. The result was health; or, indeed, life itself. In obeying the instincts we were preventing death and pre-serving life.

Have we any better guide now? The answer is, "*No*, a thousand times no!" And we never shall have.

The instincts *are* life itself, and if they are refused, or in so far as they are refused, we are engaged in "curing" life (not illness). A complete refusal of instinct life would itself be death.

What, then, is all this cure and prevention with which we are preoccupied or obsessed?

It may be that our next step along the original healthy path of instinct gratification brought us in the course of our development into conflict with other more powerful animals or powers, who were intent upon gratifying *their* instincts, even at the expense of our needs.

In a sense the law of the forest—to eat and to avoid being eaten—exists in the very cradle of culture. We discovered in the course of development that to insist upon "eating" in some instances might only result in us ourselves being "eaten" by the more powerful creatures around us. Fear set a curb upon our natural instinct lusts.

Thus it might be that our problem became, not so much how to gratify our instincts, but how to restrain them, how to put off their gratification in the face of the dangers which their drive might lead us into. Unless we can keep our fingers out of the jam those fingers will be smacked or hurt. Or, if the "jam" is "fire," even burnt off.

Now this process is a reversal of the original principle of instinct-driven activities. Instead of now employing our energies in an endeavour to gratify the instincts, we have reversed a part of that energy, and are using it against the instincts to hold them back.

In the first place, it is only fear that has induced us to do this; a fear lest, in endeavouring to get life (instinct gratification) we may merely be courting death, a fear that in striving to eat we may be running into the lion's mouth. Fear can make us too timid to live. We may become, as it were, so afraid to gratify all or any of our instincts that we spend the greater part of our energy in beating them down. Then, indeed, we are sick people.

We have been trying to "cure" or to prevent healthy life itself. We are killing ourselves so that other more powerful creatures, the powers of which we are afraid, may live.

*All this cure-nonsense is the timid person asking the more powerful "How can I suppress, or 'cure' my instincts from interfering with your wishes? How can I be a good boy, so that you will love me, spare my life and pre-serve me?"*

*Perhaps the answer is: "You cannot be good or any good if you are unduly repressed, if you have got rid of the basic instinct drive of your life."*

Instincts tend to cure themselves by gratification in one way or another. That is life. To try to cure them by any other means is working against nature, and can only result in illness.

The only qualification of this rule, and it is a further extension of it rather than an exception to it, is implied in that special mode of gratification which is achieved by displacement and sublimation. Sublimation is in general a larger and better way of achieving relief or gratification of the affectual tension originally pertaining to the instinct. It is a way of achieving it without incurring the disadvantages which may attach to direct instinct gratification. But it is limited in its scope. Only a limited proportion of the instinct tension can be so displaced and gratified without undue strain and with preservation of health, according to the degree of skill or culture we have acquired or inherited in the exercise of this mental operation. Nevertheless, it is an entirely different process from that of repression, which latter is analogous to burying the instinct tension alive, and thus attempting to smother or exterminate it. Unfortunately, this is the impractical "cure" which many sick people, and to some extent a sick world, has in its shortsightedness or anxiety endeavoured to execute.

There is only one way to cure instincts permanently. Ancient peoples recognized this when their laws provided only one cure for delinquency—beheading. Life is fundamentally instinct-driven: the only permanent cure for it is death.

The impression is emerging, and I am sure it is a correct impression, that life with its structure, instincts, and mental patterns, is very resistant to the changes or arbitrary modifications that we in our folly would wish to impose upon it. I began this chapter with an illustration to that effect. Not in one individual lifetime, but even in seventy generations, the Spaniards, in spite of repeated gruesome lessons, are still a people very prone to civil war.

Dentists have told us that dental caries can only be adequately prevented by correct feeding of the mother while she is carrying the embryo, that is to say while the germs of its teeth are being formed within her womb. Experiments in this direction might lead to the discovery that they had best be instituted several generations back, or to be practical: it may be that only if bearing mothers of several successive generations are correctly fed will we finally manage to produce a race with teeth as good as negroes or savages.

The foundations of mental health may require similar agelong treatment to produce a race relatively free from neurotic and psychotic disturbances, individual and national. Havelock Ellis has such a thesis in mind when he pins his hope of human betterment to Eugenics, selected breeding and the sterilization of the unfit.

Naturally, such grand schemes are beyond the scope of the psychotherapist. He can merely voice his conclusions that an individual life is too short for the achievement of really drastic and fundamental changes in the nature and character of any adult person. He must, often unlike the patient, resign himself to accepting the instincts and instinct-patterns as fundamental, inherited and unalterable. Fortunately, however, for his professional prestige normal health can often be restored without any alteration of these fundamentals, or on the contrary by simply getting the patient himself to cease trying to alter or smother them and to allow them to emerge from repression in their original natural form.

Fortunately for the psychotherapist, many of his patients are suffering from relatively superficial failures of adjustment and there is no need to attempt the impossible. They are merely engaged in dramatizing various conflicts and unconscious phantasies, and an alternative mode of obtaining relief and expression of these is not far to seek once their source and mechanism has been fully exposed to consciousness and brought under the direction of the Ego.

There will always be those whose trouble is of a deeper and more serious nature, those in whom the injurious changes were brought about very early in the development of their emotional patterns, and even those in whom there is an inherited tendency to morbidity. The mind of the infant is normally psychotic, and fixation at some early level or regression to it with a consequent failure of even the usual degree of Ego development is responsible for the majority of the so-called biogenic psychoses. Perhaps there will always be the schizophrenics and the cyclothymics; but, though they may fill the asylums, just as organic disease fills the hospitals, they, like their organic brethren, form a very small proportion of the sick· and suffering humanity met with in every doctor's consulting-room, and comprise less than 5 per cent of his clientele.

But even with the milder psychoses, and with the more serious during an interim period, the psychotherapist's task is not always hopeless. Protracted analysis in very skilled hands may achieve some degree of lasting improvement, and this may prove well worth while to the patient and to those responsible for him.

The psychotherapist's task will be even more difficult, if not impossible, in those cases where the individual, while inflicting discomfort upon others in his environment, is himself obtaining satisfaction from his dramatization.

Throughout the ages humanity, nations as well as individuals, has suffered at the hands of such individuals. Political and national leaders may, unknown to themselves, be indulging in the projection and dramatization of their unconscious phantasies, impelled to do so by tensions and unconscious forces and mechanisms within them, thereby obtaining intrapsychic relief and gratification for themselves, while inflicting distress and destruction upon their more repressed and less psychotic victims.

Such persons rarely enter our laboratory. They are busy using the world as their laboratory, playground or battlefield. They are unconsciously endeavouring to make the environment correspond to the patterns and phantasies of their unconscious mind. They are creating a world without to match the world within.

Far from recognizing themselves as mentally ill, such undesirables are liable to pass undetected, or even to be acclaimed by their victims, for they are employing a *normal* mechanism for the relief of their abnormal phantasies. To manipulate the environment, material and human, to correspond to one's internal state is the general endeavour of normal life, and in so far as it is successful it may be regarded as a necessary process in the maintenance of health. Further it appears that the average person is finding it rather a strain to maintain and endure a world of relative sanity. This can be the only explanation of why he so readily acclaims and supports the intolerances of leaders who are strongly determined to establish a more psychotic one. People who are capable of inflicting suffering upon their fellow beings, and this unfortunately comprises the vast majority of the human race, are either lacking in some mental quality or, still worse, are possessed of an undue proportion of the positive mental quality called sadism, or, thirdly, are victims of the uncomfortable phantasy that they themselves are in danger of destruction (castration phantasy) and in their panic must defend themselves.

The first state is merely a widespread form of mental deficiency, the last is a regrettable psychosis as uncomfortable for its possessor as for its victim, the second one is more widespread than is popularly supposed as it is almost invariably rationalized and often unconscious.

Whilst admitting that there *can* be an occasional reality basis for the infliction of death, if not of other suffering, I submit that as we are criticizing the human mind in general or mankind as a whole, and not confining our attention to one portion of it, or even to one nation, I submit that this reality basis is always secondary to the operation of one or more of the above three primary factors, and can therefore for the general purpose of our argument be ignored.

To the physician who has devoted his life to the alleviation of suffering and to the preservation of life, the spectacle of his fellow men blowing off the arms and legs and shattering the bodies and minds of their fellow men is an amazing revelation of universal mental illness. If, however, he looks for premonitory signs of this prevailing psychosis he will find them in every adult, in every infant, and in every human institution not excepting those very institutions whose avowed aim is solicitude for justice, mutual well-being and the prevention of injurious activities. Somehow or other this injury-inflicting psychosis insinuates itself into the execution of our highest ideals of justice and even of benevolence. For instance, such a cultural institution as law, particularly criminal law, in its administration, if subjected to detailed examination, is seen to inflict more suffering and cruelty, and that cold-bloodedly, than any and all of its transgressors were ever capable of inflicting singularly and collectively. Even the most benevolent of cultural institutions, that of religion, has a dark and bloody history.

Perhaps it is that under the guise of justice and benevolence the repressed hatred of man (the emotional nucleus of psychosis) can operate most freely in a form most immune from the inhibition of anxiety. The Justices in their brief authority, the Appeal Judges in their scarlet robes, and the House of Lords in its august assembly can enjoy its mental torturings and can send its minor delinquent to birching, imprisonment and execution knowing that the suffering is his and the satisfaction theirs, and confident in their immunity from retribution.

While this psychology prevails we shall have not only our minor crimes of apathies, intolerances, delinquencies, cruelties and murders, but also our major crimes of war and law. The same fundamental psychotic trend underlies them all.

Thus we see that normal life, the mirror of the mind of normal man, is just as symptomatic of the springs not only of neurosis but even of major psychosis as are the symptoms of those whose mental illness is palpable. Moreover, the former has an infinitely greater power for evil—witness our wars, not to speak of our unspeakable peacetime activities.

Sanity entails a suppression or sublimation of the primitive instinctual energy in favour of the perhaps less gratifying if not positively uncomfortable reality principle. What dog can resist the temptation and satisfaction of biting his rival, in spite of the biting he may receive in return? The instincts demand gratification in spite of reality disadvantages. Indeed, the perpetuation of human life is itself based upon this fundamental (though "insane") principle.

The gratification of the sexual instinct is responsible for much of our troubles and difficulties, though it may be regarded as a "psychosis" necessary to maintain our health and incidentally to reproduce successors of our "insanity."

Perhaps this conflict with the reality principle was originally responsible for its very considerable degree of repression—a repression which is still maintained principally by the infantile Ego, or Super-Ego, and which the adult Ego (or reason) has not yet adequately released.

This appears to have much to do with the resulting condition of strain and tension existing in the psyche, and largely responsible for the outbreak of neurotic and psychotic symptoms. It may be that it is in consequence of this state that the mind would welcome any form of relief of the tension, however psychotic or disastrous. Already the conflict within it is so intolerable that no form of external conflict could be an adequate dramatization of it. Thus to maintain a state of peace in the outer world would mean resigning ourselves to the perpetual endurance of this intrapsychic strain and conflict.

In other words, peace in the outer world can be maintained only at the expense of this inner strain, and often the price seems too much to pay. Our powers of endurance can hardly tolerate it. Our overcharged Id is itching for a bit of insanity as a deliverance.

The maintenance of this external state of peace becomes almost impossible if there are wars or rumours of wars. Any nation becomes restless if others are at war (like dogs seeing a dog-fight in progress). Their young men begin to shout for a share in the orgy and many of them volunteer for service with either side. Finally, the whole nation is swept into the avalanche. It was psychologically too difficult to keep out. In other words, wars exist because the Id is already at war and wants this dramatization, projection or mechanism of outward release for its intolerable inner tension and conflict.

*The world outside will never be either more or less mad than the hidden world within the deeper levels of the mind.* What appear to be Ego-motives are largely rationalizations. You don't rob a man because he has money, but because you have the psychology of a robber.

If we subject even the most widespread and normal sample of human behaviour to careful analysis it becomes apparent that it is not so much a necessary adjustment to reality as a dramatization, or projection into the outside world, of the unconscious phantasies and hidden conflicts which lie deeply buried within the mind of man. Such an exposition was attempted in Case XXIV in reference to our typically normal hair activities. Similarly, each and every human activity, ritual and belief, can be shown to be a reflection, as on the mirror of life, of the otherwise hidden preoccupations of the unconscious mind. The subject is so important and so persistently neglected that I propose to dedicate my next book to its comprehensive exposition.

There is no real demarcation between environment and the individual any more than there is between the individual and heredity. The environment has in the course of evolution created the mind and the mind has in turn unconsciously created its personal environment. In so far as there is war in the one there will be war of some sort in the other. Moreover, the process is a continuum, of a piece with the space-time continuum, in which the emergence and decease of individual lives are more illusionary than real, but in which an evolutionary process appears to be at work.

A necessary contingent to the replacement of diseased individuals by healthy ones is the replacement of a diseased civilization by a healthy civilization. Individual health is contingent upon world health—*and vice versa*.

Thus it will be seen that psychopathology cannot be limited to the study of a few isolated sufferers, but that it inevitably extends its field to suffering humanity, individually and collectively, and to all human habits, institutions, patterns of culture, thought and endeavour. The cure and prevention of illness in the one opens up the far wider problem of the prevention and cure of all human ills together with a recognition of world-wide mental illness.

# GLOSSARY

**AETIOLOGICAL:** Pertaining to causes.

**AFFECT:** The energy of an emotion. It may be aroused by a variety of stimuli and is capable of displacement on to concepts with which it was not originally associated.

**AMBIVALENT:** Having opposing affects, usually love and hate, existing simultaneously and often unconsciously and directed towards the same object.

**ANALYSAND:** One who is being treated by analysis.

**AUTO-EROTISM:** Erotic stimulation without resort to another person. (C/f Allo-erotism: erotism directed to another.)

**COMPLEX:** A repressed group of emotionally invested ideas.

**CONFLICT:** "War" between opposing elements in the mind.

**CYCLOTHYMIA:** A condition characterized by recurring phases of alternating elation and depression its extreme form being manic-depressive psychosis.

**DEMENTIA:** A condition of mental disintegration.

**EROTIC:** Sexual.

**EROTOGENIC:** Productive of erotic feelings.

**FETISH:** Anything which is attractive on account of its association, usually through unconscious elements, with erotic pleasure.

**IMAGO:** The phantastic image formed in infancy from an erroneous conception of a loved or hated person.

**INSTINCTS:** Innate patterns of discharge of tension.

**INTRA-PSYCHIC:** Within the mind.

**LATENCY PERIOD:** Period of life between the hypothetical end of infantile sexuality and the beginning of pubertal sexuality.

**LIBIDO:** The energy of the sexual instinct and of its psycho-sexual component instincts. It is subject to many vicissitudes. For example, it can become aim (i.e. orgasm)—inhibited and undergo unlimited displacement, even on to the person's own ego (narcissism, self love) asexual objects and abstract ideas.

**ORGASM:** The point at which erotic excitement reaches its acme and becomes involuntary. On the latter account it is suppressed by most persons in proportion to their prevailing anxiety and ill health.

**PERVERSION:** Any sexual act the object or mechanism of which is both biologically unsound and socially disapproved. Perversions are usually the manifestation of a psycho-sexual component instinct in substitution for mature genital sexuality.

**PHALLUS:** The erect penis or its image, worshipped in some religious systems as symbolizing generative power in nature.

**PHYLOGENETIC:** Pertaining to biogenic development or evolution. (C/f Onto-genetic: pertaining to the development of an individual from a fertiled ovum.)

PRE-GENITAL SEXUALITY: The infantile organization of the sexual pattern in which the component instincts and the pre-genital erotogenic zones such as oral, anal and phallic are absorbing the greater part of the libido.

PSYCHE: Mind.

PSYCHOGENIC: Originating in the mind.

PSYCHOPATHOLOGY: The study of morbidity in the psyche.

SCHIZOID: Having some of the characteristics of schizophrenia. Slighly schizophrenic.

SCHIZOPHRENIA: Split mind. A psychosis, usually in early life, characterized by repressed affect and interest with introversion and progressive dementia.

SOMATIC: Bodily, as distinct from mental. (In biology somatic would mean relating to the somotoplasm as distinct from germplasm.)

TRAUMA: A morbid condition produced by an unpleasant experience.

# INDEX